MANAGEMENT KNOWLEDGE AND THE NEW EMPLOYEE

Management Knowledge and the New Employee

Edited by
DAMIAN E. HODGSON
Manchester School of Management, UMIST

CHRIS CARTER
University of St. Andrews

Routledge
Taylor & Francis Group

LONDON AND NEW YORK

First published 2004 by Ashgate Publishing

Reissued 2018 by Routledge
2 Park Square, Milton Park, Abingdon, Oxon OX14 4RN
605 Third Avenue, New York, NY 10017

First issued in paperback 2021

Routledge is an imprint of the Taylor & Francis Group, an informa business

A Library of Congress record exists under LC control number: 2003070904

Notice:
Product or corporate names may be trademarks or registered trademarks, and are used only for identification and explanation without intent to infringe.

Publisher's Note
The publisher has gone to great lengths to ensure the quality of this reprint but points out that some imperfections in the original copies may be apparent.

Disclaimer
The publisher has made every effort to trace copyright holders and welcomes correspondence from those they have been unable to contact.

ISBN 13: 978-0-815-39037-4 (hbk)
ISBN 13: 978-1-351-15344-7 (ebk)
ISBN 13: 978-1-138-35836-2 (pbk)

DOI: 10.4324/9781351153447

Contents

List of Figures and Tables

Figures

Tables

List of Contributors

Kirstie Ball is Lecturer in Organizational Management at the University of Birmingham, UK. She has also held posts at Warwick and Aston Business Schools. With research specialisms in electronic surveillance at work, call centre management, human resource information systems and discourse analysis, she has recently published in *Organization Studies, Ethics and Information Technology*, and *Personnel Review*, and is the author of several book chapters on surveillance at work. She has been a visiting professor at Queens School of Business in Canada, and has been a core member of the ESRC's surveillance in society seminar series. She reviews for *Organization Studies, Gender, Work and Organization*, and *Personnel Review*, and is currently editing a special issue of *Gender, Work and Organization* on the topic of 'Power, Representation and Voice' following the inaugural gender sub-theme at EGOS 1999. She has also contributed to media discussions on call centre management for BBC television and radio.

Chris Carter is Lecturer in the Department of Management at St Andrews. Prior to taking up his role at St Andrews, he held positions at the Universities of Leicester and North London. Chris has published in journals such as *Critical Perspectives on Accounting, Human Relations, Organization*, and *Organization Studies*. His PhD was awarded by Aston Business School.

Stewart Clegg is Professor at the University of Technology, Sydney and the University of Aston Business School, UK, and Director of ICAN (Innovative Collaborations, Alliances and Networks), a Key University Research Centre of the University. Born in Bradford, England, Stewart Clegg migrated to Australia in 1976, after completing a first degree at the University of Aston (1971) and a Doctorate at Bradford University (1974). Previously he has held positions at the University of St. Andrews, Scotland; University of New England; University of Western Sydney, in all of which he was Professor and Head of Department, and Griffith University, Brisbane, where he was Reader. He has held Visiting Professorships at London University; Ecole des Mines, Paris; Technical University of Denmark; University of London; University of Otago; University of Leeds; Bond University; University of Brunei; University of Hong Kong; Hong Kong Baptist University; FGV Business School, Sao Paulo; University of Athabasca, Alberta; Autonomous University of Mexico; Loyola Marymount University, Los Angeles, and the University of British Columbia, Vancouver. He has written extensively on power, organizations and related matters. He has written extensively on power and organizations. His most recent books are *Trends in Japanese Management: Continuing Strengths, Current Problems and Changing Priorities*, co-authored with Toyohiro Kono (2001) and the eight-volume collection on *Central Currents in Organization Theory*, as well as *Paradoxes of Management* *and Organizations* (2002) and with Robert Westwood, *The Discourse of Organization Studies: Point/Counterpoint* (2002). He publishes regularly in journals such as the *Academy of Management Education and Learning, Organization Science, Organization Studies, Organization, Human Relations* and *Administrative Science Quarterly.*

David Crowther is Professor of Corporate Social Responsibility at the London Metropolitan University. He is a qualified accountant (FCMA, CPFA) with extensive business experience. He has authored or co-authored several books, including *Social and Environmental Accounting* (2000), *Shareholder or Stakeholder Value* (2001), *A Social Critique of Corporate Reporting* (2001), contributed to a number of edited books and numerous journal papers.

Anne-marie Greene is Lecturer in Industrial Relations at the University of Warwick Business School. She is author of *Voices from the Shopfloor: Dramas of the Employment Relationship* (2001) and co-author of *The Dynamics of Managing Diversity: A Critical Text* (2000). She has published academic articles on a range of subjects, including workplace trade unionism, paternalism, equality and diversity, and cyberunionism.

Shayne Grice currently lectures in Business Ethics and Organization Studies at the University of Otago in Dunedin, New Zealand. His research revolves around a broadly postcolonial problematic in which the limits of managing knowledge are understood in terms of concepts of hegemony, justice, and inheritance.

Damian E. Hodgson is Lecturer in Organizational Analysis at Manchester School of Management. His current interests include; governmentality and state regulation; consumption and consumerism; masculinity, discipline and resistance; globalization and management knowledge; and Foucauldian understandings of professionalism and professionalization. In the course of this work he has conducted a significant amount of research into the UK Financial Services industry and a book on this theme *Discourse, Discipline and the Subject* (2000) is published by Ashgate. He has recently published in a range of academic journals, including the *Journal of Management Studies, Gender, Work and Organization, Management Decision* and *Organization.*

Roy Jacques completed his PhD at the University of Massachusetts. He held positions at the University of Otago in Dunedin, New Zealand and at the Californian School of Professional Psychology. After a very successful career in academia, he turned his back on academic labour and is now running a coffee shop in Arizona!

Campbell Jones teaches critical theory and business ethics at the Management Centre, University of Leicester, UK, and co-edits the journal *ephemera: critical dialogues on organization* (www.ephemeraweb.org). Between 1996 and 1999 he studied and taught with a vibrant group of scholars that had gathered at the

Department of Management at the University of Otago in the far south of New Zealand. The conversation that is published here is a result of the intellectual and collegial environment that he, Shayne Grice, Roy Jacques and others enjoyed at that time.

Albert J. Mills is Professor of Management and Director of the PhD Programme in the Sobey School of Business at Saint Mary's University (Nova Scotia, Canada). His primary research interests focus on the relationship between organization and human liberation, which he has explored through numerous studies of gender and organization and the problematic of 'workplace diversity'. He is currently researching the impact of the Cold War on the development of management thought. In addition to various journal articles, Mills is the co-author and co-editor of several books, including *Organizational Rules* (1991, with Steve Murgatroyd), *Gendering Organizational Analysis* (1992, with Peta Tancred), *Reading Organization Theory* (1995, 1998 with Tony Simmons), *Managing the Organizational Melting Pot* (1997, with Michael Elmes and Pushie and Anshu Prasad), *Gender, Identity and the Culture of Organizations* (2002, with Iiris Aaltio), and *Gendered Organization and the Micropolitics of Resistance* (2004, with Robyn Thomas and Jean Helms Mills).

Julian Randall completed his Masters at the University of Stirling following a successful career as a management consultant and stayed on to teach part-time. He was Course Coordinator of the MBA course (1996-1998) and completed his PhD thesis in 2001 on enforced change at work and the psychological contract. He is currently Director of Programmes at the Centre of Business Education at the University of St Andrews. His first book, *Managing Change or Changing Managers*, will be published by Routledge in April 2004. He is currently continuing his research in the area of enforced change and individual responses in the health and public sectors.

Tim Ray is Senior Lecturer in Knowledge and Innovation at the Open University Business School, where he also directs the Management of Knowledge and Innovation Research Unit (MKIRU). After gaining his PhD in 1985, he worked at the University of Manchester on innovation and competitiveness, together with the evaluation of government sponsored initiatives to support collaborative research. Before joining the Open University in 1999, he spent seven years is Japan (initially as a visiting scholar and subsequently as an employee) based in government affiliated research organizations. His current research interests concern the processes by which the local interpretation of institutional 'rules of the game' in different contexts mediate power and knowledge relations. This focuses on how power – the capacity to achieve a difference – is enabled and constrained by tacit and explicit knowledge that is possessed by meaningfully connected individuals and groups.

Michael Rowlinson is Professor of Organization Studies at the Centre for Business Management, Queen Mary, University of London. His last book,

Organizations and Institutions: Perspectives in Economics and Sociology (1997), deals with the relationship between organizational economics, especially transaction cost economics, and organization theory, focusing on the relative importance of power and efficiency in explanations for the rise of the modern corporation, the separation of ownership from control, and divisions of labour and hierarchy. He is currently concerned with the ahistorical nature of organization studies and the atheoretical stance of business history, which he addressed in a recent article for *The Journal of Industrial History* (2001) 4(1).

Tony Tinker is Professor of Accountancy at Baruch College, City University of New York, Visiting Professor at University of Leicester and the University of South Australia, Member of the CUNY Faculty for the Development of On-Line Programs, and Fellow of the Chartered Association of Certified Accountants (national prize-winner in the final examination). He is ex-council member of the American Accounting Association and past-chair of the AAA Public Interest Section, has authored and co-authored several books, including *Social Accounting for Corporations* (1984); *Paper Prophets* (1985), and *Policing Accounting Knowledge* (1995) and published numerous academic articles. He is co-editor of *Critical Perspectives on Accounting* and the *Accounting Forum*, editorial board member of several major accounting journals, and has contributed to various public policy discussions for the BBC, CBC, Pacifica Public Radio, New York Public Radio, *Newsweek*, and the *Wall Street Journal*.

Robert Willmott previously lectured at the Universities of Birmingham and Bath. He has research interests in realist social and organization theory, new managerialism and education policy, which are reflected in his books *Education Policy and Realist Social Theory* (Routledge 2002) and *Educational Management in Managerialist Times* (Open University Press 2003).

Chapter 1

Critical Approaches to the Conceptualization of Management Knowledge: Reconsidering Jacques

Chris Carter and Damian E. Hodgson

In recent years Organizational and Management theory has witnessed a proliferation in epistemological and paradigmatic perspectives. One of the notable features of the development of Organization and Management theory has been the importation of theoretical perspectives from other disciplines, especially French philosophy. Such an assertion is borne out by the revelation that by 1995, Michel Foucault was the 7th most cited author in the journal of Organization Studies (Üsdiken and Pasadeos, 1995). The interest in poststructuralism has been further fuelled by fora such as the Critical Management Studies meetings in the UK, APROS in Australasia and the OMT division of the American Academy of Management. What is equally clear, however, is that this has led to the opening of greater fissures in the zone of consensus of organization studies. For some, this amounts to a crisis within the discipline, for instance, Jeffrey Pfeffer has argued for a robust return to functionalism. In contrast, Stewart Clegg has argued for the precise opposite:

> Such conflicts (Pfeffer) regards as dangerous, corrosive of moral authority, and destructive of professional reputation and discipline. Order is what is required. I would argue to the contrary: I would argue that intellectual communities – just as political communities – that suppress conflict do so at considerable risk to their vitality (Clegg 2001, p.11).

The poststructuralist turn has thus provoked intellectual endeavour and has attracted derision in equal measure. This collection seeks to add to current debates with Organization and Management theory engaging directly with issues of critical theory and organization. It does so by building on a workshop, convened at the University of Birmingham in late 1999 that sought to discuss the ideas set out in Roy Jacques' influential book *Manufacturing the Employee: Management Knowledge from the 19th to the 21st Centuries*. In and of itself, Jacques' book is interesting and merits attention. That said, its significance extends further in that it constitutes an attempt to theorize the development of management knowledge from an explicitly Foucauldian perspective. Simply put, Jacques attempts to understand how we are to make sense of the creation of the canon of management thought that provides the central foundations of Business School education. Jacques is well placed to comment on such issues as before entering academia he had a lengthy career as a working manager. He then took time out from being a manager to read for an MBA at the University of Massachusetts. MBA programmes of course claim to be able to help managers to manage '*better*'. Thus, unlike many other intellectual disciplines, management stakes claims about having direct links with performance in the workplace. In the United States this equates to being a 'professional' school, which among other things, means that students spend considerable time developing practical skills.

In the UK, however, the professionalization of general management took place much later than in North America. In place of getting an MBA, in contemporary times is rather akin to the acquisition of accountancy qualifications a generation ago, as it is the means of obtaining a 'business education'. The exponential take-off in such courses demands searching questions to be posed with regards to the status of management knowledge. It was this very question that led Jacques to pursue PhD studies following his Masters degree. The MBA, a self-styled 'how to do it' for managers, had little connection with Jacques' lived experience of managing. This led him to conduct a study into the history of management thought, by tracing from the 19th century to the modern day the emergence of what we know recognize as 'the employee'. His concern was to provide a genealogical account that sought to understand the various junctures and discontinuities that have led to the contemporary canon of management studies – as it is taught on MBA programmes. His argument is that what counts as management is historically specific but that management students are taught to concentrate upon transitory and superficial issues that are nonetheless represented as the transcendental problems of organizing. In particular, Jacques suggests that it is because of these limitations that 'management knowledge' as we now know it risks becoming obsolete in the face of the challenges of a postindustrial, knowledge economy.

Debate on Roy Jacques' book as the subject of the workshop provoked the development of discussion by the participating academics into asking 'how are we to understand the status and epistemological foundations of managerial knowledge?' Further, the workshop attempted to provoke debate as to how we might understand the functioning of management knowledge in contemporary work contexts? We would suggest that these questions are of direct concern to all of those researching, teaching and studying management. Yet we would also argue that all too often such questions are sidestepped in favour of the rather comfortable suggestion that management knowledge is technocratic, politically-neutral and constantly progressing. For instance, hundred years ago, British colonial administrators were prepared for their careers by being drilled in a rigorous regimen of ancient languages and classical history. This knowledge, it was held, was the 'very best that had been thought and written' and consequently was the training for a future administrator. It is easy to ridicule such notions, but it leads us to the heart of the present. More particularly, it leads us to question whether what we teach today's equivalents of the Victorian administrators, i.e. executives, consultants and so forth, will be regarded with bemusement by future generations. To the modern management academic the syllabi of the Victorians is at best eccentric, at the same time managerialists regard their knowledge as being performative: that is, being usable in the context of application. This collection goes some way to problematizing such assumptions.

One of the consequences of the close reading of Jacques is to highlight difficulties with the theoretical, methodological and empirical precepts that underpin his work. This collection highlights many areas for further debate, from the need for a greater understanding of the historical development of management knowledge, to the limits of such critiques of management practice. Other themes addressed among the papers include the political limits of management education, the control of management in a knowledge economy, the potential and limitations of discourse analysis, and management's failure to properly address issues of diversity and equality. To a varying degree, each of the contributors felt the book worthy of attention because of the contribution it makes, and in this sense the criticisms were at the same time a mark of respect for the wide ranging and provocative arguments contained within Jacques' work. We see this as entirely in keeping with the spirit of *Manufacturing the Employee* itself; as Jacques himself argues in the final chapter of this collection, 'As far as I'm concerned, it would not just be a legitimate project, but would show respect for my work and further it, for others to identify what I overlooked or misrepresented' (Jones, Grice and Jacques: 2004).

Michael Rowlinson opens the debate by addressing the perspective on history which is central to the contribution of *Manufacturing the Employee*. While applauding Jacques' recognition of the importance of 'an historical perspective' in studies of organization, Rowlinson aims to explore the various forms an 'historical' perspective might take. In particular, Rowlinson differentiates the Foucauldian, archaeo-genealogical approach of Jacques from both factual and narrative approaches to history and organizations. Although the notion of a 'factual' approach to history is highly problematic, as much of the field of business history exemplifies, there are alternative approaches which avoid naïve empiricism and eschew a simplistic belief in the power of 'historical facts'. Thus Rowlinson argues that a postmodern scepticism towards evidence and authorship has moved the field towards an engagement with deconstructionist perspectives on the nature of history. However, rather than the Foucauldian approach of *Manufacturing the Employee*, Rowlinson argues forcefully that a narrative form of deconstructionism is more likely to bring about a *rapprochement* between historians and organization theorists.

David Crowther and Anne-marie Greene continue the historical perspective in both criticizing and also building upon Jacques' understanding of the gendered nature of management knowledge in *Manufacturing the Employee*. In common with a number of other contributors to the collection, they single out specific aspects of Jacques' book for praise; in particular, his recognition of the masculinist bias of management theory, as embodied by the American Dream and other 'frontier myths' which underpin management knowledge as we now know it. However, they draw attention to a blind-spot in most histories of management, including Jacques' own – an important and frequently overlooked instance in the history of the organization of work in the US, the example of the American Shaker communities. Although frequently 'written out' of accounts of the evolution of management and management knowledge, Crowther and Greene argue that the Shaker model provides a powerful and effective example of an 'androgynous' form of organization in which gender difference is recognized without imposing a hierarchy or privileging masculine elements. This they contrast with the contemporary discourse of 'managing diversity', which frequently serves to reinforce the devaluation of feminine skills and attributes as a consequence of its foundation in US ideology of a 'society of equals'.

Albert J. Mills continues this discussion of the gendered nature of management knowledge with an empirical examination of the impact that writings on gender have made upon mainstream thought in the field of management. Reflecting Jacques argument that the management textbook is out of step with business practice, the research underlines the limited impact such work has made beyond the problematic heading of 'diversity'. Mills argues that the traditionally masculine sphere of business, shaped by an ethos of competition, remains relatively untouched by the traditionally feminine sphere, which has been consigned primary responsibility for relationship maintenance. The consequence of this tendency is felt far beyond the lecture hall; while the 'body of knowledge' of management does not predetermine the individual qualities a man or woman will bring to the organization, Mills maintains, it does indicate a powerful set of forces telling the organization member how s/he is *expected* to behave, both at work and in the broader world.

In the next piece, Tony Tinker takes up Jacques' challenge to reconsider what is meant by management education. As Jacques argues in his book, it was largely his dissatisfaction with what today counts as a 'managerial education' as epitomized by the modern MBA which led to his inquiry as to the nature and limits of 'management knowledge'. Tinker addresses this theme head-on, drawing a sharp contrast between the strictures of the MBA system and the social and political consequences of the capitalist system which it both legitimizes and perpetuates. Tinker therefore makes explicit the connections between liberal democracy, the corporate power of the world's multinationals, the casualties of globalization and a technocratic management education insulated from its wider political and social context. In conclusion, Tinker sets out a vision of how management education might be reoriented to allow students a purchase on the historical, political and sociological ramifications of management knowledge. To do otherwise, he warns, would maintain management's 'connivance in repression'.

Hodgson and Ball then attempt what they describe as a 'modest and sympathetic' critique of Jacques's work. Their criticism focuses upon the methodology employed by Jacques and in particular his conception of discourse, which he bases upon the work of both Saussure and Foucault. Discourse analysis has in recent years been a very productive methodological approach, particularly in the field of organization studies, and *Manufacturing the Employee* is an excellent example of this trend. However, the authors argue that Roy Jacques' argument is undermined as he leaves his understanding of discourse largely unarticulated. While the diversity of discourse is often seen as a strength of the approach, its ambiguity as a concept has become a matter of serious concern to a number of writers. To attempt to understand how Jacques conceptualizes 'discourse', Hodgson and Ball draw upon a taxonomy of discourse proposed by Alvesson and Kärreman (2000), and in particular their notion of 'levels of discourse'. They argue that the link between micro instances of 'discourse' (textbooks, speeches, papers cited) and a broader, universal 'Discourse' of US Management Knowledge is not explained, and that Jacques' methodological approach risks universalizing what can only ever be a partial and situated account of what constitutes 'management knowledge'.

The next contribution from Robert Willmott reflects upon the critical intent of Roy Jacques in *Manufacturing the Employee*. Jacques describes his critical position as 'more liberal than radical', and thus aspires to an pragmatic, incremental transformation of capitalist society and social relations. Willmott draws on a background in critical realism to follow through some of the implicit consequences of Jacques critique of management knowledge. Willmott is supportive of Jacques recognition of the limits of transformation and the necessity to deal with established elements of contemporary society, such as the division of labour within contemporary capitalism and the inequalities which result from this. Nonetheless, Willmott argues strongly that an effective critique of existing social and economic arrangements requires the setting out of feasible, grounded alternatives. Following Hodgson (1999), Willmott sets out a number of possible scenarios for a post-capitalist society, looking forward towards a knowledge-intensive economy and leaving behind old dichotomies of free markets versus state socialism. Without developing such a vision, he argues, Jacques' critique of management knowledge is caught between a rock and a hard place; a veiled conservatism or vain and empty utopianism.

In the next chapter, Clegg, Ray and Carter take on the global subtext of Jacques' work by considering the specifically American, indeed Anglo-Saxon, quality of much of what is accepted as management knowledge. They take as a contrast the institutional foundations of Japanese society, and in particular its implications for the development of management knowledge within Japan. In light of a carefully historicized reflection on the cultural and institutional specificity of Japan, Clegg *et al.* consider the limitations of Nonaka and Takeuchi's (1995) account of tacit/explicit knowledge. Building instead on Cook and Brown's (1999) typology, the authors propose an additional hybrid 'Mode 3' to better reflect the distinctive 'rules of the game' in a Japanese context, quite distinct from the modes of knowing characteristic of Western knowledge. In doing so, the chapter supports and develops Jacques' arguments by providing a clear challenge to universalizing epistemologies of management knowledge.

Ball and Carter take up the Foucauldian theme of Jacques' work and extend his analysis into the institutional and discursive shifts which underpin the emergence of modern 'best practice' management. Rather than the historical focus of Jacques, however, they concentrate upon an examination of discourse and practices associated with the modern-day growth of 'New Managerialism'. Taking the case of a newly-privatized public utility, the paper provides a model example of how the work of Foucault on discourse can be adapted to develop a precise analysis of the legitimation and operationalization of modern management knowledge in contemporary organizations. Through the use of social psychology, and in particular Potter and Wetherell's (1987) concept of *interpretive repertoires*, the authors analyse the narrative of a chief executive drawing upon 'New Managerialism' to reinvent and transform the organization. Around the themes of charisma, anachronism, inevitability, external alliances and empowerment, Ball and Carter offer a compelling illustration of the power of discourse, showing how popular texts, consultancies, and the various institutions of management education constitute a direct and tangible influence on the transformation of modern work organizations.

Randall develops the discursive theme of the previous chapter by reflecting on the changing construction of the employee in times of employment insecurity and enforced change at work. What distinguished the discourse of 'l'employé' in the late 19ᵗʰ and early 20ᵗʰ centuries was the shift from self-reliance to reliance upon an employer in both a material and existential sense. The 'company man', the 'hireling for life', in Jacques' terms, was the motif of an age in which loyalty and constancy came to stand for what Richard Sennett calls 'character' (1998). For an understanding of the recent transformations of the employee, it is necessary to examine the consequences of situations where the social contract is violently and unilaterally transformed, where the basic assumptions of the employee are proven to be unfounded. Randall's research points to the emergence of a new employee without the traditional reliance upon such institutional supports, and tentatively suggests a form of emancipation through insecurity.

The final paper offers a dialogue between Roy Jacques and Shayne Grice and Campbell Jones in which the range of criticisms directed towards his work are addressed clearly and directly. Here, Jacques engages directly with the criticisms and both develops his position and sets in context a number of the arguments made in *Manufacturing the Employee*. Through the debate, Grice and Jones press Roy Jacques on a range of issues; from his understanding of poststructuralism and its value, his approach to critique, the relevance of Marxist work to his thought and, fundamentally, the status of knowledge and management knowledge in the 21ˢᵗ Century.

The collection has showcased a number of contributions that taking Jacques as their starting point have engaged with concerns surrounding the status of management knowledge and theoretical perspectives that can be usefully be brought to bear to understand it. As Roy Jacques states in one of the contributions to this collection (Jones, Grice and Jacques, 2004); 'If this (debate) should turn into a case of whether Jacques, 1996, got it right or wrong *in toto*, I would find that terribly depressing. There is nothing useful that can come from a discussion like that.' We entirely concur with this position. This collection will have succeeded if it is to provoke further debate and reflection on what is and what counts as management knowledge.

References

Alvesson, M. and Kärreman, D. (2000) 'Varieties of Discourse: On the Study of Organizations through Discourse Analysis' in *Human Relations* 53 (9) pp. 1125-49.

Clegg, S. (2001) 'The Bounds of Rationality: Power/ History/Imagination' Keynote presentation to Asian Pacific Researchers in Organization Studies conference, Hong Kong Baptist University, December.

Cook, S. and Brown, J.S. (1999) 'Bridging Epistemologies: The Generative Dance Between Organizational Knowledge and Organizational Knowing' in *Organization Science* 10 (4) pp. 381-400.

Hodgson, G. (1999) *Economics and Utopia: Why the Learning Economy is not the End of History* London, Routledge.

Jacques, R. (1996) *Manufacturing the Employee: Management Knowledge from the 19th to the 21st Centuries* London: Sage.

Nonaka, I. and Takeuchi, H. (1995) *The Knowledge Creating Company: How Japanese Companies Create the Dynamics of Innovation* New York, Oxford University Press.

Potter, J. and Wetherell, M. (1987) *Discourse and Social Psychology: Beyond Attitudes and Behaviour* London, Sage.

Sennett, R. (1998) *The Corrosion of Character*, New York and London, W.W. Norton.

Shenhav, Y. (1999) *Manufacturing Rationality: The Engineering Foundations of the Managerial Revolution* Oxford, Oxford University Press.

Üsdiken B. and Pasadeos Y. (1995) 'Organizational Analysis in North America and Europe: A Comparison of Co-citation Networks' in *Organization Studies*, 16 (3) pp. 503–526.

Chapter 2

Historical Perspectives in Organization Studies: Factual, Narrative, and Archaeo-Genealogical

Michael Rowlinson

Introduction

The study of organizations is notoriously a-historical (Kieser, 1994). Critics from a variety of standpoints within organization studies argue that it would be improved if it were more historical (e.g. Brady, 1997; Jacques, 1996; Zald, 1993). I want to assess these arguments in relation to historical theory.

The arguments for an historical perspective in organization studies can be divided into three variants: factual, narrative, and archaeo-genealogical. Although these are not intended as mutually exclusive paradigms, there are tensions between them that are not sufficiently regarded within organization studies. The factual argument is that if organization studies were to take account of the facts revealed by history then a number of erroneous assumptions would be undermined (e.g. Brady, 1997). The narrative argument comes out of a sense that an engagement with history would be desirable as part of a reorientation of organization studies away from its emulation of science and towards an appreciation of the humanities (e.g. Zald, 1993).

Finally, and this is the main focus of the discussion, there is an archaeo-genealogical historical perspective derived from a Foucauldian critique of organization studies. This critique highlights the taken-for-granted and historically specific aspects of the contemporary organizational world, such as the all-pervasive 'institutional organization of our lives' and the 'generic process of organizational desexualization', which have generally been overlooked in the discourse of organization studies (Burrell, 1988, p. 25-6). The archaeo-genealogical historical perspective is exemplified by Roy Jacques' book, *Manufacturing the Employee* (1996), which combines a forceful appeal for 'an historical perspective' in organization studies with an historical account of organizational knowledge.

Before proceeding further it would be helpful to clarify some of the terms of the discussion. The reference to 'an historical perspective' is borrowed from Jacques (1996, p. viii), with the deliberate intention of making it problematic. The intention is to draw attention to ambiguities in the meaning of the term 'history' and to the potential contribution of historical theorists other than Foucault for developing an historical perspective in organization studies. As for the field of organization studies, it brings together a variety of disciplines, with major contributions having come from sociology, economics, and psychology. But since the latter two disciplines are relatively self contained, it is best to concentrate attention on organizational sociology which is characterized by greater paradigm diversity (Hassard, 1993), and is therefore more permeable to historical and philosophical critiques such as that derived from Foucault.

Factual History

The most obvious case for an historical perspective in organization studies is that neither management practitioners nor academics know very much about the history of management or management thought. For this argument to carry weight it needs to be demonstrated that 'the study of history can benefit the modern manager' (Brady, 1997, p. 161). Thus Brady, for one, claims that 'a function of history' is 'to subvert business ideology'. For example, he cites Chandler's classic work, *The Visible Hand* (1977), as evidence that 'under certain economic conditions managers are more efficient than market forces at producing and distributing consumer goods'. This allegedly serves as a corrective to the view that markets alone can co-ordinate all economic activity under any circumstances (Brady, 1997, p. 163; see also Hoskin, 1998, p. 100).

Kieser (1994) contends that historical analyses can be used as the basis for a critique of theories of organization. For example he takes the economists, Williamson (1985) and Marglin (1976), to task for their failure 'to present evidence on the motives of the actors involved' in the demise of putting-out systems of production. He maintains that their 'argumentation is not in line with the historical facts'. He also asserts that general models like theirs are susceptible to a historical critique because 'they necessarily contain assumptions on cause-event chains that are ill-specified and, therefore, not scrutinizable on the basis of historical data' (1994, p. 614, 619). Kieser's critique amounts to saying that the preference of economists for 'hypothetical' as opposed to 'actual history' (Swedberg and Granovetter, 1992, p. 15) results in a questionable treatment of historical data in the economic analysis of work organization (Jones, 1997, p. 15). As McCloskey puts it in one of his critiques of economic history:

> Economists spend a lot of time worrying whether their metaphors – they call them 'models' – meet rigorous standards of logic. They worry less whether their stories – they call them 'stylized facts,' a phrase that makes tiresome trips to the library unnecessary – meet rigorous standards of fact (1990, p. 22).

Kieser qualifies his appeal for historical analyses in organization studies by noting that since 'historical material is inexhaustible, a selection cannot be avoided', and that the 'selection as well as the interpretation of events is always in danger of reflecting the ideologies of the researcher' (1994, p. 619). Nevertheless

Kieser, in common with Brady, appears to construe history as a repository of facts which, so long as historians properly interpret them, can conveniently confirm or refute preferred or non-preferred theoretical positions in organization studies. It is just this treatment of history by non-historians which Elton, a prominent practising historian, once complained (Elton, 1967, p. 35-7).

The treatment of history as a repository of facts gives the misleading impression that history is there to be known, either through the examination of historical data, or, more likely, from the work of historians. Even from a supposedly archaeo-genealogical perspective, Shenhav and Weitz (2000) appear to concur with the view that history can provide a corrective to erroneous assumptions in management thinking, a view that is reinforced by Jacques' reference to 'reclaiming' history (1996, p. 186). Shenhav and Weitz suggest that, on the basis of original historical research, the roots of organization theory can be traced further back in time and 'go much deeper than ascribed by the classical texts' of organization studies (2000, p. 393).

The representation of an historical perspective as knowledge of selected historical facts can be interpreted as a manifestation of a failure to appreciate the ambiguity of 'history' that has long been recognized by philosophers of history. As Hegel wrote: 'In our language [Callinicos (1995, p. 4) notes that this applies to English, French, and German] the term *History* unites the objective with the subjective side… it comprehends not less what has *happened*, than the *narration* of what has happened' (quoted in White, 1987, p. 11-12). Moreover, historians usually practise a 'sleight of hand' in order to hide 'the fact that that all history is the study, not of past events that are gone forever from perception, but rather of the "traces" of those events distilled into documents and monuments on one side, and the praxis of present social formations on the other. These "traces" are the raw materials of the historian's discourse, rather than the events themselves' (White, 1987, p. 102).

What passes for history in organizational sociology, as in sociology generally, does not usually consist of original research. Instead sociologists tend to weave their interpretations of history from the studies that have already been carried out by historians (Callinicos, 1989, p. 7), as Kieser does (1994). It can hardly be expected that organizational sociologists should constantly refer to their historical work as an interpretation of commentaries on the traces of past events. But if they did so more often it would serve to remind them and their readers just how tenuous the connection is between what they write and anything that might ever have actually happened. Their interpretations of history would begin to look compromised if the necessary caveats were inserted before any mention of so-called 'historical facts' or 'evidence' (e.g. Kieser, 1994, p. 614).

If it is acknowledged that knowledge of history usually refers to the subjective side of history, that is, to the narration of history, then it implies that an historical perspective should entail an engagement with the work of historians and historiographical debates. Unfortunately that may not be obvious from the field of history that is most adjacent to organization studies, namely business history. Many business historians would be happy to endorse any assertion that knowledge of historical facts has some pedagogical value (e.g. Jeremy, 1999), since they are notably reluctant to engage with theory themselves (Hannah, 1984). Historical theory is largely ignored in business history. But business historians might be expected to line up against postmodernist arguments, along with those self-proclaimed 'professional historians' who declare that the practice of history is about 'not getting it wrong' (Marwick, 1995).

Beyond the boundaries of business history there is a literature on history and theory in which the status of historical facts is highly problematic (see Fay, Pomper and Vann, 1998). Postmodernists in particular argue that historical writing is most interesting when it generates further historiographical debate, rather than uncontested facts (Ankersmit, 1998). From this perspective it could be argued that Chandler's work (1977), for example, remains vital not because it is accepted as the last word on the rise of the American corporation but because it is still highly contested. The tensions in Chandler's theory and method leave it open to competing interpretations (see Roy, 1990; Stinchcombe, 1990).

Narrative History

As a result of its inherent ambiguity, history has almost always had to tackle epistemological questions, such as 'How can we know about the past? What does it mean to explain historical events? Is objective knowledge possible?' (Fay, 1998, p. 2). Non-historians in organization studies tend to present these epistemological issues, which are commonplace for historians (e.g. Hobsbawm, 1997, p. 186), as if they are a recent revelation (e.g. Barrett and Srivasta, 1991, p. 244). But debate in the discipline of history itself has shifted from epistemology towards a linguistic focus, 'as questions regarding the form of discourse by means of which historians describe and explain the past became the central concern' (Fay, 1998, p. 2).

In what can be termed 'deconstructionist history' it is accepted that the historian inevitably imposes a narrative structure on history (Munslow, 1997 p. 39). The most important theorists for deconstructionist history are Hayden White and Michel Foucault, who represent different responses to 'the inevitable impositionalism of the historian' (Munslow, 1997, p. 39). White is associated with the stream in postmodernism that 'is informed by a programmatic, if ironic, commitment to the return to narrative as one of its enabling presuppositions' (1987, xi), whereas in Foucauldian archaeo-genealogy anything resembling a coherent narrative is studiously avoided.

White's version of postmodernism has shifted the emphasis away from seeing archival research as the historian's craft towards a view that it is the conventions and customs of writing that constitute the craft of history (White, 1995, p. 243). Even critics among historians accept that the postmodernists' attention to history as a form of literature has reinstated 'good writing as legitimate historical practice' (Evans 1997, p. 244). White's suggestion 'that there might be a "fictional" element in the historian's text, however much he or she has tried to avoid it' (1995, p. 240), has served as a license for some of the most outstanding self-conscious historical narratives (e.g. Schama, 1989).

Judging by the extent to which their work is referred to in discussions among historians (e.g. Fay, Pomper and Vann, 1998), White is now more important for historical theory than Foucault. An indication of this is that the so-called 'linguistic turn' in the theory and philosophy of history has been traced back to the publication of White's *Metahistory* in 1973 (Fay, 1998, p. 2). Callinicos, a leading Marxist philosopher of history and a critic of White concedes, acknowledges that 'White's work is undoubtedly the decisive influence on contemporary discussion of history as narrative' (1995, p. 51).

But insofar as advocates of an historical perspective in organization studies refer to historical theory at all, it is Foucault's archaeo-genealogy that receives attention (e.g. Jacques, 1996). Unfortunately this obscures the parallels between the linguistic turn in history that draws inspiration from White's work, and the emerging critique of organization studies in which it is suggested that history represents a challenge to the prevailing determinism in theories of organization (Zald, 1993; Hirsch and Lounsbury, 1997). Zald argues that history has been excluded as a result of the rush for organization studies to be recognized as a science. He appeals for the field to be reconceptualized as a humanistic as well as a scientific enterprise. As part of the 'linguistic turn' in history, 'the question "how is history like and unlike fiction?" replaced "how is history like and unlike science?" as the guiding question of metahistorical reflection' (Fay, 1998, p. 2).

Zald's argument runs counter to the accepted view of theory in organization studies, according to which, 'theory refers to principles of organization that transcend time and space', and the only role for 'historical and comparative (that is international and/or multicultural) data' is to 'test the generalizability and utility of a theory' (Goldman, 1994, p. 623). For advocates of the version of organization theory 'that transcends time and place' the research programmes of new institutionalism and organizational ecology can be cited as evidence of a concern with 'historical issues' in organization studies (Goldman, 1994, p. 621).

Zald acknowledges that 'The easiest use of historical "facts" is to parametize variables or to add variables and context' to organizational analyses, as new institutionalists, and organizational ecologists have done. But he argues that although 'That is an advance over ahistorical generalizations … it hardly exhausts the range of ways that history and historical analyses inform theory and research' (1993, p. 520). What is more, the view of history as a variable threatens to reduce historians to a subordinate role as fact-gathering research assistants for organization theorists, as is proposed by organizational economists (see Lamoreaux, Raff and Temin, 1997).

Hirsch and Lounsbury also acknowledge that new institutionalism and organizational ecology have succeeded in reorienting organizational sociology away from cross-sectional research and towards 'the more advanced study of a smaller number of variables over long historical time periods'. But they argue that they have done so by treating 'organizations as atoms subject to the law of large numbers and other macropressures that force populations of firms into an equilibrium state'. This has been 'at the expense of understanding the uniqueness of individual organizations' from 'richly contextual case studies of single organizations' (Hirsch and Lounsbury, 1997).

Zald contends that 'the development of a historically informed organizational theory' and 'a historical approach' holds out the promise of a transformation in organizations studies (1993, p. 519). Hirsch and Lounsbury also appeal for more 'Historical studies' in order to redress the move of new institutionalism 'toward higher levels of abstraction and demise into managerial irrelevance' (1997, p. 86). If history is to fulfil the promise of transforming organization studies, making it less deterministic and more ethical, humanistic and managerially relevant, then it seems likely that type of history that is required is narrative history. This suggests that the historical theorists who are worth consulting are those such as White, who advocates narrative in history and questions whether it is ever possible to 'narrativize without moralizing' (1987, p. 25).

Archaeo-Genealogical History

For all the claims that 'Foucauldian categories and procedures ... throw fresh light on the history of the factory, management and the modern corporation', and the calls for 'detailed historical analysis' (McKinlay and Starkey, 2000, pp. 3-8), few of Foucault's acolytes in organization studies have followed him into the archives. Most Foucauldians in organization studies favour ethnographic research (e.g. Knights and Willmott, 2000). This contrasts with 'Foucault's project (and most Foucauldian projects)', which operate 'in a historical register', in parallel to contemporary, 'real-time', interpretive research (Gubrium and Holstein, 2000, p. 495). So the work of Jacques (1996) and others (e.g. Shenhav and Weitz, 2000) has to be welcomed for its recognition that Foucault's work is basically historical.

The reception of Foucault's work in organization studies has been very different to that in history. By the time of Foucault's death in 1984 historians and historical theorists had already responded to his critiques of and contributions to their discipline. Summaries of the responses to Foucault from both liberal (Merquior, 1991 [1985]) and Marxist (Poster, 1984) historians were available before his work received any serious attention in organization studies (Burrell, 1988). But advocates of a Foucauldian approach in organization studies largely ignore the damning criticisms of Foucault from the key contemporary thinkers on history, ranging from prominent practising historians, such as Elton (1991), through to historical theorists such as White (1990).

Many of the historians' criticisms of Foucault can be applied to the archaeo-genealogical historical writing inspired by Foucault in organization studies. First there is Foucault's notoriously impenetrable style. In his essay on Foucault White maintains that Foucault's writing consists of a flood of utterances which avoids narrative, and that his authority rests on a highly self-conscious style rather than 'factual evidence or rigor of argument' (White 1987, pp. 105-106). 'In fact', White continues, 'Foucault rejects the authority of both logic and conventional narrative...'.

Foucault's 'histories' are as fraught with discontinuities, ruptures, gaps, and lacunae as his 'arguments'. If he continues to fascinate (some of) us, then, it is not because he offers a coherent explanation or even interpretation of our current cultural incoherence but because he denies the authority that the distinction coherence/incoherence has enjoyed in Western thought since Plato (1987, p. 108).

Unfortunately it is Foucault's deliberately obscure style that finds favour in organization studies. The accretion of superfluous theory, such as archaeo-genealogy or social constructionism, is almost a prerequisite for the presentation of historical data in a sufficiently pretentious style. It would be gratuitous to select examples, although thankfully it can be said that Jacques (1996) is not one of them. Foucault reinforces the general antipathy towards narrative in organization studies. Archaeo-genealogy is taken as a license for scholars in organization studies to describe their speculations about the past as historical even if they do not conform to the basic conventions of history, such the provision of extensive references to historical sources or engagement with the relevant historiography.

Jacques (1996, p. 17) blames the 'truth-trap' and the emphasis on 'hypothesis-testing methodology' for 'the near exclusion of the history and sociology of knowledge' from organization studies. It is a characteristic of Foucault and archaeo-genealogical writing that 'truth' and 'facts' are treated as problematic and narrative is seen as an imposition. Much of this amounts to saying that anyone who questions the 'facts' of archaeo-genealogy has missed the point of it. But historians have taken Foucault himself to task for getting 'some of his most important facts wrong', for his 'lop-sided evaluations of historical data', and for his teleological historical explanations (Merquior, 1991, pp. 102-107). In following Foucault's methods for historical research and writing, Jacques is open to similar criticisms from a historical point of view.

At least Jacques can be credited with genuinely following archaeo-genealogy, rather than merely using references to Foucault for ornamentation. It is claimed that archaeo-genealogy allows the historian to undermine beliefs in the inevitability of the present order by reversing its images of the past. The method requires the historian to go back in time until a difference is located (Poster, 1984, p. 89). Jacques does precisely this in his use of *Work and Wealth: Maxims for Merchants and Men of Business*, a book by Freeman Hunt published in 1857. Jacques claims that *Work and Wealth* lacks anything that would be recognizable as 'management knowledge' in the late twentieth century. Therefore, Jacques argues, 'Somewhere between the 1857 publication of *Maxims for Merchants* and the 1913 publication of Andrew Carnegie's *The Empire of Business*, a new reality emerged, a new industrial common sense replaced Hunt's reality' (1996, pp. 20-27). Jacques characterizes the 'world of Freeman Hunt' as being 'Federalist' (p. 39). And albeit with all the usual provisos about periodization, a heroic periodization is offered, in which Jacques alleges that Federalist society lasted from 1790 to 1870 (p. 22).

In Federalist society it was disreputable to be a 'hireling for life'. But Federalist society was undermined in the U.S. in the late nineteenth century as employee status became more prevalent in the population, and workers had less chance of becoming independent (Jacques, 1996, p. 48). Federalist society was displaced by Disciplinary society, a society of organizations, in which the respectability of being a loyal employee needed to be established. It should be noted that this could be said to constitute a 'materialist' explanation for a shift in ideas, rather than the sort of inexplicable rupture that archaeo-genealogy is supposed to favour.

Jacques' account is fascinating, but it is questionable whether Freeman Hunt's book is sufficient evidence to sustain the historical interpretation. Especially since, following archaeo-genealogy (see White, 1987, p. 120; Merquior, 1991, p. 44), Jacques omits any discussion of Hunt's biography or significance, publication itself being taken as evidence enough of the importance of *Work and Wealth*. Which means that it is difficult to assess Jacques' claim that Hunt 'was a good reflection of the business "common sense" of his time' (1996, pp. 26-7). There is no mention of Freeman Hunt in one of the standard textbook histories of management thought (Wren, 1994). But then Jacques, again following archaeo-genealogy, does not engage with the historiography of management thought, or other fields of historiography for that matter.

Take one of Jacques themes, 'Protestant perfectionism'. According to Jacques the American Dream has been reshaped over time, but remains within the same Puritan/Quaker framework that it emerged from in the eighteenth century (1996, p. 21). Jacques traces the 'Puritan/Quaker vision' to mid-seventeenth century England (p. 33), a time and place that constitutes one of the most contested periods in historiography. Yet the only source on English Quakers that Jacques cites is Reay (1985), a follower of the renowned Marxist historian Christopher Hill, whose own work is hardly uncontroversial (see Elton, 1991, pp. 20-3).

Instead of engaging with historiography, Jacques chooses to highlight the inadequate treatment of history in mainstream organization studies textbooks, such as Robbins (1990), which is characterized as 'linear, progressive, teleological and truth-centered' (1996, p. 14). Critical or Marxist histories are said to be 'no less linear, progressive, teleological and truth-centered', than the mainstream textbooks (p. 15), which is an unduly harsh assessment. It could be argued that Jacques fails to distinguish between his critique of organization studies for being a-historical, and an analysis of the rhetoric of competing historical metanarratives, such as Alfred Chandler's monumental work, *The Visible Hand* (1977), or Harry Braverman's *Labour and Monopoly Capital* (1974). When Jacques does mention Chandler, it is merely as a source of historical information, rather than historiographical debate.

Jacques uses two ruses to side step any discussion of the claims of his own metanarrative, which is what his grand periodization amounts to, compared to competing metanarratives. First there is the usual retreat into relativism, so that he claims that he is not presenting his own 'story as superior or these others as "incorrect"' (1996, p. 15). Then he claims that 'Unlike both managerialist and critical histories, which attempt to tell the truth about organizations', his own story 'documents the development, not of organizations, but of knowledge about organizations' (p. 19). This reverses the more familiar criticism of Braverman, and Marx, which is that they take the pronouncements of capitalist ideologues, such as Andrew Ure, Charles Babbage and Frederick Taylor, at face value as evidence of the actual labour process (Elbaum *et al.*, 1979). In other words Jacques is content to analyse the pronouncements of capitalist ideologues rather than the actual labour process.

Jacques warns against 'overly deterministic views of social change' and is critical of deterministic 'pseudo-economic models such as those of population ecology' in organization studies (1996, p. 189). However, Jacques' choice of Foucault as a mentor for writing history makes it difficult for his call for an historical perspective to be aligned with other historical critiques of determinism in organization studies. Jacques hints at unease with his own position when he writes that 'belief in the self-determining individual may be an anachronistic nuisance, but unless human intentionality has the potential to make *some* difference, there is little point in writing or reading books such as this' (p. 189).

It is difficult to reconcile a Foucauldian approach in organization studies with an appeal to 'human intentionality', or for an historical perspective that can be used to identify opportunities for effecting social change (Jacques, 1996, p. viii, 189), when Foucault himself did so much to decentre the sovereign subject and to locate texts in discourses rather than reading them as the outcome of conscious intention. As White observes,

> If we were to follow what Foucault claims to be his own critical principles, we should not be able to refer the whole body of texts, the oeuvre, to any presiding authorial intention, to any originating event in the life of the author, or to the historical context in which the discourse arises (1987, p. 108).

Archaeo-genealogy is probably more compatible with the social constructionism of the new institutionalists (see Shenhav and Weitz, 2000), rather than narrative accounts of human intentionality, insofar as both dissolve the conscious human actor into discourse or institutions (Hirsch and Lounsbury, 1997, p. 84). So, notwithstanding the archaeo-genealogical objections to such questions, it is worth asking why the work of Foucault is so attractive to an author such as Jacques. There is a hint when Jacques reveals that in his business school teaching position he 'quickly learned that power was a peripheral topic and one the savvy management scholar avoided lest s/he be branded insufficiently soft on Marxism' [*sic*, Jacques presumably means that the savvy management scholar should avoid being branded soft on Marxism, or appearing insufficiently hard on Marxism] (p. 1996, xi). What better way to distance oneself from Marxism, while still appearing radical, than to claim, as Jacques does, that, 'like the work of Foucault', his own 'ideology advocates questioning the *status quo*, but it does not to do so within an established "radical" context of seeking to replace one system with another' (pp. xvii).

The welcome for Foucault in organization studies from Jacques and others is a manifestation of the reception from erstwhile radicals for postmodernism, which gained momentum during the 1980s. As Callinicos recalls, this reception:

> ... represented a depoliticization of radical theory, and its aestheticization, so that the critique of bourgeois society was transformed into striking a knowing, ironic attitude towards both the defenders of the status quo and those still benighted enough to wish to overthrow it (1995, p. 180).

Radical thought has been on the defensive since the 1970s, 'compelled to slough off its last Utopian skins under pressure from a growing critique of social constructionism' (Merquior, 1991, p. 158). The displacement of humanistic critiques of the capitalist labour process by Foucauldian analyses of organizational knowledge in organization studies is but one expression of the trend towards the obfuscation of historical metanarratives in which human intentionality plays a leading role.

Conclusion

If organization studies is to acquire an historical perspective then it needs to be recognized that history does not consist of a repository of facts that can be called upon to test or illustrate theories of organization. An historical perspective in organization studies needs to take account of historiographical debates and historical theory. This means that the alternative forms that an historical perspective might take require elaboration. If it is hoped that an historical perspective will facilitate a reorientation of organization studies, then this will probably entail the incorporation of ideas from deconstructionist history, of which there are two main strands, narrative and archaeo-genealogical. There are several reasons why a narrative historical perspective, drawing on White (1987), might be preferred to an archaeo-genealogical historical perspective, derived from Foucault, as a means of reorienting organization studies.

If it is hoped that an historical perspective will facilitate a dialogue between organization studies and historians, then Foucault is hardly the best historical theorist to choose as a mentor, given the longstanding antipathy towards Foucault from practising historians (Poster, 1984, p. 73). While it could hardly be said that White has been unconditionally welcomed by practising historians (Marwick, 1995), it is White rather than Foucault who provides the basis for contemporary debates in historical theory (Fay, Pomper and Vann, 1998). Historians fear that Foucault's version of deconstruction will turn history into endless interpretation of interpretation at the expense of original research, whereas White's advocacy of narrative has restored respect for writing as an essential element of the historian's craft (Evans 1997, p. 98).

If organization studies is to become more historical, then a narrative perspective derived from White is more likely to facilitate reflection on the conventions that separate the genres of writing in history and organization studies. To be fair to Foucault, even if his 'arguments' are virtually incomprehensible, some of his 'histories' are fairly 'straight', as White concedes (1987, p. 140). To that extent Foucault has something in common with most other historians, who usually keep their history separate from their reflections on historical theory. Whereas in organization studies it seems that any presentation of historical data has to be framed by a philosophical essay on the nature of truth and reality. White's version of deconstructionist history is also to be preferred to Foucauldian archaeo-genealogy because it offers the prospect of analysing the rhetoric of both the managerialist and critical metanarratives of management and organization, such as Chandler (1977) and Braverman (1974).

Finally, it is difficult to reconcile Foucauldian archaeo-genealogy with the advocacy of history as a way of facilitating a more ethical or humanistic orientation in organization studies, given Foucault's animosity towards humanism. If an historical perspective is envisaged as a counter to determinism in organization studies, then it is probably narrative history that is required. As Callinicos puts it:

> A theory of history which rejects the idea of inevitability ... needs narrative historiography to gain insight into the situations in which events decisively took one course rather than another (1995, p. 210).

Historians from a variety of persuasions are becoming more interested in narrative and counterfactual history as a counter to determinism in their own discipline (Ferguson, 1997). This may open up opportunities for dialogue with scholars from organization studies who are also concerned to question determinism. But dialogue will be impeded if organization studies becomes too wedded to any of the French philosophers, such as Derrida and Foucault who are anathema to many English-speaking historians, both of the Anglo-Saxon empiricist variety (e.g. Elton, 1991) as well as those of a more Marxian hue (e.g. Hobsbawm, 1997, p. 288 note 8; Callinicos, 1995, p. 180).

References

Ankersmit, F.R. (1998) 'Historiography and Postmodernism' in B. Fay, P. Pomper, and R.T. Vann (eds.) *History and Theory: Contemporary Readings* Oxford, Blackwell.

Barrett, F.J., and S. Srivasta, (1991) 'History as mode of inquiry in organizational life' in *Human Relations* 44(3) pp. 231-254.

Brady, F.N. (1997) 'Finding a History for Management' in *Journal of Management Inquiry* 6(2) pp. 160-167.

Braverman, H. (1974) *Labour and Monopoly Capital* London, Monthly Review Press.

Burrell, G. (1988) 'Modernism, Post Modernism and Organizational Analysis 2: The Contribution of Michel Foucault' in *Organization Studies* 9(2) pp. 221-235.

Burrell, G. (1998) 'The Contribution of Michel Foucault' in McKinlay, A. and Starkey, K. (eds.) *Foucault, Management and Organization Theory* London, Sage.

Callinicos, A. (1989) *Making History* Cambridge, Polity Press.

Callinicos, A. (1995) *Theories and Narratives: Reflections on the Philosophy of History*, Cambridge, Polity Press.

Chandler, A.D. (1977) *The Visible Hand: the Managerial Revolution in American Business* Cambridge, Harvard University Press.

Elbaum, B., W. Lazonick, F. Wilkinson, and J. Zeitlin (1979) 'Symposium: the Labour Process, Market Structure and Marxist Theory' in *Cambridge Journal of Economics* 3, pp. 227-30.

Elton, G.R. (1967) *The Practice of History* London, Fontana.

Elton, G.R. (1991) *Return to Essentials: Some Reflections on the Present State of Historical Study* Cambridge, Cambridge University Press.

Evans, R. (1997) *In Defence of History* London, Granta.

Fay, B. (1998) 'Introduction: The Linguistic Turn and Beyond in Contemporary Theory of History' in Fay, B., P. Pomper, and R.T. Vann (eds.) *History and Theory: Contemporary Readings* Oxford, Blackwell.

Fay, B., P. Pomper, and R.T. Vann (eds.) (1998) *History and Theory: Contemporary Readings* Oxford, Blackwell.

Ferguson, N. (ed.) (1997) *Virtual History: Alternatives and Counterfactuals* London, Papermac.

Goldman, P. (1994) 'Searching for History in Organizational Theory: Comment on Kieser' in *Organization Science* Vol. 5(4) pp. 621-623.

Gubrium, J.F. and Holstein, J.A. (2000) 'Analyzing Interpretive Practice', in N.K. Denzin and Lincoln, Y. S. (eds.) *Handbook of Qualitative Research* (2nd Edition), London, Sage.

Hannah, L. (1984) 'Entrepreneurs and the social sciences' in *Economica* 51 pp. 219-234.

Hassard, J. (1993) *Sociology and Organization Theory: Positivism, Paradigms and Postmodernity* Cambridge, Cambridge University Press.

Hirsch, P.M. and Lounsbury, M. (1997) 'Putting the Organization Back Into Organization Theory: Action, Change and the "New" Institutionalism' in *Journal of Management Inquiry* 6(1) pp. 79-88.

Hobsbawm, E. (1997) *On History* London, Weidenfield and Nicolson.

Hoskin, K. (1998) 'Examining Accounts and Accounting for Management: Inverting Understandings of "the Economic"' in McKinlay, A. and Starkey, K. (eds.), *Foucault, Management and Organization Theory* London, Sage.

Jacques, R. (1996) *Manufacturing the Employee: Management Knowledge from the 19th to 21st Centuries* London, Sage.

Jeremy, D. (1999) 'Do Managers Need Business History? Business History Workshop' British Academy of Management Conference, Manchester Metropolitan University, England.

Jones, S.R.H. (1997) 'Transaction Costs and the Theory of the Firm' in *Business History* 39 pp. 9-25.

Kieser, A. (1994) 'Why Organization Theory Needs Historical Analyses – and How This Should be Performed' in *Organization Science* 5(4) pp. 608-620.

Knights, D., and Willmott, H. (2000) *The Reengineering Revolution: Critical Studies of Corporate Change* London, Sage.

Lamoreaux, N.R., Raff, D.M.G. and Temin, P. (1997) 'New Economic Approaches to the Study of Business History' in *Business and Economic History*, 26(1) pp. 57-79.

McCloskey, D.N. (1990) *If You're So Smart: The Narrative of Economic Expertise* Chicago, University of Chicago Press.

McKinlay, A. and Starkey, K. (1998) 'Managing Foucault: Foucault, Management and Organization Theory' in McKinlay, A. and Starkey, K. (eds.), *Foucault, Management and Organization Theory* London, Sage.

Marglin, S. (1976 [1974]) 'What do Bosses Do? The Origins and Functions of Hierarchy in Capitalist Production' in Gorz, A. (ed.), *The Division of Labour and Class Struggle in Modern Capitalism* Brighton, Harvester.

Marwick, A. (1995) 'Two Approaches to Historical Study: the Metaphysical (including Postmodernism) and the Historical' in *Journal of Contemporary History* 30 pp. 5-35.

Merquior, J.G. (1991) *Foucault* (2nd Edition) London, Fontana.

Munslow, A. (1997) *Deconstructing History* London, Routledge.

Poster, M. (1984) *Foucault, Marxism and History* Cambridge, Polity.

Reay, B. (1985) *Quakers in the English Revolution* London, Temple Smith.

Robbins, S.P. (1990) *Organizational Behavior* London, Prentice Hall.

Roy, W.R. (1990) 'Functional and Historical Logics in Explaining the Rise of the American Corporation' in *Comparative Social Research* 12 pp. 19-44.

Schama, S. (1989) *Citizens: A Chronicle of the French Revolution* Harmondsworth, Penguin.

Shenhav, Y. and Weitz, E. (2000) 'The Roots of Uncertainty in Organization Theory: A Historical Constructivist Analysis' in *Organization* 7(3) pp. 373-401.

Stinchcombe, A. (1990) *Information and Organizations* Berkeley, University of California Press.

Swedberg, R. and M. Granovetter, (eds.) (1992) *The Sociology of Economic Life* Oxford, Westview Press.

White, H. (1987) *The Content of the Form: Narrative Discourse and Historical Representation* London, John Hopkins University Press.

White, H. (1995) 'Response to Marwick' in *Journal of Contemporary History* 30 pp. 233-246.

Wren, D. (1994) *The Evolution of Management Thought* Chichester, John Wiley and Sons.

Zald, D. (1993) 'Organization Studies as Scientific and Humanistic Enterprise: Toward a Reconceptualization of the Foundations of the Field' in *Organization Science* 4(4) pp. 513-528.

Chapter 3

Deconstructing the Employee: A Critique of the Gendered American Dream

David Crowther and Anne-marie Greene

Introduction

One of the principal tenets of the colonization of organizational thought by American notions of idealism is predicated in the concept of the American Dream. One platform of this Dream is based upon the notion of the frontier (Jacques, 1996) with its implications of limitless resources and the ability to attain the 'good life' without the subjugation of one's fellow men.[1] Thus the Dream can be actualized by all, without the need for competition, merely through industry and application and regardless of gender, race or any other social category. The closing of that frontier might have initially appeared to negate this promise of bounty for all, but in fact it merely led to the seeking of new frontiers; these arose through the prospect of colonization of other parts of the world, the possibilities of extension into space, and the development of cyberspace. Thus the frontier continues open for colonization and only requires the exertion of effort for the fruits to be manifest. As Jacques (1996, p. 24) states: 'America *means* escape from the limits of zero-sum; on the frontier, everyone can have more than their share.'

At the same time a further platform of this Dream is based upon the ideals of the family and its associated values, symptomized by the concept of 'Mom's apple pie'. The ideal of the family necessarily implies the idea of the separation of work from the family, with work being for men while the establishment and maintenance of the family was for the women. In this way therefore women are written out of the benefits of the limitless frontier, except through their association with the men who are destined, depending upon their efforts, to reap the rewards of their industry. For Jacques (1996) therefore the world of work becomes a masculine world, which for him is focused upon the organization, as the organization exists to accumulate the benefits which exist from frontier extension. He states:

> Male businesses centred on character underwent a masculinization into practices centred on scientific objectivity and Darwinian competition ... .This is not to say that relational practices[2] have been eliminated from organizations. They have, however, become relatively invisible because they do not constitute objects of knowledge, the basis for reward or a source of authority (Jacques, 1996, pp. 177-178).

More recently however the discourse of organizational theory has been extended to include the ideas of masculine and feminine. Although the terms 'male' and 'masculine', as well as 'female' and 'feminine', are used interchangeably, Burke and Nelson (1998, pp. 227-228) argue that 'there is a critical distinction between maleness [or femaleness], as a biologically determined state, and masculinity [or femininity], a socially constructed state'. Indeed, West and Zimmerman (1991) see gender as an 'achieved status' constructed through social, cultural and psychological means. For West and Zimmerman (1991), gender is the product of social interaction or 'social doings' within the context of a larger social system. Thus, men and women acquire 'appropriate' sex roles through socialization. These sex roles embrace a set of attitudes, behaviours and attributes that are seen as normal or appropriate for a man or a woman (Burke and Nelson, 1998).

Since masculinity and femininity are socially constructed, then the views of males and females of these sex roles is likely to vary. Cheng (1996), for example, acknowledges variations in what men see as constituting masculinity as a function of their age, social class, race, sexual orientation, and intelligence, among other factors. Gender is also seen as dynamic, yet constrained by history and culture (Burke and Nelson, 1998). For Kimmel (1996, p. 120) gender is 'a constantly changing collection of meanings that we construct through relationships with ourselves, with each other and with our world'. Nevertheless, research appears to reveal commonality in what are seen as the characterizing features of masculinity and femininity; masculinity is associated with task and instrumentality, femininity with emotions and interpersonal relationships (Bem, 1974).

Organizational life is characterized by gendered structures and systems (Collinson and Hearn, 1995; Mills and Tancred, 1992). Given the historical hegemony of males within organizations, it is not surprising that research has highlighted a masculine bias in organizations that favours men while limiting the progress and developmental opportunities for women (Burton 1992; Maier 1992). Indeed this bias is reflected in the rituals of organizational behaviour which can be traced back (Campbell 1997) in time to the superseding of the hunter-gatherer way of life by the seed planting and growing way of life of primitive tribes. This change in societal organization effectively resulted in the supplanting of men as the principal food collectors by women, and resulted in the development of male rituals to both occupy the time of men and to separate them from women. This separation necessarily implied superiority as only the males could participate in these rituals. This superiority of maleness, through inclusion of it in the rituals of separation, can be traced through history in the rites of the Christian church and the medieval guild system to the rites of organizational existence in the present. These rites continue to exclude women and thereby preserve male hegemony.

We extend upon Jacques' (1996) analysis, exploring the utility of the androgynous ideal in management knowledge discourses. First, we present an alternative viewpoint, exploring a significant arena of management knowledge missing from Jacques analysis, that of the American Shaker communities. This provides an alternative to the patriarchy of Fordist management practices, indicating an egalitarian separation of work between the genders (Conway and

Crowther, 1999) and a model of more androgynous management. We then move the analysis forward to the 1990s, where we discuss the implications of our foregoing analysis for a recent transplant of American management knowledge; the construction of 'managing diversity' as a new way forward for equal opportunities and equality policies within management practice (Kandola and Fullerton, 1994; Liff, 1996; Webb, 1997, Kirton and Greene, 2000). In its 'difference' approach, 'managing diversity' attempts to play down the importance of gender differentials, and is therefore, in essence, an attempt to provide an androgynous management model. However, we offer a critique of this latest American management 'fad', indicating the detrimental effects on the experience of women in the workplace, which derive from its continued patriarchal discourse and neglect of the historically situated gender relations which underlie management practice.

The Shaker Experience

For Jacques (1996), one of the forces for the development of the American Dream was that of religion, with various religious groups migrating from Europe to the freedom on the new world. He classifies such diverse groups as Protestants and Quakers, and goes on to state that they were anti-democratic, hierarchical and motivated to create their individual ideas of a perfect society in which they had freedom to practice their beliefs. Of the Quakers in particular he states:

> Rather than removing status differences, the vision of these empirical Utopians was a society without the extremes of aristocratic privilege or subproletarian poverty (Jacques, 1996, p. 34).

In this way therefore, he views these religious migrants as being in perfect accord with the ideals of the American Dream but subsumes their ideals within the general masculinity of his analysis of the development of American organizational life. Our analysis however shows that one of these movements escaping from European persecution is indeed significant to an understanding of alternatives to the masculine ideals of the Dream. This group is the Shakers, who are ignored by Jacques (1996), except for a passing mention (p. 58) of them as an 'anti-industrial communistic experiment'. This is, in our view, a serious omission from this analysis, as the Shakers point the way to an alternative method of structuring society and its organizations which challenges the conventional gendering of that society.

The Shakers form an interesting and instructive arena for studying organizational form. At one level, possibly the ultimate gendering of an organization and its activity can be evidenced by the Shaker communities (Andrews 1953; Andrews and Andrews 1974). In these communities all work was gendered to such an extent that the men and women within the community not only undertook separate tasks but also completely separated their lives and activities within the community. Thus within a Shaker community the men and women lived in parallel with each other to such an extent that the communal buildings constituted mirror images of themselves, with one half inhabited by men and the other half inhabited by women. Indeed this separation is manifest in the ultimate through an invisible line running down the centre of the building beyond which a member of the community would not step into the other domain. This separation was also evidenced in the hierarchy of the organizational structure whereby two distinct hierarchies co-existed alongside each other – one for men and the other for women – with neither being superior to the other. The Shakers can therefore be considered to be both highly gendered in their organizational structure and also highly androgynous, as the biological component of sex was removed from their organizational life. What is significant however about the Shakers is that this divide of duties and of life was not hierarchical in that no work was considered to be of higher value than any other. Thus the paths followed by men and by women were different[3] but equal. Consequently, the organization of the communities also involved double hierarchies with one man and one woman as the joint leaders of each community.

In terms of considering the economic development of life in pursuance of the American Dream it is important to recognize that the Shakers were highly effective as an organization in their time. They were not anti-industrial but were responsible for a number of inventions in terms of economic activity, such as the invention of the washing machine. They were also responsible for both the development of herbal medicine and the development of a pre-packed distribution system for seeds. Moreover they developed means of production which were predicated in the saving of labour and were responsible for the creation of furniture and devices which were not just aesthetically pleasing but highly functional and efficient. For them the limitless resources of an open frontier did not lead to profligacy but to the efficient use of both resources and human effort. This model therefore provides an example of the efficacy of androgyny in organizational life, which is built upon the establishment of a completely androgynous mode of operation predicated in separate development. Thus the Shakers can be considered to depict both the ultimate in gendering and the ultimate in degendering of organizational life.

This mode of organizing had demonstrable benefits for the Shakers and for the development of the American Dream but has been written out of modern analyses and therefore is not deemed worthy of even a mention by Jacques (1996). Such a model does not lend itself to the cultural mores of the modern time and modern organizational theory. It therefore has become necessary to reconsider the feminization of organizations, rather then to consider this androgynous model. Thus in the present Burke and Nelson (1998, pp. 232-233) argue that 'men believe that this masculine model of management, rewarded in organizational structures, is the best and right way to manage' and yet they see this situation as problematic in a number of ways: firstly, as a consequence, feminine approaches to management are devalued; secondly, female managers who are required to imitate male behaviour encounter a double-bind since they are also criticized for behaving like males; and thirdly, masculine styles of management also limit the behaviours of men. Burke and Nelson note that:

Masculine management tends to be associated with qualities of average/typical managers, whereas androgynous management – a combination of both masculine and feminine behaviours – is often associated with qualities of effective managers – [and] is potentially advantageous since it allows individuals the freedom and flexibility to exhibit male- or female-typed attributes in response to a given situation (1998, p. 234).

From a feminist perspective, androgynous management has a part to play in addressing the undervalued role of women in organizations. From a managerialist perspective, androgynous management has the potential to improve organizational effectiveness by embracing femininity, and this was significant during a period of the development of the American Dream.

'Managing Diversity': The New Androgyny?

The interest in looking at the Shaker form of management is that threads of its ideal androgynous model can be found in more modern forms of management discourse. As an example, we examine the recent emergence of the 'managing diversity' discourse. Discussions of 'diversity' are explored by Jacques (1996), most notably looking at the difficulty of submerging diversity discourses within the existing gendered notions of management knowledge. For example, given the ideal of the American Dream: 'in a society of equals, how does one legitimate difference?' (Jacques, 1996, p. 72).

Jacques (1996) notes that diversity emerged as a topic for organization studies in the late 1980s, with the main theme being that people are essentially equal once individual differences (such as race, gender, disability) are controlled for. In its most recent incarnation as 'managing diversity', the term is located in the USA from 1987, when an influential report, *Workforce 2000,* by Johnston and Packer, identified the increasing heterogeneity of the American workforce, pointing to the fact that by the year 2000, white male employees would make up a minority of new entrants to the labour force (Kandola and Fullerton, 1994). At the heart of the 'managing diversity' discourse is the belief that organizations should recognize differences rather than deny or dilute them (Liff, 1996). There is a move away from the idea that different groups should be assimilated to meet an organizational norm. The employer is expected to be committed to creating a workplace which facilitates the inclusion of different social categories and enables everyone to contribute in their own way, to the business (Webb, 1997). In this way, rather than difference being viewed negatively, there should be a recognition of the inherent strengths of employees based on their cultural background, gender or age, or differential experience (Chen, 1992). Difference is thus viewed positively, looking at the benefits to the organization, which could derive from different perspectives and approaches and seeing that differences should be nurtured and rewarded rather than suppressed (Liff and Wajcman, 1996). This essentially distinguishes the managing diversity discourse from older liberal and radical equal opportunities approaches to equality and inequality (Kirton and Greene, 2000; Jewson and Mason, 1986; Cockburn, 1989).

The 'managing diversity' discourse, can be viewed as androgynous, in that there is a shift in emphasis from social groups to a focus on individuals, such that 'managing diversity' does not recognize the collective force of disadvantaged groups such as those based upon gender. In other words, all differences are viewed on the same or similar terms; none are seen as more salient than others in leading to disadvantage in the workplace. Kandola and Fullerton's (1994) definition of the 'Managing Diversity' approach makes the case that a wider range of differences are taken into consideration than liberal or radical equal opportunities approaches. However, such differences are viewed equally, so that personality or characteristics such as 'workstyle' are seen as being as significant as, and independent of, gender or ethnicity (Kirton and Greene, 2000). This not only fits with the 'society of equals' view of the American Dream, but in the case of gender differences, can be seen as androgynous, in that, as with the Shakers, there is no hierarchy; both male and female, masculine and feminine are to be equally valued.

However, it is interesting then to debate whether such an androgynous discourse is to be seen as a positive force in gaining greater equality in organizations. Firstly, in line with Jacques (1996), it is difficult to legitimate the diversity discourse if American society is seen as one of equals. Such assertions therefore imbue the 'managing diversity' discourse, continuing to uphold the American Dream of equality, implicitly presupposing that equality already exists so that difference can be celebrated. This in essence is one of the central problems with the diversity discourse as it has been popularly disseminated. As Thomas (1990) points out, you cannot 'manage diversity' unless you have a diverse workforce to begin with; in other words, that equality of outcome already exists and is testified to in a fair distribution of jobs, rewards and resources. One major difficulty with the 'Managing Diversity' approach therefore, is that it is introspective, focusing more on the movement of people *within* organizations rather than the problems existing in the wider labour market (Miller, 1996). There are obviously more factors involved in the perpetuation of disadvantage, than direct discrimination at entry level to organizations. Wider workplace values and fundamental human assumptions are very difficult to manage. Just as there are inherent contradictions between the American Dream of equality and the American 'Reality' of inequality, so too are these inherent contradictions filtered through into the managing diversity dream.

Secondly, given the incongruence between difference and equality within the American Dream, the emphasis on difference within the managing diversity discourse may have detrimental implications. There are inherent dangers in that emphasizing the differences which exist could be used to reassert inferiority and justifiable exclusion (Webb, 1997). Indeed, Webb uses a quote from Cockburn (1991, p. 219), which points out that there is little room for difference *not* to be constructed as something inferior, stating 'the dominant group know you are different and continue to treat you as different, but if you yourself specify your difference, your claim to equality will be null'. Thus a diversity approach may give ammunition to those who feel that being 'different' to the dominant norm, disqualifies members of certain groups from equality, allowing differences to be used in a way which is detrimental to equality (Liff, 1996). In support of this viewpoint, recent research indicates the importance of group identity and membership in supporting the struggle against unfair discrimination (Greene and Kirton, 2000).

Discussions elsewhere of the implications of the denial of the importance of collective disadvantage (in the case of gender, the androgynous nature of the discourse) are salient here. We agree with a view that the campaign for equality needs the force of political and collective action to have any profound or lasting effect (Greene and Kirton, 2000; Dickens, 1997). What an emphasis on differences between individuals does is to weaken the ties that people have through common experience that provide the necessary support to push for action (Greene and Kirton, 2000), essentially leaving people alone and isolated in their struggle (Cockburn, 1989). Rather than being empowering then, the ideal model of 'Managing Diversity' is disempowering, dissolving collective identity and strength.

The extent of practice of 'managing diversity' is also limited (Webb, 1997). Whilst a 'managing diversity' approach has been claimed by numerous organizations in Britain and the USA, there is a lack of evidence indicating the success of such an approach. Indeed Webb (1997) finds that, while her case study firm proclaimed a 'managing diversity' philosophy, the policies introduced offered no challenge to the structure and culture of the organization. In fact, in contrast to the rhetoric, the policies tended to reflect more of a 'sameness' agenda, where recruitment and training were open to all, and managers saw the lack of women responding, and continued occupational sex segregation, as evidence of women's choices, rather than recognizing the role of the existing culture in constructing barriers. Rees (1998) states that in practice, there can be short and long agendas (Cockburn, 1989) of 'managing diversity'. There is a need for organizational cultures to be 'transformed', building upon the politics of difference. But this is clearly no easy task, especially when organizations face myriad pressures such as from competition in the market or from periods of recession. Thus many organizations simply have polices of 'tinkering' or 'tailoring' existing initiatives and procedures which do not challenge the inherent inequalities within the structures, systems and cultures. Overall, Webb (1997) claims that what 'Managing Diversity' tends to mean is market-driven and politically unthreatening equal opportunities, which fits more with the wider trends towards flexibility.

Such a lack of transformation is recognized by Jacques;

> Even in a hypothetical, 'androgynous' world, where gender disparities between men and women in the workplace were completely remedied, this devaluation of the 'feminine' sphere of domestic labour and relational work would be untouched. In the masculinized workplace of the industrial society, women and men can be equalized *only be giving both the status of men* (1996, p. 85, original italics).

Such assertions stand as current criticisms of the 'managing diversity' discourse (Webb, 1997; Liff, 1996; Kirton and Greene, 2000) exactly as they did for other management knowledge discourses by Jacques (1996).

Conclusion

The American Shaker communities challenge the conventional 'American Dream', rendering gender differences as neutral, and removing the hierarchy from domestic and public spheres of work. However, this is made possible because the Shakers deliberately removed themselves from conventional American society and consequently from the American Dream. While management knowledge discourses of diversity (within the wider politically neutral discourse of human resource management) take on such androgynous rhetoric, it is unworkable, and in direct contradiction with the dominant society in which it is supposed to be utilized. Therefore, managing diversity, as a discourse, is neither successful in advancing the equality agenda, nor in challenging the existing status quo, indeed it can be seen as positively detrimental to those most disadvantaged in society.

Management knowledge discourses implicitly uphold structures and organizations that perpetuate and collude with, the masculinized American Dream. Challenging inequality within modern industrial society requires a transformative challenge tantamount to the separation from society utilized by the Shakers. As Jacques states:

> To 'do diversity' seriously would mean rethinking the dominant philosophy and methodology of organizational science to accommodate, not simply other *data*, but other *ways of understanding data* (1996, p. 173, original italics).

However, there appears little evidence as yet that such a transformation is possible, or even desired by the proponents of such management knowledges. We conclude therefore that, despite the evidence from the Shaker mode of organizing, androgynous organizational forms remain excluded from the mainstream of organizational theory due to the dominance of the ideals of the American Dream.

Notes

[1] The word men is used deliberately as this discourse, coupled with the concept of family values, effectively excludes women from any participation in the benefits arising from this limitless frontier.

[2] He had previously stated that relational responsibility is the role assigned to women.

[3] Indeed these paths were physical as well as spiritual, with different paths trodden by the members of the communities according to their sex.

References

Andrews, E.D. (1953) *The People Called Shakers* New York, Dover Publications.

Andrews, E.D. and Andrews, F. (1974) *Work and Worship among the Shakers* New York, Dover Publications.

Bem, S. (1974) 'The Measurement of Psychological Androgyny' in *Journal of Personality and Social Psychology* 42 pp. 155-162.

Burke, R.J. and Nelson, D.L. (1998) 'Organizational Men: Masculinity and its Discontents' in *International Review of Industrial and Organizational Psychology* 14 pp. 225-271.

Burrell, G. (1984) 'Sex and organizational analysis' in *Organization Studies* 5 pp. 97-118.

Burton, C. (1992) 'Merit and Gender: Organizations and the Mobilization of Masculine Bias' in Mills, A.J. and Tancred, P. (eds.) *Gendering Organizational Analysis* Newbury Park, CA, Sage.

Campbell, J. (1997) *The Mythic Dimension: Selected Essays 1959-1987* New York, Harper Collins.

Cheng, C. (1996) *Masculinities in Organizations* Thousand Oaks, CA, Sage.

Cianni, M. and Romberger, B. (1997) 'Life in the Corporation: A Multi-Method Study of the Experiences of Male and Female Asian, Black, Hispanic and White Employees' in *Gender, Work and Organization*, 4(2).

Cockburn, C. (1989) 'Equal Opportunities: the Long and Short Agenda' in *Industrial Relations Journal*, Autumn pp. 213-225.

Cockburn, C. (1991) *In the Way of Women* Basingstoke, Macmillan.

Collinson, D.L. and Hearn, J. (1995) 'Men Managing Leadership? Men and Women of the Corporation Revisited' in *International Review of Women and Leadership* 1 pp. 1-24.

Conway, S. and Crowther, D. (1999) 'Shaking the Masculine Organization: Inspirations from History and Science Fiction for the De-gendering of Organizations', paper presented to Science Fiction and Organization Conference; Leicester; Sept 1999.

Dickens, L. (1997) 'Gender, Race and Employment Equality in Britain: Inadequate Strategies and the Role of Industrial Relations Actors' in *Industrial Relations Journal* 28(4) pp. 282-289.

Greene, A.M. and Kirton, G. (2000) 'Managing Diversity: A New Way Forward? A Trade Union Perspective' paper presented to the British Academy of Management Conference (BAM2000), Edinburgh, September.

Jacques, R. (1996), *Manufacturing the Employee: Management Knowledge from the 19th to the 21st Centuries* London, Sage.

Jewson, N. and Mason, D. (1986), 'The Theory and Practice of Equal Opportunities Policies: Liberal and Radical Approaches' in *The Sociological Review* 34(2) pp. 307-34.

Kandola, R. and Fullerton, J. (1994) *Managing the Mosaic: Diversity in Action* London, Institute of Personnel and Development.

Kimmel, M.S. (1996) *Manhood in America* New York, Free Press.

Kirton, G. and Greene, A.M. (2000) *The Dynamics of Managing Diversity: A Critical Text* London, Butterworth-Heinemann.

Liff, S. (1996) 'Two Routes to Managing Diversity: Individual Differences or Social Group Characteristics' in *Employee Relations* 19(1) pp. 11-26.

Maier, M. (1992) 'Evolving the Paradigms of Management in Organizations: A Gender Analysis' in *Journal of Management Systems* 4 pp. 29-45.

Mills, A.J. and Tancred, P.S. (1992) *Gendering Organizational Analysis* Newbury Park, CA, Sage.

Thomas, R. (1990) 'From Affirmative Action to Affirming Diversity' in *Harvard Business Review*, March.

Webb, J. (1997) 'The Politics of Equal Opportunity' in *Gender, Work and Organization*, 4(3) pp. 159-167.

West, C. and Zimmerman, D.H. (1991) 'Doing Gender' in Lorber, J. and Farrell, S.A. (eds.) *The Social Construction of Gender* Sage, Newbury Park, CA pp. 13-37.

Chapter 4

Feminist Organizational Analysis and the Business Textbook[1]

Albert J. Mills

Introduction

Male dominance of business has not remained unchallenged, particularly in regard to discriminatory practices. There have been numerous challenges to workplace inequities that have resulted in important changes in employment legislation throughout industrial society. Similar challenges have developed within business education, with the growth of feminist organizational analysis (e.g., Ferguson, 1984), including women in management approaches to managing (e.g., Henning and Jardin, 1977). Nonetheless, Jacques (1996) and others (Collinson and Collinson, 1997; Maier, 1997; Martin, 1996; Martin and Collinson, 2002) contend that, business practice continues to be dominated by masculinist discourse. This is evidenced in a number of recent studies of the cultural values and nuances of organizations (cf. Bruni and Gherardi, 2002; Wicks and Bradshaw, 2002), projected images of particular companies (Benschop and Meihuizen, 2002), media images of business as a whole (Sharp, 2003), and workplace segregation and occupational identity (Greene *et al.*, 2002).

Perhaps, as Jacques (1996) counsels, we should not be surprised that masculinist discourse continues to dominate organizational realities. Pointing out, 'women in the workplace have achieved organizational prominence to the degree that they have been able to work within the norms of that organization', Jacques (1996, p. 178) goes on to ask, 'How the industrial transformation of society has interacted with gendered sex role socialization to marginalize, not women, but the entire domain of relational practice?' Part of the search, according to Jacques, is to be found in processes of social codification whereby certain activities become viewed as inappropriate to the workplace. Thus, the problem of such things as employment equity and gender identity at work 'cannot be solved by increasing the numbers of women in the workplace if both men's and women's workplace credibility is contingent upon the suppression of "domestic" and "feminine" relational practices' (Jacques, 1996, p. 179).

In the search for how certain gendered codifications develop this chapter examines three intersecting aspects of current business discourse – organizational change programmes, the development of feminist theories of organizational analysis and their respective representation in the business text.

As a number of scholars have observed, management theory of the past twenty-five years has been dominated by popular theories of organizational change (Abrahamson, 1996; Jackson, 2001; Kieser, 1997). This has reflected the widespread adoption by companies of corporate culture change programmes, Total Quality Management (TQM), Business Process Reengineering (BPR) and, more recently, Balanced Scorecard and Six Sigma programmes. The rapid adoption of each of these programmes in turn has led some organizational scholars to question their viability as mere fads and fashions (Abrahamson, 1996; Kieser, 1997). Helms Mills (2003) contends that what we are witnessing is an 'imperative' of change, whereby managers feel almost compelled to be seen as on the cutting edge of change, and thus as 'good' leaders, by adopting the newest change programme. She suggests that, despite its detractors within academia, the imperative of change is encouraged through the complex relationships between 'educators, prophets, and missionaries', by which she means, respectively, business professors, consultants, and change agents (Helms Mills, 2003, pp. 106-111). Managers make sense of their change environment through exposure to the heralded 'successes' of practices in other companies through such things as popular 'how to' books, management consultants, and the legitimacy of management training and education.

In the later regard the textbook occupies a central position within the process of management education. For most North American business students their first introduction to management and workplace behaviour is through a textbook. It is through the business textbook that students gain their first glimpse of the theorized employee. I say 'theorized' because clearly students will have some experience of employees per se but not systematic ways of viewing the employee as such. I also say 'glimpse' because recent evidence suggests that the individual has all but disappeared from organizational studies (Nord and Fox, 1996). Indeed, the notion of the (ideal) employee is inferred through discussion of various privileged behaviours and structuring arrangements. Such inferences are themselves framed in a way that encourages the student reader to see his or her self as *the manager* of the various work processes, in control of the elusive employee. It is through the textbook that a range of theories and practices are distilled and simplified as an introduction to the 'business world'. It may not be the only influence on the fledgling manager, employee or future business educator but it will be an important influence given the significance of the textbook within processes of business education.

In distilling current management research for textbook production organizational change has been one of many developments for consideration by the textbook author. Over the same period of thirty years a number of other developments in management research have vied for attention, including the development of feminist critique and the growth of feminist organizational analysis (Mills and Tancred, 1992). In this chapter analysis of 128 North American business textbooks compares the extent to which feminist theories of organization and mainstream theories of organizational change are incorporated into textbook production of 'the business world' and what conclusions can be drawn.

Gendering Organizational Analysis Revisited

The 1992 edited collection, *Gendering Organizational Analysis* set out to reveal the gendered character of organizational analysis. Through selected previously published texts and new contributions, the collection presented a picture of organizational analysis as malestream, framed by a masculinist view of reality, in a field dominated by male researchers, and male oriented research. The collection documented the 'sex structuring of organizations'; 'sex power differentials' and the problem of organizational research; the marginalization of the female researcher; the 'neglect of gender' in organizational research; 'sex' as an organizational problematic; the relationship between organization, gender and culture; work and 'sex-role spillover'; state bureaucracy and gender discrimination; women and masculinist perceptions of management and managing; masculine bias and merit; and women and cultures of resistance. Moving beyond feminist accounts focussed on dichotomous notions of women and men in organizations, the collection included chapters dealing with issues of post-feminism and race. The primary aim of the collection was to contribute to a growing body of feminist organizational analysis that was forcing a rethink of the field.

This retrospective seeks to assess developments within organizational analysis over the last twenty-five years. In particular the chapter will examine the influence of feminism on mainstream organizational analysis, in particular the extent to which feminist research informs construction of the business textbook. Strategies for improving feminist intervention in mainstream organizational analysis are identified and discussed.

Feminism and the Mainstream

Feminist analyses of organization are not new. More than a quarter of a century has passed since the publication of Acker and Van Houten's (1974) feminist critique of mainstream organizational analysis, and more than two decades since the publication of Kanter's (1977) study of the relationship between gender and organizational structuring. Indeed the last quarter of the Twentieth Century witnessed a tremendous flowering of feminist studies of organization and a strong presence of feminist researchers within the Academy of Management and, to a much lesser extent, the Administrative Sciences Association of Canada (ASAC) In 1992 *Gendering Organizational Analysis* (Mills and Tancred, 1992) attempted to reflect and to further a field of study that had come of age.

Thus, as we review the central outlets of mainstream studies of organization and management (e.g., academic journals, business text books, etc.) we should expect to find feminist organizational analysis reflected in the comments, references and subject-matter of numerous theorists. That this is far from the case raises serious concerns and a need for review.

Gender and the Management Text

There is good news and bad news. A 1999 review of '107 widely used North American business texts published between 1959 and 1996' concluded that, 'the typical business or management text constitutes a narrative that is built around a white, male, liberal American view of reality' (Mills and Helms Hatfield, 1998, p. 37). That is clearly the bad news, especially given the fact that:

> Of the 107 texts reviewed, the overwhelming majority – including 18 published in the 1990s – have little (65) or nothing (37) to say about women, gender or even sex differences. Only five texts (...) discuss the issue of gender in any depth... The majority of references to gender differences are introduced by way of discussion of employment equity legislation or the 'growing number of women in the work force' – with women being depicted in each case as a departure from the male work norm; something of note for male managers... (Mills and Helms Hatfield, 1998, p. 55).

The good news is that the majority of post-1990 business texts include 'a fuller discussion of gender', but even this is tempered by the fact that these texts 'fail to discuss the implications for understanding organizational behaviour (e.g. the effect of gender on culture, motivation, stress, communication, etc.) And even among the better texts, gender – along with race, age, sexual preference and ethnicity – is becoming subsumed under 'diversity' and problematized anew' (Mills and Helms Hatfield, 1998, p. 56).

Moreover, an in-depth analysis of six business texts published between 1992 and 1996 and widely in use in North America, found that:

> Where it is discussed at all, gender is seen ... as something that strictly pertains to women and, as such, an aberration from the norm – something to be dealt with, managed, or prepared for. Nevertheless, the indexes of two of the texts fail even to include any reference to women and the remaining ones devote less than 20 out of a total of approximately 2900 pages (0.7 per cent) to discussing women. One of these works uses less than 35 lines to discuss such issues as employment equity, 'female leadership styles', the number of women in the workforce, female self employment, and sexual harassment. Another text devotes 4 (0.6 per cent) of its nearly 700 pages to discussing women and mentoring, female advancement in a bank, workplace diversity, and issues of gender and equity, leadership, negotiation and stereotyping. The two more comprehensive texts devote a little more than one percent of their pages to gender issues, but in both cases gender is equated with women, and women are equated with organizational difficulties. In none of the texts are men, males or masculinity discussed as organizational issues or problems. Employment equity, sexual harassment and workplace diversity, for example, are viewed as 'problems' associated with women (Mills and Simmons, 1999, p. 20).

Feminist Research and the Business Text

Most North American business students are introduced to specific subjects by way of a textbook. The standard textbook attempts to summarize and explain in simple terms a range of studies, analyses and findings within the field of study. In business, commerce or administrative studies, students learn about management and organization through such diverse subject areas (and associated texts) as introduction to business, management, organizational behaviour, organizational theory and human resources management. Although textbooks purportedly address many of the key issues, findings, and debates within a field, analysis reveals that they, in fact, tend to reflect the dominant paradigm to the exclusion of others. For example, Burrell and Morgan's (1979) groundbreaking work on organizational paradigms discussed at length the contribution of a range of approaches that they went on to group under four paradigms; functionalist, interpretive, radical humanist and radical structuralist. Feminist critiques of Burrell and Morgan (1979) question the absence of a feminist paradigm (Hearn and Parkin, 1983). More recent accounts suggest the existence of feminist, postmodernist and racio-ethnicity paradigms (Mills and Simmons, 1998) Notwithstanding, the student of today will be hard pressed to find discussion of anything beyond the 'functionalist' approach in the pages of the business textbook.

To discover the extent to which feminist organizational analyses have affected management thinking, I undertook content analysis of 128 business textbooks published between 1960 and 2000. I particularly examined 100 texts published since Virginia Schein's (1973) early work on managerial sex role stereotyping.

For the first stage of the research, a list was established of key feminist works in the field of organizational analysis. The list of 57 references, constructed by a single researcher, was not intended to be an all-inclusive reference list, but rather some measure of the extent to which feminist research is cited in mainstream business textbooks. To ensure a broader reflection of feminist organizational analyses, several internationally prominent feminist scholars, who publish in English, were asked for their suggestions: 'Which, in your opinion, are 5 of the more significant feminist studies of organization/management to appear in the last 25 years?' Interpretation of the question was left up to respondents. Thirteen feminist scholars replied (five from the United States, two each from Sweden, Canada, and the United Kingdom, and one each from Finland and the Netherlands) While most suggested five article or book titles, some suggested the generic work of certain authors. Excluding overlapping references, this generated a list of eighty-four journal and book titles and fourteen named authors (see Appendix 1) to be used as the basis for tracing feminist work within mainstream business texts. Again this list was to serve only as a guide to the extent to which selected feminist work is referenced.

For the second stage of the research, the indexes of a number of selected business texts and journals were analyzed. The objective was to gauge: a) whether or to what extent (selected) feminist research is cited, and b) how soon after publication (selected) feminist research get cited in business texts.

For the third stage, a list was drawn up of theoretical approaches (e.g., population ecology, Business Process Reengineering) and specific theorists (e.g., Herbert Simon, Michael Hammer) that had affected mainstream organizational and management analysis (see Appendix 2). The goal was to track: a) the extent to which they are referenced in business textbooks, and b) the time frame from publication of a selected mainstream theory to its referencing in a business text.

For the fourth stage, a count was done of the top five referenced authors in the indexes of each business textbook.

The last two stages allow for comparison of the textbook treatment of selected mainstream theories and feminist work in the field of management and organizational study.

Results: Positive Trends

Content analysis indicated that:

- Feminist organizational research is being cited in mainstream business texts.
- Citations to feminist organizational research are increasing in numbers, particularly since the early 1990s.
- Feminist researchers, albeit in only a few cases, do make the list of top five, referenced organizational analysts.

Table 4.1 indicates the extent to which selected feminist works were cited in business texts. In the 100 selected business texts published since 1973, citations to the work of Rosabeth Moss Kanter (1977; 1979) occur in just under half, while citations to the work of Virginia Schein (Brenner *et al.*, 1989; Schein, 1973, 1975) occur in almost one-quarter. In addition, the work of Anne Morrison and her colleagues (Morrison *et al.*, 1987) is cited in 8 per cent of business texts, Deborah Tannen (1990; 1994) in 5 per cent, and each of Carol Gilligan (1982), Gary Powell (1988) and Barbara Gutek (1980, 1987, 1988; Tsui and Gutek, 1984) in 4 per cent. A further twelve feminist studies are cited in 1–3 per cent of the selected post-1973 business texts. In two specific business textbooks, Rosabeth Moss Kanter and Nancy Adler were among the top five most often cited organizational researchers (although the references were, for the most part, not to their explicitly feminist research).

Table 4.1 Feminist Research Cited in 100 Selected Business Texts since 1973

Feminist Authors [Total number of business textbooks referencing these authors]

Kanter, 1977, 1979 [47]	Adler [3]	Hochschild [1]
Schein, 1973, 1975 [22]	Mills and Tancred [2]	Maier [1]
Morrison *et al.* [8]	Abella [1]	Martin [1]
Tannen [5]	Acker and van Houten [1]	Mumby and Putnam [1]
Gilligan [4]	Brenner *et al.* [1]	Smircich [1]
Powell [4]	Burrell [1]	Task Force on Barriers
Gutek, 1980, 1987,	Harriman [1]	to Women [1]
1988 [3]		Tsui and Gutek [1]

Table 4.2 indicates that it is becoming increasingly more likely to find some reference to feminist research in the pages of the standard business text. Although prior to the early 1980s few or no references to (selected) feminist work could be found in the pages of the business text, by 1987 at least half of all business texts made some reference, however small, to feminist research. This figure rose to around two-thirds by 1992 and has since stayed at that level.

Table 4.2 Percentage of Selected Business Text Books in a Given Period that Cite Feminist Organizational Research

[a] Time Period	[b] Number of Business Text Books Reviewed	[c] Number from column 'b' that cite feminist research (%)	
1973-77	6	0	(0)
1978-82	9	2	(22)
1983-87	24	12	(50)
1988-92	33	21	(67)
1993-98	28	18	(65)
Total: 1973-98	100	53	(53)

Compared with twenty-five years ago, the business texts devote more attention to issues of gender. At the very least then, gender has become part of the broader discourse of organizing and organization. The reasons for this are not hard to find. They include the impact of the women's movement on legislation; the growing number of women with university business degrees who are joining the ranks of management;[2] and, one would hope, the influence both of women-in-management organizations and the body of feminist scholarship within organization and management studies. Indeed, 'employment equity legislation' and the 'growing number of women in the workforce' are the two most referenced issues in textbook discussions of gender. Moreover, at least one more recent text has, albeit in a limited and confusing way, referenced the influence of feminism within organizational analysis:

> The student of organizations needs to be an active evaluator of new theories and facts about how organization works. To this end each individual needs to understand the methods of modern science as well as postmodern approaches. These latter approaches include poststructuralism, deconstruction of texts, and feminism (Field and House, 1995, p. 666).

Limitations and Concerns

Further analysis shows that such optimism concerning the influence of feminist scholarship on the business textbook is premature. At least four main concerns must be addressed:

- The majority of selected feminist work was not cited in any business textbook.
- A substantial number of business textbooks continue to ignore gender.
- The great majority of those business textbooks that cite feminist research do so in a cursory manner.
- Business textbooks take longer to cite feminist organizational research than research from other mainstream organizational approaches.

Several key feminist works, indeed the majority of those termed 'influential' by feminist organizational analysts, were totally ignored by the authors of business textbooks. For example, Joan Acker's (1992) *Gendering Organizational Theory* one of the most referenced works by feminist organizational scholars, is completely ignored in business textbooks. And where, we may ask, is the post-feminist work of Marta Calás and Linda Smircich? Where, too, is the work of Cynthia Cockburn, David Collinson, Kathy Ferguson, Jeff Hearn, Judi Marshall, Rosemary Pringle, Stella Nkomo, and a multitude of others?

A little less than half (47 per cent) of the 100 selected business textbooks cited *no* feminist research. Even in the last decade of the twentieth century, then, one third of all business textbook authors saw fit to exclude any reference to feminist organizational analysis (see Table 4.2); many of those do not even reference gender, women, sexual preference, or sexual harassment (Mills and Helms Hatfield, 1998, p. 55) Indeed, in at least one case, that of Field and House (1995), reference to feminist research simply disappeared in a later edition of the textbook: Field and House, for instance, included reference to 'other approaches to organizational science' and the role of feminist research, but dropped this discussion entirely from the later edition (see Field, 1998).

In any event the citation of feminist research is extremely limited: often only a single author is cited. For instance, seventeen textbooks refer only to the feminist research of Kanter, a further six reference only the work of Schein, while one text makes reference only to the feminist work of Harriman. Thus, those twenty-four business textbooks account for 43 per cent of the fifty-three books that include references to feminist work. A further sixteen textbooks (28.5 per cent) cite no more than two of the selected feminist works. The average number of feminist citations for all fifty-three textbooks is just over 2 per textbook.

As for the impact of *individual* feminist studies on the business textbooks, only the work of Kanter (1977, 1979), Schein (1973,1975), Tannen (1990), and Morrison *et al.* (1987) has made any discernable impression (see Table 4.1) As Table 4.3 (column d) indicates, Kanter's 1977 and 1979 works were cited, respectively, by 23 per cent and 31 per cent of all relevant textbooks (i.e., those published after the feminist work's publication date; see column c); Schein's 1973 and 1975 works were cited, respectively, in 18 per cent and 13 per cent of relevant textbooks; and the newer and less referenced work of Tannen and Morrison *et al.* were cited, respectively, nonetheless, respectively cited in 12.5 per cent and 10 per cent of relevant textbooks. Apart from the two specifically Canadian studies (Abella, 1984; Task Force on Barriers to Women in the Public Service, 1990), only Powell (6.5 per cent) and Mills and Tancred (6 per cent) exceed 5 per cent. All the remaining feminist studies are referenced in 5 per cent or fewer of the relevant textbooks.

Table 4.4 provides a point of comparison between the citing of feminist research and that of other (mainstream) theoretical approaches in business textbooks. The table indicates that mainstream approaches fare better than feminist research. Management By Objectives (MBO), for example, is cited in more than three-quarters of all relevant textbooks (see columns c and d) Campbell *et al.*'s 'expectancy theory', Burns and Stalker's 'contingency theory', and Adams' 'equity theory' fared almost as well, with respective citations in 73.5 per cent, 71.5 per cent and 70 per cent of relevant textbooks. Organization Development (OD), Organizational Culture, and Business Process Reengineering (BPR) were cited in 60 per cent or more of the relevant selected texts. Three other approaches – Path-Goal Theory (58 per cent), Quality of Working Life (54 per cent), and Clayton Alderfer's 'Existence, Relatedness and Growth' Theory (50 per cent) – were cited in at least half of business texts, with two others – TQM at 47 percent, and Diversity Management at 46.5 percent – not far below the 50 per cent mark. With the sole exception of Diversity Management, all these mainstream approaches were more heavily referenced than the work of the most cited feminist scholar – Rosabeth Moss Kanter (see Table 4.1).

Even those theories that were relatively ignored in selected business texts, including Population Ecology (10 per cent) and Organizational Learning (9 per cent), are more often cited than the great majority of selected feminist scholarship. Only New Institution Theory, with 4 per cent of potential citations, comes close to the low referencing experienced by feminist scholars; even here, however, it does better than the 12 (48 per cent) of the 25 feminist studies that received citations.

In a similar vein, a considerable time lag occurs between the publication of the feminist works and their citation in a business textbook. Table 4.3 indicates that it is often several years before a feminist work is recognized in a business textbook and even then only fleetingly so. Work by Harriman (1985), Smircich (1983)[3] and Brenner *et al.* (1989), for example, was quickly noted but never again cited. Mills and Tancred (1992), and Mumby and Putnam (1992), fared only slightly better, being cited once more after early recognition. The exception is the work of Kanter (1977, 1979), which, was cited relatively quickly after three and four years respectively, and often. Even the relatively well-referenced work of Schein (1973, 1975) appears to have needed six to eight years to make some impact.

Table 4.3 Impact of Selected Feminist Organizational Studies on 100 Business Textbooks Published Since 1973

[a] Feminist research referenced in Table 4.1	[b] Year of publication	[c] Potential number of business textbooks that could cite research	[d] Number of citations (d as % of c)		[e] Year when research first cited in a business textbook	[f] Time lag (years) from column b to column e
Schein	1973	100	18	(18)	1981	8 years
Acker and van Houten	1974	99	1	(1)	1998	24 years
Schein	1975	99	13	(13)	1981	6 years
Kanter	1977	95	22	(23)	1980	3 years
Kanter	1979	91	28	(31)	1983	4 years
Gutek	1980	91	1	(1)	1993	13 years
Gilligan	1982	87	4	(4.5)	1993	11 years
Hochschild	1983	85	1	(1)	1995	12 years
Smircich	1983	85	1	(1)	1986	3 years
Tsui and Gutek	1984	79	1	(1)	1990	6 years
Abella	1984	18[4]	1	(5.5)	1995	11 years
Burrell	1984	79	1	(1)	1998	14 years
Harriman	1985	77	1	(1)	1987	2 years
Morrison *et al.*	1987	63	8	(12.5)	1990	3 years
Gutek	1987	63	1	(1)	1993	6 years
Powell	1988	61	4	(6.5)	1992	4 years
Adler	1988	61	3	(5)	1995	7 years
Gutek	1988	61	1	(1)	1993	5 years
Brenner *et al.*	1989	54	1	(2)	1992	3 years
Tannen	1990	50	5	(20)	1993	3 years
Task Force on Barriers to Women	1990	14[5]	1	(7)	1998	8 years
Martin	1990	50	1	(2)	1998	8 years
Maier	1991	39	1	(2.5)	1998	7 years
Mills and Tancred	1992	33	2	(6)	1995	3 years
Mumby and Putnam	1992	33	1	(3)	1995	3 years
						Average time lag = 7 years

Table 4.4 Impact of Selected Mainstream Approaches to Organization Analysis on 128 Business Textbooks Published Since 1960

[a] Theoretical Approach	[b] Year of publication in which the approach was introduced [main author]	[c] Potential number of business textbooks in which reference could be cited	[d] Number of citations (column d as % of column c)	[e] Year when approach was first cited in a business textbook	[f] Time lag (years) from column b to column e
Management By Objectives (MBO)	1954 [Drucker]	128	98 (76.5)	1969	At least 9 years[6]
Contingency Theory	1961 [Burns and Stalker]	127	91 (77)	1972	11 years
Equity Theory	1963 [Adams]	126	88 (70)	1963	0 years
Organization Development (OD)	1969 [French]	125	83 (66)	1973	4 years
Expectancy Theory	1970 [Campbell *et al.*]	125	92 (73.5)	1973	3 years
Existence, Relatedness and Growth (ERG) Theory	1972 [Alderfer]	125	63 (50)	1976	4 years
Path-Goal Theory	1974 [Mitchelland House]	122	71 (58)	1976	2 years
Organizational Culture	1974 [Eldridge and Crombie]	122	77 (69)	1976	2 years
Quality of Working Life (QWL)	1975 [Dickson]	121	65 (54)	1981	6 years
Population Ecology	1977 [Hannan and Freeman]	116	12 (10)	1984	7 years
Organizational Learning	1981 [Huber]	112	10 (9)	1981	0 years
Institution Theory	1983 [DiMaggio and Powell]	111	4 (4)	1990	7 years
Total Quality Management [TQM]	1988 [Juran; Demming]	81	38 (47)	1988	0 years
Business Process Reengineering (BPR)	1993 [Hammer and Champy]	43	26 (60)	1994	1 year
Diversity Management	1993 [Foster *et al.*]	43	20 (46.5)	1993	0 years
					Average time lag =3.7 years

Tables 4.3 and 4.4 enable comparisons to be made between the time lags of selected feminist and mainstream theories. Whereas the average feminist theory takes about seven years to be cited, mainstream approaches are recognized in almost half that time. In the latter case, six approaches were cited in two years or less after their first publication; only Harriman's work comes close to that time frame. And unlike Harriman's work, all six mainstream theories were cited on multiple occasions. Nonetheless, it is fair to say that the time lag between several feminist and mainstream studies was comparable. Eleven of the former took five years of less to be cited compared with ten of the latter. Notwithstanding, it is quite remarkable that Acker and van Houten's (1974) prominent study of 'sex power differentials' took almost a quarter of a century to be noticed and Hochschild's (1983) study of emotion work took twelve years to gain one small reference.

In short, feminist organizational analysis has made some impact on the business textbook in the last twenty-five years, but the process has been pitifully slow and inadequate. To quote the reaction of a young female MBA student to a middle-aged male classmate's comment that 'women have come a long way in 40 years': she said 'I don't have 40 years'.

What Does This Tell Us And Where Do We Go From Here?

This preliminary analysis supports Jacques' (1996) contention that management education too often fails to critically engage with management practice. This is especially the case with textbook production, which occupies an important space in the process of business education. Analysis of major North American textbooks suggest that textbook production is intimately linked to isomorphism and the reproduction of safe, similar and legitimate practices (DiMaggio and Powell, 1991).

It is relatively easy to see how the process works. In the North American classroom business professors and students alike expect to use a textbook as the central reading for any undergraduate (indeed, graduate) course. Here we have normative isomorphism. There are also expectations of what the textbook should cover, and should include an introduction to many of the 'major' theories and studies in the field, which, despite Burrell and Morgan's (1979) far reaching critique, is typically defined as that which is functionalist or 'managerialist' (Mills and Simmons, 1999) Coercive isomorphism is embedded in the long established standardization of business education, which rarely allows room for experiment and change (read critical approaches to management). The standardization process has accelerated in recent years with the growing influence of the American Assembly of Collegiate Schools of Business (AACSB) This body plays a powerful role in the accreditation of business schools in the United States and Canada, with accreditation depending on the implementation of a number of standardized practices. Mimetic isomorphism comes into play as the would-be author sets out to produce a saleable textbook. He or she immediately comes up against a number of conservative forces; not least of which is the assumption that textbook learning is unproblematic. The author may have radically new ideas for a textbook but has to get past the big publishing houses that produce most of the business textbooks. The publishers are looking for something that has the widest appeal rather than what is radically different. In the end, it would seem, it is far easier and quicker for the author to mimic the best selling textbooks in the field. Without denigrating the efforts of honest business educators, it has to be said that the pressure to reproduce a standardized text is enhanced by the fact that tens of thousands of dollars may be at stake; best selling textbook authors stand to make $100,000 plus in a given year.

The relative absence of feminist studies of organization within the business text is, thus, not unexpected but is just part of the problem. Discussion of gender has been incorporated into a malestream discourse that tends to speak in a male voice and which subordinates humanist concerns (e.g., issues of self-esteem, discrimination, etc.) to a focus on organizational outcomes of profitability, effectiveness, and growth.

An example of male voice can be found in the text book by Randolph and Blackburn (1989, pp. 155-7). Included in an exercise that tests 'attitudes people have about women in business'. The authors state that '(t)he scores ... will provide some indication of how comfortable a person is with women in managerial positions. Since women are entering management in greater numbers, attitudes about them as managers are important and should be understood'. A more recent version of this problem can be found in the 1995 text of Field and House. The authors, despite devoting space to issues of gender, comment that:

> Females are evolutionarily adapted to bear and nurture children. Besides the ovaries, uterus, and breast milk ducts, female arms have a curve that seems to make easier the carrying and breast feeding of young infants. A male arm, when displayed out from the body, palm up, is straight at the elbows whereas the female arm has a bend at the elbow. This biological difference is undoubtedly ignored on unknown by a male who when playing catch with a female says she 'throws like a girl' (Field and House, 1995, p. 2).

It is not quite clear what we are supposed to do with this information.

Part of the 'male voice' problem stems from a paucity of female textbook authors[7] and North American business school Deans[8] and faculty members[9] of North American business schools.[10] Indeed, in Canada, if we compare the percentage of female business faculty members with the percentage of female faculty as a whole,[11] the percentage of female business faculty members is lower at all ranks, except that of assistant professor. Part of the solution is the age-old strategy of working to ensure that more female faculty are hired and promoted within our universities. Part of the solution is also to encourage more of our existing female faculty, particularly feminist scholars, to take up the challenge of writing their own business textbooks.[12] As well, however, as many colleagues as possible should be encouraged to contact publishers to complain about the neglect of gender and the outmoded sexist style of today's textbooks.

But if the discourse remains focussed primarily on profitability and efficiency, the addition of more women's 'voices' will not solve the problem. Indeed, as has been argued elsewhere (Mills and Simmons, 1999), the field of business studies is dominated by a narrow functionalist or managerialist perspective. In effect, the few feminist works incorporated into the discourse are usually made to fit, rather than question, that paradigm.

An example of the subordination of gender to business outcomes can be found in Hellriegel, Slocum and Woodman's (1995, pp. 7-8) comment: 'One management challenge is to help people understand diversity so that they can establish productive relationships with people at work. For example, Hewlett-Packard conducts workshops for all employees in which the emphasis is on educating and encouraging managers to understand culturally different employees and to create an environment that will foster productivity.' Clearly, in the absence of an influential feminist discourse, discussion of gender is being pursued within the narrow framework of 'diversity' and 'diversity management', thereby conflating a range of human needs and problems into a single 'problem' area. As Table 4.4 indicates, diversity management has become a significant discourse within management education in recent years.

As has been argued elsewhere, 'This celebration of diversity is to be applauded' rather than condemned out of hand, as '(it) certainly stands in sharp relief to the recent period in North American history when race segregation and the exclusion of women from countless occupations was viewed as normal' (Prasad and Mills, 1997, p. 5). Clearly, a number of problems with this discourse need to be engaged. For one, the discourse is centred on organizational outcomes, i.e., the celebration of diversity is secondary to bottom-line outcomes. Second, it frames gender (and race, age, etc) as a problem to be managed. Third, it lumps together issues of gender, race/ethnicity, sexual preference, age, disabilities, etc.; and fourth, it focuses the issues as a problematic for the white male manager. Nevertheless, it is a discourse where gender and race can be discussed and where feminist researchers can take issue and enter into the debate.

The unspoken question in all of this is the relevance of feminist studies to organizational analysis. Are we developing enough of the 'right kind of work to illuminate the problem of organizational development? Has the lack of 'usable' feminist research caused it to be ignored within the mainstream? Certainly a number of women-in-management adherents have been making the case for some time.

On the other hand, do feminists need to concern themselves with organizational analysis as a field of study? Isn't it, in fact, a field framed by a fundamentally masculinist bias, i.e., the dominant focus is on improving the operations and outcomes of organization. Indeed some feminists within the field have argued that organizational analysis is one of the most masculinist of the sociological specialties and therefore particularly tough for feminist scholarship to make inroads' (cf. Tancred-Sheriff and Campbell, 1992). We might also, therefore, question whether textbooks, with their oversimplification and selected distillations of a complex field of study are a viable educational tool for feminist work. It could be argued that organizational analysis encourages a masculinist style of discourse that avoids concern with feeling and an emotional attachment to selected issues. To quote Jacques (1996, p. 178), the representation of certain practices (e.g., relational practices) 'do not simply disappear. They are subject to systematic organizational practices through which they "get disappeared"'.

And, finally, assuming that feminists still feel the need to engage in organizational analysis, there is the enduring question of gender vs. women's voice (Calás and Smircich, 1992; 1996). In short, how do we combine the problem of questioning the gendered frameworks in which 'women' and 'men' are constructed with the need to challenge the impact of those frameworks on women? This issue has proved particularly problematic in textbook discussions, with their emphasis on the contributions and outcomes for 'real' or essential people. That is not to argue for an essentialist perspective that panders to the managerialist discourse; rather it is a call to reflect on how feminists can advance the political problem of equity that, to a certain extent, asks for the locating of 'essential women' in discriminatory contexts. A good example is the decision by the Women-in-Management Division of the Academy of Management to rename itself the Gender and Diversity Division. The aim was to circumvent a strong focus on women-in-management research that had strengthened the notion of essential women and, arguably, contributed to discriminatory images of ingrained sex differences. Some argued that the change would obfuscate the feminist project of 'women's liberation', by removing 'women' from the title of the new division and linking gender with the broader concerns of 'diversity'. Others argued that, in fact, the change encourages a broader concern with the intersections of race, ethnicity, and gender, thereby moving away from the narrower, more problematic concern with racially neutral i.e. 'white' women.

Notes

[1] This chapter has been adapted from Gendering Organizational Analysis – A Retrospective, which appeared in Feminism(s) Challenge the Traditional Disciplines (13-25). Montreal: McGill Centre for Research and Teaching on Women Monograph (1).

[2] For example, in Canada the percentage of business and commerce Ph.D. students has risen from 29.7 per cent in 1992-3 to 34.7 per cent in 1994-95 (Statistics Canada, 1995; CAUT Bulletin, 1996. According to one estimate, the percentage of middle and senior managers in Canada who are female rose from 16 per cent in 1971, to 25 per cent in 1981, and to 39 per cent in 1991 (MacLean's magazine, Oct. 4, 1993).

[3] This was an article of organizational culture and does not reference gender.

[4] As a Canadian Royal Commission Report, its contents might more likely be reported in business textbooks with a Canadian focus. On that basis, the potential referencing is reduced from 79 to 18 textbooks.

[5] This was also a specifically Canadian report as well. Thus, the number of business texts that might reasonably be expected to reference the report is reduced from 50 to 14.

[6] Although MBO dates back to 1954 the time lag has been weighted to take account of the lack of pre-1960 textbooks in the sample.

[7] Of the 107 textbooks reviewed by Mills and Helms Hatfield (1999, p. 62) only one was solely authored by a woman, and six others had female co-authors.

[8] In Canada less than five per cent of business school deans are women, an improvement on 1987 when the figure was less than two per cent (Mills and Simmons, 1999, p. 180).

[9] In Canada women constitute around 18 per cent of all business professors, including 7 per cent of full professors, 16 per cent of associate professors, 29 per cent of assistant professors, and 39 per cent of lecturers.

[10] This is certainly the case in Canada but may be less so in the United States.

[11] Women constitute 23.1 per cent of all Canadian professors; 11.1 per cent of professors, 26.4 per cent of associate professors, 56.8 per cent of assistant professors, and 40.9 per cent of lecturers.

[12] In the United Kingdom Fiona Wilson (1995) and Elisabeth Wilson (2001) – no relation – have made important contributions to this process.

References

Abella, R.S. (1984) *Equity in Employment. A Royal Commission Report* Ottawa, Ministry of Supply and Services Canada.

Abrahamson, E. (1996) 'Management Fashion,' in *Academy of Management Review* 21(1) pp. 254-285.

Acker, J. (1992) 'Gendering Organizational Theory,' in A.J. Mills and P. Tancred (eds.) *Gendering Organizational Analysis* pp. 248-260 Newbury Park, CA, Sage.

Acker, J. and van Houten, D.R. (1974) 'Differential Recruitment and Control: the Sex Structuring of Organizations,' in *Administrative Science Quarterly* 9(2) pp. 152-163.

Benschop, Y. and Meihuizen, H.E. (2002) 'Reporting Gender: Representations of Gender in Financial and Annual Reports,' in I. Aaltio and A.J. Mills (eds.) *Gender, Identity and the Culture of Organizations*, pp. 160-184 London, Routledge.

Brenner, O.C., Tomkiewicz, J. and Schein, V.E. (1989) 'The Relationship between Sex Role Stereotypes and Requisite Management Characteristics Revisited,' in *The Academy of Management Journal* 32(3) pp. 662-669.

Bruni, A. and Gherardi, S. (2002) 'En-gendering Differences, Transgressing the Boundaries, Coping with the Dual Presence,' in I. Aaltio and A.J. Mills (eds.) *Gender, Identity and the Culture of Organizations*, pp. 21-38. London, Routledge.

Burrell, G. and Morgan, G. (1979) *Sociological Paradigms and Organizational Analysis* London, Heinemann.

Calás, M.B. and Smircich, L. (1992) 'Using the "F" word: Feminist theories and the social consequences of organizational research,' in A.J. Mills and P. Tancred (eds.) *Gendering Organizational Analysis*, pp. 222-234. Newbury Park, CA, Sage.

Calás, M.B. and Smircich, L. (1996) 'From 'The Woman's' Point of View: Feminist Approaches to Organization Studies,' in S.R. Clegg, C. Hardy and W.R. Nord (eds.) *Handbook of Organization Studies*, pp. 218-257. London, Sage.

Collinson, D.L. and Collinson, M. (1997) ''Delayering Managers': Time-Space Surveillance and its Gendered Effects,' in *Organization* 4(3) pp. 375-407.

DiMaggio, P.J. and Powell, W.W. (1991) 'The Iron Cage Revisited: Institutional Isomorphism and Collective Rationality in Organizational Fields,' in W.W. Powell and P.J. DiMaggio (eds.) *The New Institutionalism in Organizational Analysis.*, pp. 63-82. Chicago, University of Chicago Press.

Ferguson, K.E. (1984) *The Feminist Case Against Bureaucracy* Philadelphia, PA, Temple University Press.

Field, R.H.G. (1998) *Human Behaviour in Organizations: A Canadian Perspective* (2nd Edition) Scarborough, Ont., Prentice-Hall Canada.

Field, R.H.G. and House, R.J. (1995) *Human Behavior in Organizations. A Canadian Perspective* Scarborough, Ont., Prentice Hall.

Gilligan, C. (1982) *In A Different Voice: Psychological Theory and Women's Development* Cambridge, MA: Harvard University Press.

Greene, A.-m., Ackers, P. and Black, J. (2002) 'Going Against the Historical Grain: Perspectives on Gendered Occupational Identity and Resistance to the Breakdown of Occupational Segregation in Two Manufacturing Firms,' in *Gender, Work and Organization* 9(3), pp. 266-285.

Gutek, B. and Larwood, L. (eds.) (1987) *Women's Career Development* Newbury Park, CA, Sage.

Harriman, A. (1985) *Women/Men, Management* New York, Praeger.

Hearn, J. and Parkin, P.W. (1983) 'Gender and Organizations: A Selective Review and a Critique of a Neglected Area' in *Organization Studies* 4(3), pp. 219-242.

Hellriegel, D., Slocum, J.W. and Woodman, R.W. (1995) *Organizational Behavior* St. Paul, MN., West.

Helms Mills, J.C. (2003) *Making Sense of Organizational Change* London, Routledge.

Henning, M. and Jardin, A. (1977) *The Managerial Woman* New York, Anchor/Doubleday.

Hochschild, A.R. (1983) *The Managed Heart* Berkeley, CA, University of California Press.

Jackson, B. (2001) *Management Gurus and Management Fashions* London, Routledge.

Jacques, R. (1996) *Manufacturing the Employee: Management Knowledge from the 19th to 21st Centuries* London, Sage.

Kanter, R.M. (1977) *Men and Women of the Corporation* New York, Basic Books.

Kanter, R.M. (1979) 'Power Failure in Management Circuits' in *Harvard Business Review* 57(4), pp. 65-75.

Kieser, A. (1997) 'Rhetoric and Myth in Management Fashion,' in *Organization* 4(1), pp. 49-74.

Maier, M. (1997) '"We Have to Make a Management Decision": Challenger and the Dysfunctions of Corporate Masculinity.,' in P. Prasad, A.J. Mills, M. Elmes and A. Prasad (eds.) *Managing the Organizational Melting Pot: Dilemmas of Workplace Diversity*, pp. 226-254. Newbury Park, CA, Sage.

Martin, P.Y. (1996) 'Gendering and Evaluating Dynamics: Men, masculinities, and management,' in D.L. Collinson and J. Hearn (eds.) *Men as Managers, Managers as Men: Critical Perspectives on Men, Masculinities and Management*, pp. 186-209. Newbury Park, CA, Sage.

Martin, P.Y. and Collinson, D. (2002) '"Over the Pond and across the Water": Developing the field of "Gendered Organizations"' in *Gender, Work and Organization* 9 (3) pp. 244-265.

Mills, A.J. and Helms Hatfield, J.C. (1998) 'From Imperialism to Globalization: Internationalization and the Management Text,' in S.R. Clegg, E. Ibarra and L. Bueno (eds.) *Theories of the Management Process: Making Sense Through Difference*, pp. 37-67. Thousand Oaks, CA, Sage.

Mills, A.J. and Simmons, T. (1999) *Reading Organization Theory: Critical Approaches to the Study of Behaviour and Structure in Organizations*, (2nd Edition) Toronto, Garamond Press.

Mills, A.J. and Tancred, P. (eds.) (1992) *Gendering Organizational Analysis*, Newbury Park, CA, Sage.

Morrison, A., White, R. and Van Elsor, E. (1987) *Breaking the Glass Ceiling*, Reading, MA, Addison Wesley.

Mumby, D.K. and Putnam, L.L. (1992) 'The Politics of Emotion: a Feminist Reading of Bounded Rationality' in *Academy of Management Review*. 17(3), pp. 465-486.

Nord, W. and Fox, S. (1996) 'The Individual in Organizational Studies: The Great Disappearing Act?,' in S. Clegg and C. Hardy (eds.) *Handbook of Organizational Studies*, pp. 148-175 Thousand Oaks, CA, Sage.

Powell, G. (1988) *Women and Men in Management* Newbury Park, CA, Sage.

Prasad, P. and Mills, A.J. (1997) 'Managing the Organizational Melting Pot: Dilemmas of Diversity at the Workplace.,' in P. Prasad, A.J. Mills, M. Elmes and A. Prasad (eds.) *Managing The Organizational Melting Pot: Dilemmas of Workplace Diversity*, pp. 3-27. Thousand Oaks, CA, Sage.

Randolph, W.A. and Blackburn, R.S. (1989) *Managing Organizational Behavior*, Boston. MA, Irwin.

Schein, V.E. (1973) 'The relationship between sex role stereotypes and requisite management characteristics among female managers' in *Journal of Applied Psychology* 57, pp. 89-105.

Schein, V.E. (1975) 'Relationships between sex role stereotypes and requisite management characteristics among female managers' in *Journal of Applied Psychology* 60, pp. 340-344.

Sharp, C.D. (2003) 'Projected Ideal and Presented Reality: What a Foucauldian Perspective on Appearance in the Workplace Tells Us About Corporate Discrimination'. Unpublished PhD thesis, Department of Management, University of Calgary.

Smircich, L. (1983) 'Concepts of Culture and Organizational Analysis' in *Administrative Science Quarterly* (28), pp. 339-358.

Tancred-Sheriff, P. and Campbell, E.J. (1992) 'Room for Women: A Case Study in the Sociology of Organizations,' in A.J. Mills and P. Tancred (eds.) *Gendering Organizational Analysis*, pp. 31-45. Newbury Park, CA, Sage.

Tannen, D. (1990) *You Just Don't Understand: Men and Women in Conversation* New York, William Morrow.

Tannen, D. (1994) *Talking 9 To 5* New York, William Morrow.

Task Force on Barriers to Women in the Public Service. (1990) *Beneath The Veneer* (Vol. 1) Ottawa: Minister of Supply and Services, Canada.

Wicks, D. and Bradshaw, P. (2002) 'Gendered Value Foundations that Reproduce Discrimination and Inhibit Organizational Change,' in I. Aaltio and A.J. Mills (eds.) *Gender, Identity and the Culture of Organizations*, pp. 137-159. London: Routledge.

Wilson, E.M. (2001) *Organizational Behaviour Reassessed: The Impact of Gender* London/ Thousand Oaks, CA, Sage.

Wilson, F.M. (1995) *Organizational Behaviour and Gender* London, McGraw-Hill.

Appendix 1: Key Feminist Organization Research and Researchers

Authors
Joan Acker
Kathryn Bartol
Ella Bell
Judith Butler
Marta Calás
David Collinson
Joyce Fletcher
Barbara Gutek
Judi Marshall
Joanne Martin
Albert Mills
Stella Nkomo
Gary Powell
Linda Smircich

Appendix 2: Selected Mainstream Theories

Business Process Reengineering (BPR)
Contingency theory
Diversity management
Equity theory
ERG theory
Expectancy theory
Institution Theory
Management by Objectives (MBO)
Organization Development (OD)
Organizational Culture
Organizational Learning
Path-goal leadership theory
Population Ecology
Quality of Working Life
Total Quality Management (TQM).

Chapter 5

Ending the Velvet Revolution: Managing the Re-Education of Vaclav Havel

Tony Tinker

Introduction

The September 2000 meeting of the World Bank and International Monetary Fund in Prague posed a quandary for the Czech President, Vaclav Havel. Having led the velvet revolution in a mass non-violent ejection of communism in favor of liberal democracy, the former playwright and dissident was now protecting 14,000 global financiers from 20,000 protestors with 11,000 police and 5,000 soldiers.

The Prague meeting was primed beforehand by a lighting-rod statistic (courtesy of the United Nations Development Agency) that 19,000 children die each day as a result of unpayable debt. Managers of Western-based global business rely on the World Bank and IMF to contrive new ways to recover debt (it falls to their sister organization – the WTO – to come up with ever more creative laws, contracts, and enforcement mechanisms for ensuring that the debt is incurred in the first place).[1] These three institutions are the principle architects of the New World Order. Their function is to establish the infrastructure of a market economy whereby conditions for profitable trading relations are guaranteed (Polanyi, 1957).[2]

Management Re-education

MBA-type education maintains a Chinese wall between its management technology of financial appraisals, cash flow analysis, etc, and its more gruesome consequences of poverty and deprivation. Like B52 pilots, they operate in an eerie arcade-game world, inured to the heart-wrenching impact of their 'hits'. Occasionally however, reality elbows its way into the fiction. Jenson and Meckling (the doyens of the 'Finance Revolution' in business schools) did at least question the moral and ethical basis for property rights. Unfortunately, instead of acknowledging their roots in institutional conflict and coercion, they resorted to a spurious grounding offered for 'all' human rights: that they were 'natural' (Jensen and Meckling, 1980; Tinker, 1988).[3]

In a more recent 'blast-from-the-past', we have witnessed the unseemly spectacle of ex-dictator Augusto Pinochet, hop-skip-and-jumping across the Heathrow tarmac, out of the arms of British justice -on grounds of poor health. For students of management, the squalid saga did not end here. More than compassion moved Home Secretary Jack Straw to release Pinochet. A trial in Britain would have further exposed CIA complicity in the Pinochet regime (something that wouldn't do much for the 'Special Relationship'). It has long been known that the CIA assisted in the overthrow of Chile's democratically elected government of Salvador Allende (who had the temerity to propose nationalizing the U.S. mining interests in Chile – acquired during gentler, colonial times). However, even this, and the tragedy of the thousands who 'disappeared' under Pinochet's rule, would not normally be enough to divert Home Secretary Straw's unswerving commitment to human rights. The CIA was also implicated in more than the assassination of American citizens – murdering a disposable aid worker (the subject of the Jack Lemon movie, *Missing*) and a car bombing in Washington that killed Chilean diplomat Orlando Letelier, and his American assistant, Ronni Moffitt (Franklin, September 28–October 4, 2000).[4] They also helped-out in kidnapping a general in the Allende government who opposed American policy.

Sequels to the Pinochet Affair occurred in the management literature in the 1970s and the 1980s. Stafford Beer (Visiting Professor at the Manchester Business School, and Ex-President of the Operations Research Society) was assisting the Allende government's economics minister in installing a system's model of the economy that provided for widespread participation by the peasantry.[5] Beer was vilified at the time by American Corporations, who declared that his Operations Room 'just couldn't work'. Later, in the 1980s, British academics added to the chorus by branding the Chilean experiment as 'academic totalitarianism' that would slide, inexorably, into a Gulag (Checkland, 1999; Jackson and Willmott, 1988).

Farewell to Democracy

The liberal democratic ideal was tarnished long before Seattle. The dead letter of campaign finance reform in the U.S. Congress, the recent parade of influence-peddling scandals in the U.K., Australia, Germany, France, and the U.S., and nagging statistics on low-voter turnout, all gave fair warning that extra-parliamentary action was inevitable. America is now the land of one political party with two heads, and must now turn to the Buchanan mutation to tell, 'how it is', who describes the unregulated free market as:

> ... sold as globalization, and that Reaganism with its twin sister, Thatcherism, creating fortunes among the highly educated, but in the middle and working classes, generating anxiety, insecurity and disparities. ..Tax cuts, slashing of safety nets and welfare benefits, and global free trade.. . unleashing the powerful engines of capitalism that go on a tear. Factories and businesses open and close with startling speed. Companies merge, downsize and disappear, and the labour force must always be ready to pick up and move on... The cost is paid in social upheaval and family breakdown... Conservatism is being confronted with its own contradictions for unbridled capitalism is an awesome destructive force (Elahi, 1999, p. 15).

American corporations are not working too hard to sustain the enchanting spell of liberal democracy. Commenting on data published by the Center for Responsive Politics (http://www.opensecrets.org), Mokhiber and Weissman note that, 'For all but the ideologically committed or deluded few who believe corporations and their executives make contributions out of a sense of civic obligation, there can be little doubt that the U.S. campaign finance system is fundamentally corrupt, and corrupting' (Mokhiber and Weissman, 2000).

The WTO meeting in Seattle was an exemplar of 'best management practice'. Although the WTO is an intergovernmental body, its dispute resolution panels in Seattle were closed sessions where national governments had no decision-making powers. Direction came from companies and industry bodies; such as the International Chamber of Commerce (ICC) and the Trans-Atlantic Business Dialogue (TADB). Industry lobbying dwarfed anything achieved by the NGO lobby in a wide range of ecological and social problems, ranging from the plunder of ancient forests to the ravages of storms driven by climate change.

American corporate executives gave the lead in showing how to deploy the democratic process to best effect. Boeing, for example, is a major benefactor from the increasing international airfreight trade that currently nets the firm $40bn a year and is expected to triple in the next 20 years. Boeing's CEO, Phil Condit, co-chaired the Seattle Host Organization that sought out corporate sponsorship for the opening session of the talks. Boeing itself contributed more than $250,000 – and thus obtained five seats at the top (dinner) table with trade ministers. Monsanto is also a major benefactor of increased trade and a stronger WTO. Monsanto's chairman, Robert Shapiro, is the chair of the U.S. President's Advisory Committee for Trade Policy and Negotiations. Mickey Kantor, US trade representative for much of the Uruguay Round of GATT talks, and the person responsible for leading WTO assault against the EU ban on beef hormones, is a board member of Monsanto. He served as the trade counsel for the US wheat industry at the Seattle talks. (Juniper, 1999).

Patents, Copyrights, and Debt Repayment

As the shock troops for staking out new frontiers for capitalist social relations, the World Bank, IMF, and WTO follow in hallowed footsteps. These institutions are installing a panoply of judicial, cultural, and coercive arrangements for securing a return for capital with minimal risk. Software, music, seeds, and a basket-load of other products are being parcelled up into a judicial-economic form, much the same fashion as Church lands were massively redistributed during the French and English revolutions, and public land was privatized during the great enclosure movements of 16th and 17th Century England (Turner, 1984). Property, once held for common-usage by poor village communities, was given private title that could then be transferred, much like the commodification now underway in rural Peru, Indonesia, Brazil, China and Mexico.[6]

Establishing property relations in fixed property (land) is usually the opening salvo in establishing capitalist social relations. However, property in labour (labour power) is far more vital (indeed intrinsic) to capitalism (Marx, 1977).[7] This involves not merely controlling the labour processes but also the products of labour. Patents and copyrights (immediate concerns of the WTO and indirectly, the World Bank and IMF) are only part of this problem for corporate management. Ownership is worthless unless there is control over access and usage that can be exchanged for a price in the marketplace (i.e., capital can be valorized). There are many instances where product innovations have been withheld from the marketplace until a technology for regulating access and usage have been devised (software and electronic publishing are recent examples).

The conflictual underpinnings of property relations are the dark secret of management education and research. Yet these are exactly the relations that protesters in Seattle, London, Los Angeles, Melbourne, and Prague sought to reassert. They highlighted the struggle between the juggernaut of property rights, and people's right to a 'decent living'. A decent living involves more than what is found in the store. Those on the streets understood that their formal means of political expression – liberal democracy – is now on the ropes. They reject the tacit assumption that liberal democracy exists in an independent and incorruptible political sphere, and recognized that it's sanctity has now been violated by an unholy union between corporate and political estates. The World Bank, the IMF, and WTO are the love children of this unholy union. Government is no longer by-or-for the people; it is a subsumption 'of' the people.

Accumulation versus The People

There are an increasing number of schisms between market-oriented corporate management and the peoples who make up the World's population. It has fallen to the World Bank, IMF, and WTO to finesse these perils. For instance, publishers have had the ability to deliver textbooks, journal articles, and other documents, in an electronic form, at a fraction of the hardcopy cost, for several years now. These products were withheld from the market, pending the erection of the legal and technical 'enclosure' fences and toll booths, to control access and collect user charges. Vital medical research, aimed at developing screening methods and cures for congenital diseases, has been curtailed or abandoned under threat of prosecution for infringement of newly registered property rights. American laboratory directors received letters from lawyers, acting for biotechnology companies, ordering them to cease clinical tests designed to red-flag breast cancer, Alzheimer's disease, and a variety of other illnesses. Athena Diagnostics Corporation advised these laboratories that it had 'acquired exclusive rights to certain tests in the diagnosis of late-onset Alzheimer's disease'. Testing elsewhere infringes that patent. Athena was willing to perform the tests itself for $195 per specimen – more than twice the price previously charged by university medical laboratories, and putting the cost of the test beyond the means of many researchers operating on government grants (Borger, 1999, p. 4).

The regressive impact of these legal threats is likely to retard medical research world-wide under WTO rules. The threat to medical research is considered so ominous that a group of American doctors and scientists issued a protest saying that, 'The use of patents or exorbitant licensing fees to prevent physicians and clinical laboratories from performing genetic tests limits access to medical care, jeopardizes the quality of medical care, and unreasonably raises its cost' (Ibiden). Half the laboratories in a survey in California and Pennsylvania said they had stopped work on developing screening because they knew a patent had been licensed or was pending. Scientists who had pioneered work in isolating and identifying genetic deformities linked to serious diseases feared that the pace of research and the spread of ideas has been stultified by the threat of being sued by patent license holders (Ibiden).

Implications

Vaclav Havel's re-education is likely to be completed well before those in academia. Mainstream management teachers and researchers treat business as a realm that is independent from politics, the state, and the economy. The reduction of management education to a technocratic consciousness ensures that political and social precepts remain unexamined pre-analytic acts (MacPherson, 1972; Lowe and Tinker, 1984). This self-inflicted myopia guarantees management's connivance in repression (Tinker, 1984).

What kind of educational curriculum would begin to properly prime students for these issues? First, cases about a 'Corporate World Upside Down' would add a contemporary urgency to the curriculum; provided they contained an (ethnographic) empathy with the victims of efficiency (rather than just with its exponents). This 'history' could be told for each of the functional areas of management (marketing, strategy, finance, accounting, personnel, etc). Second, an introduction to dialectical analysis and praxis would not only endow students with political acuity, but also breed a philosophical scepticism as to the conservative precepts of Cartesian and empiricist analysis (Tinker *et al.*, 1982; Tinker, 1999). And last, a primer in social analysis, and the manner in which 'the social' preconditions phenomena covered in each the disciplinary areas.

As of now, relatively greater awareness was to be found in the streets of Prague and Seattle than in academe. Protestors are closer-to (integral to) the 'real' contradictions and are not hogtied by the niceties of 'parliamentary cretinism'. U.S. unions, once bedfellows of the CIA in sabotaging overseas union movements and Left- Wing governments, are increasingly assuming a leadership role on issues ranging from human rights to global trade. In Seattle, they laid the groundwork for what may become a 'Peoples Alliance' or an 'Historical Bloc' (Nimtz, 1999; Marx and Engels; 1847; Gramsci, 1971). It is too early to pronounce that this is the manner in which the dialectic will unfold, but the genie is out of the bottle. Liberal democracy is on the rack, and it is no longer a question of if it will snap, only when, and how.

Notes

[1] Among the World Bank's debt repayment "success stories" are Zambia and Uganda. The former – a beneficiary of the Bank's "Heavily Indebted Poor Country Initiative" – spent $222 on debt repayment, and half as much on health care. Uganda, devoted $55 million on debt repayment and $102 on health care (Todaro, 2000).

[2] The sophistication of this global-judicial strategy of the WTO, IMF and World Bank contrasts markedly with their apparent naïveté in sending the Russian economy into free-fall – claiming that they were unprepared for the task of building institutions to support market relations.

[3] As Orlando Paterson argues regarding slavery, human rights such as liberty, fraternity, and equality are not socially ineluctable, but are won through struggle (Paterson, 1980; Tinker on Naturalizing).

[4] We are, of course, still waiting for a Harvard International Business case study based on the movie, *Missing*.

[5] The work is described in Beer's books, *Platform for Change* (1974) and *Brain of the Firm* (1972).

[6] As such, it can then be bought, sold, owned privately, and its access and usage restricted.

[7] The mass migration from the countryside to the town, establishing a reservoir of 'tree' wage labour, was an antecedent to capitalism's inauguration in 18th Century England and (say) 20th Century China.

References

Checkland, P. (1999) *Systems Thinking, Systems Practice* London, Wiley.
Franklin, J. 'CIA 'Helped Set Up Pinochet's "Secret Police"', Guardian Weekly, September 28–October 4, 2000, p. 5.
Beer, S. (1972) *Brain of the Firm* London, Penguin.
Beer, S. (1974) *Platform for Change* London, John Wiley.
Borger, J. (1999) The Guardian Weekly 23 December 1999, p. 4.
Elahi, (1999) The Guardian Weekly, 2 December-1999, p. 15.
Gramsci, A. (1971) *Selection from the Prison Notebooks* London, Lawrence and Wishart.
Jackson N. and Willmott, H. (1987) 'Beyond Epistemology and Reflective Conversation: Towards Human Relations' in *Human Relations* 40(6), pp. 361-380.
Jenson, M.C., and Meckling, W.H. (1980) 'Can the Corporation Survive?' in Buckley, J.W. and Weston, J.F. (eds.) *Regulation and the Accounting Profession* Belmont, CA, Lifetime Learning Publications, Wadsworth.
Juniper, T. (1999) The Guardian Weekly 17 November 1999, p. 12.
Nimtz, A. (1999) 'Marx and Engels: The Unsung Heroes of the Democratic Breakthrough' *Science and Society* 63 (2) Summer, pp. 203-231.
Macpherson, C.B. (1972) *The Real World of Democracy* New York, Oxford University Press.
Marx, K. (1847) *The Communism of the Rheinscher Beobachter* MECW: 6.

Marx, K. (1977) *Capital: A Critique of Political Economy* (Volume One) New York, Vintage Books.

Mokhiber, R. and Weissman, R. (2000) 'Withering Democracy' http://www.corporatepredators.org.

Paterson, O. (1980) 'Slavery as Social Death' in *New Left Review* August.

Polanyi, K. (1957) *The Great Transformation: The Political and Economic Origins of Our Time*, Boston, Beacon Press.

Tinker, A.M. Merino, B. and Neimark, M.D. (1982) 'The Normative Origins of Positive Theories: Ideology and Accounting Thought' in *Accounting, Organizations and Society* 167-200.

Tinker, A.M. (1984) 'Theories of the State and the State of Accounting: Economic Reductionism and Political Voluntarism in Accounting Deregulatory Theory' in *Journal of Accounting and Public Policy* 3, pp. 55-77.

Tinker, A.M. (1988) 'Panglossian Accounting Theories: The Science of Apologizing in Style' in *Accounting, Organizations and Society* 13 (2) pp. 165-189.

Tinker, A.M. (1999) 'The Hegelian Logic of Critical Research: Understanding Professor Yoshinori Shiozawa' in *Accounting, Auditing and Accountability Journal* 12(1).

Tinker, A.M. and Lowe, E.A. (1984) 'One-Dimensional Management Science: The Making of a Technocratic Consciousness' in *Interfaces* 14 (2) pp. 40-55.

Todaro, L. 'The Promise of Prague' in *Village Voice* 10 October 2000.

Turner, M. (1984) *Enclosures in Britain* London, Macmillan Press.

Chapter 6

Problematizing Discourse Analysis: Can We Talk About Management Knowledge?

Kirstie Ball and Damian E. Hodgson

Introduction

Proponents of discourse analysis argue with some justification that 'the study of discourse is emerging as one of the primary means of analysing complex organizational phenomena and engaging with the dynamic and often illusive features of organizing' (Oswick, Keenoy and Grant, 2000, p. 1115). However, there is a serious danger in the field of Organization Studies (and in social science more generally) of what has been referred to as 'discourse babble', a term used by Henriques *et al.* to highlight the 'extravagant vagueness concerning the limits of application of the term' (1984, p. 105). In *Manufacturing the Employee* (1996), Roy Jacques purports to offer a historical discourse analysis of management knowledge in North America. His work draws upon evidence through which we can construct temporally-bounded dominant cultural discourses, and examples of more specific translations of the similarly bounded discursive practices, which contributed to the construction and production of management knowledge from the 19th to the 21st century. His objective, as we see it, is to problematize current conceptions of 'black boxed', normalized elements of management knowledge by analysing how they are culturally, politically and, above all, historically produced. The work attempts to illuminate the discursive and episodical nature of this production.

In this paper, which attempts a modest and sympathetic methodological critique of Jacques' work, we make several assertions concerning his project, which are, admittedly, embedded in the same current and historical discourses he attempts to problematize. It is structured as follows. We begin with an exposition of Jacques' method and objectives: what he purports to do, and how he does it. We then offer the following critique. Given the recent emergence of 'organizational discourses' as a unit of analysis, and the indiscriminate explosion of work which claims to 'do' discourse analysis in management studies, we suggest that his methodological articulation is brief at best. Second, we argue that his explicit use of the Saussurean definition of 'discourse', and allusion to concepts of Saussurean linguistics is at odds with his emergent discourse analytic strategy which appears to draw upon

Foucault's archaeological and genealogical methods. In particular we focus our argument on the distinction between 'discourse' and 'Discourses', and the practical difficulty in understanding how they are related. In conclusion we offer an alternative conception of discourse analytic work which may guide future intellectual journeys of this nature.

Management Knowledge as Discourse

Since the 1990s there has been an explosion in the use of discourse analysis in management studies. The field has now produced its fifth conference on 'Organizational Discourses', from which have emerged a number of special issues and books addressing the importance and emergent nature of a focus upon 'discourse' in organizational analysis. Whilst the notion of discourse has seduced many a qualitative researcher it is acknowledged that this field of study is fraught with methodological and epistemological problems, namely that:

> ...it has few clear parameters and, as a field of study, it incorporates a variety of diverse perspectives and methodologies reflecting its multidisciplinary origins (Grant, Keenoy and Oswick 1998, p. 2).

Loose definition, diversity and richness thus constitute the field, and its territory has only recently been mapped in any systematic sense (Alvesson and Kärreman, 2000). This is reflected in Jacques' work. Jacques sets out by telling us that he is using a Saussurean conception of discourse alongside the Foucauldian archaeological/genealogical method of discourse analysis. The latter refers to the idea that organizational worlds should be studied both *archaeologically*; as being shaped and constructed through time, according to a set of historically developed 'grand discourses' which constitute social order; and *genealogically*; as local systems of power relations wherein constitutive discourses are mobilized in live social ordering.

This double-edged approach necessitates a deep analysis of evidence, from extra-organizational data in the case of the former, to accounts of micro-social processes in respect of the latter (see, for example, Ball and Wilson 2000). Jacques' analysis is packed with textual artefacts which are serve as a rich resource to the discourse analyst. He begins by presenting a table of management texts from the early twentieth century, and observes that their titles and subject matters are little different from the current range of available management texts. The significance of this observation is the subject matter of the rest of the book: the emergence of managerialist discourse and the significance of *l'employé* are set against more wide ranging social changes associated with the construction and demise of 'Federalist reality', in North America from its early colonial history to the beginning of the twentieth century.

Chapters three and four are at pains to construct this reality, largely drawing upon its contemporary texts such as that of De Tocqueville's 'Democracy in America' (1835) and Hunt's 'Maxims for Merchants' (1857) and occasional live speech fragments from committee meetings. Jacques observes that Federalism in general contained a specific discourse which addressed (and constituted) the identity of the merchant/business person, emphasizing aspects of the individual's moral character. These earlier chapters are, in our view, constructed using a conventional, temporally-linear historical narrative. This is contrasted, in later chapters with the emergence of the 'manufactory', larger organizations, more, and more diverse, employees and the consequential need for 'works management' (1996, p. 50).

This need generated the emergence of the multi-faceted *employé* – an individual whose identity was positioned as 'the good worker', 'the permanent worker', the organization's worker', 'the subordinate', 'the task worker', 'the wage worker', 'the typologized worker', 'the ignorant, childlike, encoded self' and (unsurprisingly) 'the divided self' (1996, p. 70). He builds this multiple identity by reference to newspaper reports (Martin, 1877), memoirs (Morris, 1920), interviews (Garson, 1977), diaries and social commentaries (Borsodi, 1929). These positions of the business person (the manager-employee or worker-employee) were now constituted within a discourse of service, rather than within a discourse of character, with only 'the professional' identity emerging as a direct throwback to the earlier, dominant character discourse. With the subject(s) of management knowledge defined, the book then proceeds to historically and politically locate its development.

Jacques' method and evidence produces a not altogether unexpected mix of levels of analysis, evidence and data, and he deftly integrates them into a generally convincing narrative. However, we would like to make a closer examination of Jacques' conceptualization and use of the terms 'discourse' and 'discourse analysis' to highlight continuing problematics in this field of study.

Jacques' Use of Discourse Analysis

Jacques is explicit in his work that he is attempting a discursive analysis of management knowledge, although his definition of discursive analysis is perfunctory beyond brief references to the work of Saussure and Foucault. This is particularly unfortunate as the notion of 'discourse' is typically inadequately defined, and the breadth of the term can mask a number of fundamental epistemological and ontological differences. There is indeed a danger in the field of Management (and social research more generally) of what has been referred to as 'discourse babble'. This vagueness leads Henriques *et al.* to ask where the limits of this concept of 'discourse' lie; 'Is everything discourse? Are all practices and all subjects captured within the expansive nets of the discursive?' (1984, p. 105). Not only is the concept of discourse often ill-defined, but competing terminology such as 'culture' (Kunda, 1992), 'ideology' (Benson, 1973), 'knowledge' (Knights and Morgan, 1994), 'institutions' (DiMaggio and Powell, 1991), 'rationalities' (Parker, 1995), 'narratives' (Law, 1994) all appear to cover very similar territory.

Concerns over the ambiguity, indeed the methodological laxity, of much of the work describing itself as addressing 'discourse' has recently led to a number of articles attempting to offer some perspective on the field as a whole. To attempt to clarify both Jacques' position and its shortcomings, we will draw on the paper by Alvesson and Kärreman in which they attack the use of 'discourse' 'to cover up muddled thinking or postponed decisions on vital analytical matter' (2000, p. 1129) by attempting to establish a taxonomy of discourse analysis.

For Alvesson and Kärreman (2000), a key dimension by which conceptions of discourse may be differentiated is their Analytical Level i.e. between, on the one hand, localized, context-specific discourses and, on the other, generic, universal 'epochal' discourses, which they denote as 'Discourse'. Between these extremes, they suggest it might be able to distinguish between a range of 'ideal-typical' approaches:

(1) a micro-discourse approach, involving the detailed study of language use
(2) a meso-discourse approach, 'going beyond details of the text and generalizing to similar local contexts' (Alvesson and Kärreman, 2000, p. 1133)
(3) a Grand Discourse approach, which orders and integrates a range of 'discourses' and finally
(4) a Mega-Discourse approach, addressing a universal, if historically-situated, set of vocabularies, such as 'masculinity', or 'globalization'. In general they characterize this dimension as ranging from 'Myopic' to 'Grandiose' notions of discourse.

The enterprise undertaken by Alvesson and Kärreman is timely, and in differentiating conceptions of discourse they underline the importance of specifying the relation between levels of discourse. They rightly highlight the tension between approaches which focus on 'discourses' and those concerned with examining 'Discourse'; 'Investigations of the local construction of discourse treat discourse as an emergent and locally constructed phenomenon, while the study of Discourses usually starts from well established a priori understandings of the phenomenon in question' (Alvesson and Kärreman, 2000, p. 1134). This is not to imply that 'discourse' and 'Discourse' should be seen as incompatible; however, the distinction underlines the vital question posed by Alvesson and Kärreman:

> How does one in empirical work proceed from encounters with texts (documents, interview talk, observed talk) to make summaries and interpretations of wider sets of discourses including aggregations of a variety of elements, an integrated framework of vocabularies, ideas, cognition, and interrelated with these, practices of various kinds? In short: To what extent – and if so, when and how – can we move from discourses to Discourse(s)? (2000, p. 1146).

The distinction between these approaches exists not only as a philosophical commitment, but equally is evident in the type of material considered as elements of discourse. Hence the study of 'discourses' in the most *myopic* sense limits itself to readings of text/conversation with little or no connection drawn to surrounding social and power relations (cf. Schegloff, 1997) referred to by Alvesson and

Kärreman as 'the trap of linguistic reductionism' (2000, p. 1145). The danger is neatly summed up by Parker; 'Language may be the medium for all forms of enquiry into (the) social world, but it does not follow from that premise that language is all there is' (1995, p. 557). While most research based on discourse analysis claims that it would be a mistake to see discourse as simply concerned with language, the work itself often does not reflect this, implying that the social world essentially consists simply of talk and text, with material practices a secondary effect. This is often the case in approaches based in the linguistic tradition, where theory, action and communication are conflated into one term. Stubbs, for example, in his text *Discourse Analysis*, accepts that 'the terms text and discourse require some comment, since their use is often ambiguous and confusing' before going on to say 'I do not propose to draw any important distinction between the two terms (...) they often simply imply slight differences in emphasis, on which I do not base any important theoretical distinction' (1983, p. 9). This should be contrasted with more sociologically-inclined accounts, such as that of Norman Fairclough, who makes an important distinction here; 'whereas all linguistic phenomena are social, not all social phenomena are linguistic (...) discourse refers to the whole process of social interaction of which a text is just a part' (1989, p. 23). Language does indeed reflect social contingencies and acts as a medium for their reproduction and reconstitution, and as such is therefore a key focus for social research. Nonetheless, society is not *reducible* to language and linguistic analysis, and the restrictions of language as a human construct rather than as some transcendent, universal base matter must therefore be appreciated in all forms of social research.

It is at this point, then, that we reintroduce Jacques conception of discourse. Jacques seeks to avoid 'the trap of linguistic reductionism' by drawing on both Saussurean and Foucauldian notions of discourse. He defines his position by stating; 'Discourse can be interpreted to mean "what can be said". This differs from focusing on what *is* said. While the *site* of discursive analysis is language, discourse is a relationship between bodies, meanings, power and language [Foucault]. Through the process of discursive relationships, material events are related to the words through which they attain meaning [Saussure]' (Jacques 1992a, p. 87 cit. Jacques 1996, p. 19, original emphases). He later states:

> A discursive approach to social reality focuses on knowledge and language. What can be said is both an indication of social values and a powerful shaper of social action. Experience that does not reflect the values embedded in discourse may as well not exist because it has no social effect (Jacques, 2000, p. 67).

This definition of discourse has three implications. First, that discourse analysis is concerned with language use beyond the utterance or sentence; second, that it is concerned with an articulation of materiality and social relations, and third, that it is concerned with the dialogic quality of communication. Nevertheless, in light of the framework set out by Alvesson and Kärreman, Jacques' conception of discourse can be seen to be both all-embracing and simultaneously undifferentiated. In particular, his conception appears to incorporate both 'discourse' and 'Discourse', both the myopic and the grandiose notions of discourse. Consequently, he fails to address the essential question 'To what extent (...) can we move from discourses to Discourse(s)?' (or from Discourse(s) to discourse(s)?). We see this problem as resulting from his unproblematized juxtaposition of Saussurean and Foucauldian ideas, and between 'early' Foucault and 'late' Foucault. In the following sections we discuss these juxtapositions before moving on to questions of 'discourse' and 'Discourse'.

Saussure and Foucault: Strange Bedfellows?

Saussure's 'semiological' approach underpins a significant development in the field of linguistics; that language should be seen as *constitutive* rather than *representational*. Saussure was the father of structural linguistics – he saw language as 'a system that has its own arrangement' (1974:22). For Saussure, words attain meaning purely from their relationship to other words, not on their form. Thus, we cannot derive meaning or interpret the significance of something without comparing it to other similar things. Language, therefore, is nothing but differences between the elements that constitute the system. Furthermore, the system is not something that is 'out there' waiting to be discovered: Saussure distinguished between *parole* – individual speech, and *langue* – which referred to the 'sum of impressions deposited in the brain of each member of the community, almost like a dictionary of which identical copies have been distributed to each individual' (1974:19). This is similar, although not identical to Chomsky's distinction between *competence* (the speaker-hearer's knowledge of the language) and *performance* (the actual use of the language in speech situations).

Clarification of this distinction occurs in Saussure's discussion of the speech circuit: this concerns the arbitrary linking of linguistic resource and linguistic sound to produce a conversation. Imagine a conversation between two individuals, A and B. A opens the conversation and articulates part of their linguistic resource (concepts) by associating it with a linguistic sound (sound image). This sound image is unlocked and spoken by A to B, who then connects the sound image with its associated concept and speaks back to A. The concept becomes the signified, and the sound image becomes the signifier. *Competence, langue, concept* and *signified* focus on what can be said, whereas *performance, parole, sound image* and *signifier* focus on what is said. Language thus becomes a purely ideal, self-contained phenomenon whose articulation is based upon the speech circuit. Saussure postulated that the relationship between signified and signifier was arbitrary – in other words, that sign and signifier pairings are socio-historically contingent. For Saussure, this also becomes the underlying principle by which social practices are explained.

Hence Saussure's approach, in highlighting the arbitrariness of the link between signifier and signified, indicates the role played by language in giving shape to 'reality' through signification. As Henriques *et al.* explain, 'The argument is not that words determine but that those practices which constitute our everyday lives are produced and reproduced as an integral part of the production of signs and signifying systems' (1984, p. 99). This semiological conception of language built upon the focus on language in 20th century philosophy (Wittgenstein, 1953; Winch, 1958) and paved the way for what has been described as the 'linguistic turn' in social studies and in particular in the development of a social constructionist perspective in the social sciences.

Saussure's principle of arbitrariness is used by Jacques in his discussion of the identity of 'l'employé'. In the multiplicity of positions which we described earlier, there is necessarily no fundamental connection between the term 'employee', for example, and the physical individual to which the term refers. Moreover, the identification of someone as an 'employee' reflects social conventions and does not reflect the essential nature of the person but rather a social orthodoxy of classification (Jacques, 1996). Thus, in Saussurean terms, the term 'employee' itself only has meaning insofar as it can be classified as different from other signifiers such as 'employer', 'unemployed', 'worker', 'customer' and so on.

However, we would argue that the relationship between speakers, and their language use in terms of signs and signifiers is not as dyadic as Saussure would have us believe. Saussurean linguistics does not address the nature of social relations other than by default. A reliance on Saussurean linguistics and notions of discourse may tell us what can be said, but it does not illuminate central questions concerning who gets to say what, how, to whom, why, and whose version becomes accepted as 'truth'. Saussure may have had grandiose aspirations to 'Discourse', but more frequently his analysis merely concerns local 'discourse'. For an understanding of 'Discourse', we turn to Jacques' use of the work of Michel Foucault.

Foucault Contra Foucault

A major weakness in Jacques position stems from his tendency to regard Foucauldian work as a coherent and consistent corpus. Foucault repeatedly stresses the hypothetical and tentative nature of much of his writings. He explains that 'the notion common to all the work that I have done since *Histoire de la Folie* is that of *problematization*' (Foucault, 1988, p. 257 emphasis added), and states that the role of the intellectual is 'to question over and over again what is postulated as self-evident, to disturb people's mental habits ...' (Foucault, 1988, p. 265). This approach is celebrated by numerous commentators on Foucault:

> For (Foucault) uncertainty causes no anguish ... He advances hypotheses with the delight that others reserve for the revelation of truth ... As he remarks in an interview ... the uncertainty is genuine, not a rhetorical device. He compares his last book to a Gruyère cheese, with holes in which the reader can install himself (Sheridan, 1980, pp. 222-3).

This view of his oeuvre is reflected by Burrell, who denies that Foucault's work can be, nor that he intended it to be, integrated into an overarching 'Grand Theory';

'In the place of widely-held views, he substituted tentative hypotheses which invite, indeed beg for, heated discussion and debate' (Burrell, 1988, p. 222). Further evidence can be found in several of Foucault's interviews, which echo one of Foucault's most quoted phrases, 'Do not ask who I am and do not ask me to remain the same: Leave it to our bureaucrats and our police to see that our papers are in order' (Foucault, 1972, p. 17). Thus unsurprisingly, a retrospective consideration of his work indicates a clear shift in philosophy from the structuralist early work, in which history may be divided into epistemes, to the later work which attempts to rectify the implicit determinism by focusing on tactics, subjugated knowledge and the capillary, ascending operation of power.

In Foucault's earlier work (1975; 1977) his emphasis is firmly on discourses as large-scale power/knowledge regimes, defined as epistemes, such as the discourse of medicine, or of humanism, whereby individuals are constituted as objects through calculation and normalizing judgement. Foucault's structuralist background is evident in his attempts to demonstrate the hegemony of such regimes at particular historical junctures, and the position Foucault adopts in his major early works frequently obscures the potential for the resistance to and transformation of such regimes. This tendency persists in the work of Foucault most frequently cited in managerial debates, *Discipline and Punish* (1977), where the focus is on the growth of a specific form of power, disciplinary power, and the discourses which accompany and embody it. Poster, for instance, argues that Foucault himself is 'tempted by the totalizing impulse at several points in his text (*Discipline and Punish*)' (1984, p. 103). Similarly, McNay notes of this work, 'Despite his assertions to the contrary, Foucault in fact produces a vision of power as a unidirectional, dominatory force which individuals are unable to resist' (McNay, 1992, p. 40). This determinist tendency, in Alvesson and Kärreman's framework, can be seen as a reliance upon more 'grandiose' understandings of discourse; micro-discourses are merely the epiphenomena of grander Discursive shifts, towards the 'disciplinary society', for instance. It is no coincidence that Jacques reproduces the notion of the emergence of the disciplinary reality. along with similar epochal shifts; from pre-Federalist to Federalist reality, for instance. Thus Jacques can state:

> Somewhere between the 1857 publication of 'Maxims for Merchants' and the 1913 publication of Andrew Carnegies 'The Empire of Business', a new reality emerged, a new industrial common sense replaced Hunt's reality, erased any popular awareness that it had ever existed and placed its logic in the realm of the nonsensible (1996, p. 27).

At the same time, however, when clarifying his arguments in various other writings and interviews, Foucault is explicit in underlining the existence and subversive potential of subjugated discourses within such regimes (see, for instance, Foucault, 1980). The change of focus in Foucault's later work (1977; 1985; 1986) was accompanied by an overdue empirical focus on the operation of subjugated discourses. Thus the grand Discourses, such as disciplinary power, are now described by Foucault as 'great anonymous, almost unspoken strategies'

(Foucault, 1980, p. 95) constituted from the bottom up. His position is made clear in an interview, where he states:

> If you ask me "Does this new technology of power take its historical origin from an identifiable individual or group of individuals who decide to implement it so as to further their interests or facilitate their utilization of the social body?" then I would say "No". These tactics were invented and organized from the starting points of local conditions and particular needs. They took shape in a piecemeal fashion, prior to any class strategy designed to weld them into vast, coherent ensembles (Foucault, 1980, p. 159).

The key point here is the lack of co-ordination, the lack of an organized force deliberately manipulating power relations in society across time. Nonetheless:

> There is a logic to the practices. There is a push towards a strategic objective, but no-one is pushing. The objective emerged historically, taking particular forms and encountering specific obstacles, conditions and resistances. Will and calculation were involved. The overall effect, however, escaped the actors' intentions, as well as those of anybody else (Dreyfus and Rabinow, 1982, p. 187).

The local actors, therefore, are clear of what they are doing and why. The development of these local initiatives into a larger strategy is demystified succinctly by Foucault; 'People know what they do; they frequently know why they do what they do; but what they don't know is what they do does' (Foucault, quoted in Dreyfus and Rabinow, 1982, p. 187). This shift in position is in a sense a reversal; rather than being able to 'read' the emergence of discourses from the development of Discourse, Foucault now posits the interaction of numerous discourses to enact major Discursive change. As we believe that it is clear that Foucault's work is not seen as a coherent and consistent corpus, we problematize Jacques' method because of the lack of space he devotes to this issue. Accordingly, the close juxtaposition of Foucault and Saussure is equally problematic if we take this into consideration.

How Can We Talk of Management Knowledge?

The above critique of *Manufacturing the Employee* is in a sense a recognition of the endeavour undertaken by Jacques; the writing of a disruptive and problematizing poststructuralist history of American management knowledge. In doing so, his work reflects the argument that 'we are nothing but our history, and therefore we will never get a total and detached picture of who we are or of our history' (Dreyfus and Rabinow, 1982, p. 122). However, by decomposing the notion of discourse adopted by Jacques, we mean to highlight some of the inconsistencies and difficulties involved in the project, in particular that his reliance upon Saussurean notions of discourse and Foucauldian notions of discourses/Discourses is potentially problematic without addressing the questions of how the two may be related. Similarly, we also ask whether the apparent distance between these two ideas as expressed in the Alvesson and Kärreman framework is a problem.

For example, the array of evidence presented and the discussion he advances attempts to cut through the levels of analysis implicit within the Foucauldian framework. However, in chapter six where disciplinary technologies, techniques and emergent fields of management knowledge are discussed, analysis is kept, apart from a few anecdotes, firmly at the institutional level. Maybe this is unsurprising, given that the aim of this book was to highlight the surface of emergence of the field of management knowledge, to problematize and politicize it as historically located. The very fact that management knowledge was emergent means that coherent datasets demonstrating the richness of social relations in the workplace simply would not exist to be analysed as part of this project. We see his tendency towards a temporally-linear historical narrative as symptomatic of this, and from within text we find his examination of any link between discourse and Discourse unsophisticated in nature.

In our discussion of Saussurean linguistics and Foucauldian analysis, we tried to show that the direction of the relationship between discourse and Discourse differs: Saussure focuses on discourse, and makes general claims about Discourse; whereas early Foucault focuses on Discourse, with discourses having a small role to play. In later work, the situation is reversed. Thus a number of clichés may describe Jacques position: is he 'falling between two stools?', 'having his cake and eating it?'. Can he make generalizable claims about Discourse from his local evidence, whilst, at the same time explain the local relations he describes as being located within grander Discursive trends? Like Alvesson and Kärreman assert, their link here is assumed, rather than articulated, but we acknowledge that the extent to which it can be explored is circumscribed by the available evidence.

So how can we talk about 'Management Knowledge'? We would assert that if we are to do so with the poststructuralist commitments similar to those of Jacques, it is important to do so with an acute sense of our own history, and with as much methodological and epistemological reflexivity that space allows. If we are going to place Saussure and Foucault, both early and late, in close proximity, and if we are to place them in a taxonomy as differentiated approaches pertaining to either discourse or Discourse, then it is imperative for discourse analysts and theorists to consider the nature and direction of their relationship, but to do so without being accused of either rampant realism or relativism. To avoid the traps inherent in these positions, as either over-categorizing apparent fluidity between levels of analysis or promoting the use of depthless social ontologies. A discussion of 'paradigm wars' is beyond the scope of this paper, but we are conscious of our own academic formation within the business school environment, and it is a debate which is unavoidable. There is as yet no solution to this problematic, but we call for reflexivity on the part of those employing discourse analytic strategies. Whilst we have taken up the majority of space in this chapter critiquing the methodology with which Jacques makes his assertions, he has an important message for the practising manager, and for organizations who treat knowledge and its management as an issue of value. Jacques highlights that forms of management knowledge have a history, and embedded within this history are issues of power, which govern what can be said, what is said, and what is accepted as true. So whilst we as academics are concerned with how best these processes might be known, practitioners and policymakers may want to reflect more deeply on the historically embedded content of what is known and learnt in their specific contexts, what comes to be accepted as normal, what gets discounted and why. It is for this reason that we remain sympathetic to Jacques project: we use it as a platform to call for reflexivity upon one's situated knowledge (Haraway, 1991) as a member of the business school private organizational, or professional knowledge community.

References

Alvesson, M. and Kärreman, D. (2000) 'Varieties of Discourse: On the Study of Organizations through Discourse Analysis' in *Human Relations* 53 (9) pp. 1125-49.

Ball, K. and Hodgson, D. (2001) 'Knowing Your Limits: Organization Studies and Discourse Analytic Technologies' Paper presented to *Critical Management Studies Conference*, UMIST, Manchester, July 2001.

Ball, K. and Wilson, D.C. (2000) 'Power, Control and Computer-Based Performance Monitoring: Repertoires, Resistance and Subjectivities' in *Organization Studies* 21 (3) pp. 539-565.

Benson, J.K. (1973) 'The Analysis of Bureaucratic-Professional Conflict: Functional versus Dialectical Approaches' in *The Sociological Quarterly* Vol. 14 pp. 376-394.

Burrell, G. (1988) 'Modernism, Post Modernism and Organizational Analysis 2: The Contribution of Michel Foucault' in *Organization Studies* Vol. 9 (2) pp. 221-235.

DiMaggio, P.J. and Powell, W.W. (1991) 'The Iron Cage Revisited: Institutional Isomorphism and Collective Rationality in Organizational Fields,' in W.W. Powell and P.J. DiMaggio (eds.) *The New Institutionalism in Organizational Analysis.*, pp. 63-82. Chicago, University of Chicago Press.

Dreyfus, H.L. and Rabinow, P. (1982) *Michel Foucault: Beyond Structuralism and Hermeneutics* Brighton, Harvester Press.

Fairclough, L. (1989) *Language and Power* London, Longman.

Foucault, M. (1972) *The Archaeology of Knowledge* London, Tavistock.

Foucault, M. (1975) *The Birth of the Clinic: An Archaeology of Medical Perception* London, Tavistock.

Foucault, M. (1977) *Discipline and Punish: The Birth of the Prison* Harmondsworth, Penguin.

Foucault, M. (1979) *The History of Sexuality Volume I: An Introduction* London, Allen Lane.

Foucault, M. (1980) *Power/Knowledge-selected interviews and other writings 1972-1977* Gordon, C. (ed.) Brighton, Harvester Press.

Foucault, M. (1985) *The History of Sexuality Volume II: The Use of Pleasure* Harmondsworth, Penguin.

Foucault, M. (1986) *The History of Sexuality Volume III: The Care of the Self* Harmondsworth, Penguin.

Foucault, M. (1988) *Politics, Philosophy, Culture: Interviews and Other Writings 1977-1984* Kritzman, L.D. (ed.) London, Routledge.

Grant, D. Keenoy T. and Oswick, C. (1998) (eds.) *Discourse and Organization* London, Sage.

Haraway, D (1991) *Simians, Cyborgs and Women: The Reinvention of Nature* New York, Routledge.

Henriques, J., Hollway, W., Unwin, C., Venn, C. and Walkerdine, V. (1984) *Changing the Subject: Psychology, Social Regulation and Subjectivity* London: Methuen.

Jacques, R. (1995) *Manufacturing the Employee: Management Knowledge from the 19th to 21st Centuries* London, Sage.

Jacques, R. (2000) 'Theorizing Knowledge as Work: the Need for a "Knowledge Theory of Value"' in *Managing Knowledge* Prichard, C. Hull, R. Chumer, M. and Willmott, H. London, Macmillan.

Knights, D. and Morgan, G. (1994) 'Organization Theory, Consumption and the Service Sector' in Hassard, J. and Parker, M. (eds.) *Towards a New Theory of Organizations* London, Routledge.

Kunda, G. (1992) *Engineering Culture* Philadelphia, Temple University Press.

Law, J. (1994) 'Organization, Narrative and Strategy' in Hassard, J. and Parker, M. (eds.) *Towards a New Theory of Organizations* London, Routledge.

McNay, L. (1992) *Foucault and Feminism: Power, Gender and the Self* Cambridge, Polity Press.

Parker, M. (1995) 'Critique in the Name of What? Postmodernism and Critical Approaches to Organization' in *Organization Studies* Vol. 16 (4) pp. 553-564.

Poster, M. (1984) *Foucault, Marxism and History: Mode of Production versus Mode of Information* Cambridge, Polity Press.

Saussure, F. de (1974) *Course in General Linguistics* London, Fontana.

Schegloff, E (1997) 'Whose text? Whose context?' in *Discourse and Society* 8/2 pp165-187

Sheridan, A. (1980) *Michel Foucault: The Will to Truth* London, Tavistock.

Stubbs, M. (1983) *Discourse Analysis: The Sociolinguistic Analysis of Natural Language* Oxford, Blackwell.

Winch, P. (1958) *The Idea of a Social Science* London, Routledge.

Wittgenstein, L. (1953) *Philosophical Investigations* Oxford, Blackwell.

Chapter 7

Explanatory Critique, Capitalism and Feasible Alternatives: A Realist Assessment of Jacques' *Manufacturing the Employee*

Robert Willmott

Introduction

In general, the positive (descriptive and explanatory) and the normative (critical and evaluative) sides of critical social science are imbalanced: if critical social science is to become more successful it must address normative theory (Sayer 1995). Jacques is not alone here. Historically, Marxism has explicitly eschewed normative theory. However, in his preface, Jacques refers to the metaphor of the invisible hand as 'one of the central icons used to defend the positive social value of corporate capitalism'. A paragraph or so later, he assumes – reasonably – that the main purpose of inquiry is to identify the little which can be changed, to assess the limits of the possible and to anticipate the consequences of various actions. He then argues that:

> Societies are not voluntaristic in the sense that they can be rationally planned, but a central component of social action has to do with taking responsibility for one's choices and acting purposefully in relation to one's values […] we must create a more comprehensive forum for discussing the problems of tomorrow by articulating the ways that today's problems are constrained by *yesterday's* … (Jacques, 1995, pp. ii-ix).

Finally, he argues that the very point of explanatory critique is to facilitate useful action. By 'useful action', I take it that he means the aim of reducing illusion and freeing people from domination. I would not dispute any of this. That we may only be able to identify 'the little which can be changed [for the better]' shows that we cannot escape assessment of the feasible alternatives that derive from prior social, cultural and economic conditioning. Jacques is well aware of the untenability of rational planning, for example. He assures us that his critical account does not yield to prediction (presumably because he accepts that society is an open system). Furthermore, his account 'seeks to throw into relief the fault lines and points of leverage marking the points at which intentional action is most likely to have results' (1995, p. 14). Indeed, his book is *practical* 'because it seeks to change work practices by changing the way we think about what can be changed and what possibilities exist for those involved in change' (*idem.*).

However, Jacques does not map out, even in general terms, the alternative social arrangements implied by his recognition of prior conditioning and generic critique of 'management knowledge' of *l'employé*. In essence, we are not dished up what is promised. Indubitably, his correct claim that advanced economies cannot be rationally planned underscores the problems of state socialist planning, for example. Here, reference to Hayek's 'epistemological problem' and to the allocational efficiency of market mechanisms would usefully serve to underscore the (dangerous) myopia of those crude Marxist approaches that dogmatically assert the feasibility of rational central planning. More crucially, it would also show that non-capitalist economies could not avoid *ex post* regulation. However, any assessment of feasibility depends crucially upon an adequate theoretical analysis of concrete socio-economic systems. In this regard, Jacques falls at the first hurdle, since, following Foucault, his analysis is (reductively) discursive, that is, it focuses solely on knowledge and language (see also Jacques 2000). Contrary to Jacques, language and knowledge are not exhaustive of the social.

In contradistinction to Jacques' Foucauldian reductionism, an adequate assessment of feasibility enjoins a realist social ontology. Accordingly, the first section of this article briefly delineates some of the basic tenets of a critical realist social ontology. The second section defines capitalism, which Jacques conspicuously fails to do. Here, following Hodgson (1999), it is argued, *inter alia*, that Marx ignored non-capitalist elements, thereby ignoring the problem of necessary impurities, which has important implications for alternative socio-economic systems. The third section explicates the nature of disaggregative analysis, which is predicated upon a realist ontology. The fourth section addresses the nature of division of labour, knowledge and Hayek. The fifth section discusses the range of plausible future scenarios proffered by Hodgson. The concluding section underscores the need for normative theory.

Critical Social Realism: Stratification and Emergence

My own research (Willmott 1999, 2000a, 2000b, 2001, 2002) utilizes the realist 'morphogenetic approach' as developed by Archer (1995). Morphogenesis is the methodological complement of transcendental realism (see Bhaskar 1975, 1989). However, for the purpose of this article, I do not wish to dwell upon all of the key features of critical social realism.[1] This section will delineate the rudiments of a stratified social ontology, which forms the springboard of my critique and underpins disaggregative analysis of concrete socio-economic systems. In brief, critical realism is a philosophy of and for the social sciences. It is mainly concerned with ontology, with being, and has a relatively open stance towards epistemology (Sayer 2000). Critical realism distinguishes between the real, the actual and the empirical. As Sayer notes, when critical realists refer to the real, this is not in order to claim privileged knowledge of it but to note two things. Firstly, the real is whatever exists, be it natural or social, regardless of our fallible epistemological grasp. Secondly, the real is the realm of objects, their structures and powers. Such (natural or social) objects 'like minerals or ... like bureaucracies ... have certain structures and causal powers, that is, capacities to behave in particular ways, and causal liabilities or passive powers, that is, susceptibilities to certain kinds of change' (Sayer, 2000, p. 11).

Whereas the real refers to the structures and powers of objects, the actual refers to what happens if and when those powers are activated, to what they do. Here, Sayer provides the example of the Marxist distinction between labour power and labour, where the capacity to work derives from irreducible physical and mental structures whilst labour involves the exercise of this capacity. The empirical is defined as the domain of experience. As Sayer argues:

> In distinguishing the real, the actual and the empirical, critical realism proposes a 'stratified ontology' in contrast to other ontologies which have 'flat' ontologies populated by either the actual or the empirical, or a conflation of the two. Thus empirical realism assumes that what we can observe is all that exists, while 'actualism' assumes that what actually happens at the level of events exhausts the world, leaving no domain of the real, of powers which can be activated or remain dormant (Sayer 2000, p. 12).

Furthermore, Sayer notes that critical realism argues that the world is characterized by emergence, i.e., situations in which the conjunction of two or more features of aspects gives rise to new phenomena, which have properties that are irreducible to those of their constituents, despite their necessary dependence. Sayer refers to the standard (physical) example of water, whose emergent properties are quite different from those of its constituents, hydrogen and oxygen (see Willmott 2000a, 2002, for social examples of emergent properties and an elucidation of the differentiation of the real, actual and empirical).

As Lawson notes, social systems involve 'dependencies or combinations [that] causally affect the elements or aspects, and the form and structure of the elements causally influence each other and so also the whole' (1997, p. 64). Equally, Hodgson takes Friedman to task for his 'conceptual blindness to emergent properties of the system that transcend individuals. There properties, furthermore, are necessary for the very survival of the capitalist system that he [Friedman] advocated' (Hodgson 1999, p. 69). Indeed, 'Where many market individualists go wrong is in seeing an atomistic subjectivism as a necessary theoretical foundation of any argument for markets' (ibid., p. 73). Hodgson explicitly adopts a stratified social ontology. Furthermore, he also provides a transcendental realist argument for what he calls the 'impurity principle', as we shall see shortly.

Finally, realism rejects the (Humean) 'successionist' view of causation, which views causation in terms of regularities among sequences of events. Social structures are composed of internally relates elements, whose causal powers, when combined, are emergent from those of their constituents. Thus, hierarchical structures might enable delegation, division of tasks, surveillance and efficient throughput of work (Sayer 2000). For realists:

Causation is *not* understood on the model of regular successions of events, and hence explanation need not depend on finding them, or searching for putative social laws... What causes something to happen has nothing to do with the number of times we had observed it happening. Explanation depends instead on identifying causal mechanisms and how they work, and discovering if they have been activated and under what conditions... explaining why a certain mechanism exists involves discovering the nature of the structure or object which possesses that mechanism or power... the price mechanism depends on structures of competitive relations between profit-seeking firms producing for markets, and so on (Sayer 2000, p. 14).

Consistent regularities only occur in closed systems. The social world is intrinsically open, such that the same causal power can produce different outcomes and different causal mechanisms can produce the same result. Furthermore, it is precisely because society is an open system that the future is open. Indeed, it is on this basis that Hodgson is able to consider possible non-capitalist future developments (or what he terms long-term 'scenario planning'). As we shall see later, scenario building is not idle speculation, 'but the investigation of *plausible future causal chains*, stemming from the conditions and forces of the present' (Hodgson 1999, p. 180, original emphasis). Here, deterministic or probabilistic modelling is rejected because of the insurmountable difficulties in making forecasts in complex, adaptive open systems.

Capitalism and Necessary Impurity

Recently, Jacques commented:

> ... I am again reminded that while my colleagues who are ... primarily interested in understanding from a radical perspective – that is, a willingness to return to the roots of knowledge and conceive of the good society *de novo* – I am less bold. Perhaps it is because I write from the USA, where alternatives to conservatism – let alone capitalism – are extremely marginal. Perhaps it is for other reasons. Nonetheless, I think it would be fair to say that my goals are more liberal than radical and, as a consequence, my assumptions incorporate certain capitalist relationships because I do not imagine any likely future outside of them (2000, p. 235).

Yet we are not told what such capitalist relationships consist of; in fact, in *Manufacturing the Employee* no definition of capitalism is provided. This is a pity, since a rejection of capitalism does not enjoin conceiving of the good society *de novo*. However, following Hodgson, capitalism is essentially a type of market system involving extensive private property, capital markets and employment contracts. For Marx, it is generalized commodity production:

> It is generalized in a double sense, first because under capitalism most goods and services are destined for sale on the market, that is, they are commodities ... Second, because under capitalism one type of item is importantly a commodity: labour power, or the capacity for work. In other words, an important feature of capitalism is the existence of a labour market in which labour is hired by an employer and put to work according to

the terms of the contract. Within capitalism, there are markets for both capital and labour power, and these have crucial regulatory functions for the system as a whole. However, markets and private property are necessary but not sufficient features of capitalism: not all market systems are capitalist systems (Hodgson 1999, p. 121).

Marx ignored all the non-capitalist elements when analysing the capitalist system. This, Hodgson points out, was because he believed that commodity exchange and the hiring of labour power in a capitalist firm would become increasingly widespread, displacing all other forms of economic co-ordination and productive organization. As he puts it:

> Confidence in the all-consuming power of capitalist markets was Marx's justification for ignoring impurities in his analysis of the alleged essentials of the capitalist system. Such impurities were regarded as doomed and extraneous hangovers of the feudal past, eventually to be pulverized by the ever-expanding market. Just as capitalism and commodity-exchange were assumed to become all-powerful, the Marxian theoretical system was built on these structures and relations alone (Hodgson 1999, p. 125).

Now, Hodgson argues that 'impurity' *necessarily* characterizes all socio-economic systems. In other words, every socio-economic system must rely on at least one structurally dissimilar subsystem to function. As he puts it:

> There must always be a co-existent plurality of modes of production, so that the social formation as a whole has the requisite structural variety to cope with change. Thus if one type of structure is to prevail (e.g. central planning), other structures (e.g. markers, private corporations) are necessary to enable the system as a whole to work effectively ... In particular, neither planning nor markets can become all-embracing systems of socio-economic regulation. In general, it is not feasible for one mode of production to become so comprehensive that it drives out all the others (Hodgson 1999, p. 126).

Thus, the utopias of both the traditional (radical) left and of the neo-liberal right are unfeasible partly because they do not incorporate the fundamental importance of structural variety in any complex socio-economic system. For Hodgson, the impurity principle is a theoretical guideline, predicated upon ontological considerations. Whilst he does not make use of such phraseology as transcendental realism, Hodgson's impurity principle is quintessentially transcendentally realist. As he argues, the impurity principle 'concerns much more than the empirical existence of impurities. Above all it concerns their functional necessity for the system as a whole. [This recognition] ...is entirely absent from the writings of Marx and his followers ...' (Hodgson 1999, p. 127). *Crucially, a corollary of the impurity principle is that an immense variety of forms of any given socio-economic system can exist: an infinite variety of forms of capitalism is possible* (Hodgson 1999, p. 130).

The above would help Jacques clarify what precisely alternative (non-capitalist) social relationships might comprise. The salient point here is that radical views that demand abolition of markets and private property fail to understand that some elements of private commodity exchange are necessary to sustain innovation and diversity. In sum, (feasible) alternative scenarios enjoin that we spell out the nature of capitalism in order to assess which elements can be changed, attenuated, replaced or expunged. Non-capitalist social relations should not be confused with unfeasible radical-left programmes that decry market regulation and the price mechanism. Indeed, as we shall see in a moment, advanced division of labour necessarily results in inequalities that are independent of class. In other words, market socialism cannot avoid the power imbalances and inequalities that derive from division of labour.

Disaggregative Analysis and Counterfactuals

One needs to stick to the distinction between immanent possibilities for change (feasibility) and their contingent realization (that is, mobilization). If one plays down the former, the slide towards fatalism is inexorable. However, in light of Jacques' pessimism above, I want to reaffirm that even if enough people are willing to try to realize certain desired end-states, viz. non-capitalist social relations, such end-states are feasible. As Sayer (1995) argues, there are some promising alternatives. One would be naïve not to agree with Alvesson and Willmott's point that 'While critical reflection is rarely a sufficient condition of [emancipatory progress], it is generally a necessary element ...' (1996, p. 14). I am not (implicitly) reproving Jacques for not having provided us with a 'blueprint'. Instead, the aim is to think through the likely tendencies or mechanisms of different forms of political-economic organization. This does not mean conceiving of the society *de novo*. On the contrary, the materiality of the past provides us with a delimited range of possibilities (as Jacques also acknowledges). The crucial task is to disaggregate socio-cultural conditioning in order to consider whether particular elements of political-economic systems can exist only in combination with one set of other elements or whether they can also coexist with other sets. It thus assesses the validity of abstractions.

To recapitulate, the social ontology adopted here is a stratified one, where structure and culture are held to be emergent properties irreducible to agency yet causally efficacious. Both external (contingent) and internal irreducible social and cultural relations and forms constitute the social world. Abstract analysis is used to establish whether relations are external or internal. Marxists such as Bertell Ollman (1971, 1990) have argued that the social totality is internally related. This immediately forfeits analysis of parts of capitalist economies that may operate in similar fashion in post-capitalist ones. However, the contingency of sexism and racism underscores the untenability of the universal internal social relations ontology. As Sayer (1995, p. 27) points out, a realist approach is open to the possibility that features found within capitalism, such as markets or an advanced division of labour, could exist outside capitalism, and possess causal powers irreducible to those of the unique powers of capitalism, such as minority private ownership of the means of production.

For Alvesson and Willmott:

... emancipation is not a gift to be bestowed upon employees but, rather, is an existentially painful process of confronting and overcoming socially and psychologically unnecessary restrictions. The latter include a broad range of phenomena extending from sexual and racial discrimination to dependency on a consumerist lifestyle for self-esteem (1996, p. 162).

In the abstract, capitalism does not presuppose sexism and racism and vice versa. This points towards the immanent possibility for capitalist economic organization along non-sexist and non-racist lines, since race ideologies and sexist beliefs are contingently related. Indeed, sexist practices can be expensive. Careful abstraction from concrete social reality is clearly immensely useful in this respect. Despite the tendency for radical theorists to abstract the exploitative internal capital/labour relation, capitalism in the inclusive sense is much more than this as we have seen above in our discussion of the impurity principle and thus caution needs to be exercised. In discussing contingent and necessary relations, we can say that some relations are asymmetric. For example, money can exist without capitalism but not vice versa; markets can be considered separately from capitalism but not vice versa. As we have seen, the capital/labour relation is symmetric, since each presupposes the other and cannot exist without the other. As Sayer puts it:

A disaggregative approach ... requires particular care over how we abstract. Abstractions may leave out that which is only contingently related to the phenomena under consideration [e.g. capitalism and sexism], but if they leave out essential features which make a significant difference to the process of interest then serious misunderstanding may result (1995, p. 31).

One of the key failings of past radical political economy approaches is the reduction of concrete reality to the capital/labour relation, thereby ignoring the intractability of an advanced division of labour. As Sayer argues, the explanations offered by radical political economy can be further assessed by considering the counterfactuals that they imply. If we say *x* was responsible for *y* then we imply that in the absence of *x*, *y* would not have existed or happened. If this is the case then we know something is wrong with the explanation. Counterfactual questions may help us see that mechanisms or conditions other than *x* could have been responsible for *y* or at least could have been jointly responsible, with *x*, for *y*.

Thus, if it were claimed or assumed that the hierarchical organization of large-scale production were purely a function of its capitalist social character, then asking whether non-capitalist large industry could be organised non-hierarchically would help to support Marx's view that hierarchy and supervision in such industry are also, in part, technically unavoidable (*idem.*).

It is by asking counterfactual questions that we can establish what is contingent or necessary. Sexism and racism exemplify contingency vis-à-vis capitalism. Indeed, in comparison with the United Kingdom, the existence of better anti-discrimination laws in the United States underscores the fact that its capitalist organization *qua* capitalist operates efficiently. Furthermore, the fact that both capitalism and market socialism generate macro-economic problems shows that their social relations of production are irrelevant and that they share some other feature that generates such problems (market regulation, for example).

But Managers are Employees! Division of Labour, Knowledge and Hayek

I have referred to the materiality and intractability of an advanced division of labour. This is often played down or ignored in radical political economy. Jacques discusses the increase in division of labour, specifically the rise of the 'professional' as part of the 'manufacture of *l'employé*'. He emphasizes the fact that managers were (and are) generically employees. This seems to be something of a conundrum for him. Whatever the reason, he does not address the implications of the growing division of labour and associated dispersal of knowledge vis-à-vis feasible alternatives to capitalist relations. What needs to be recognized is the materiality and intractability of division of labour, which is irreducible to private ownership. It seems that Jacques is unhappy with the inequalities generated by the growth of *l'employé*. But he also (rightly) recognizes that central planning is not the answer. Given his concern with epistemology, it is a pity that we are not offered an analysis of the material and informational properties of an advanced division of labour. He does, of course, deal with knowledge in the 'World Three' sense (Popper 1979) – especially management textbooks and their ideological import. But we are not offered even a brief discussion of Hayek's 'epistemological problem', planning, markets and the intractability of division of labour. (It is not unreasonable to expect this, since Jacques introduces political economy and the issue of rational planning in his preface.)

Planning and the Materiality of Division of Labour

The latter are crucial for assessing feasible alternative social arrangements to capitalism. If we take as our starting point the long debate between socialism and capitalism. It is often characterized as one of planning versus markets. As Hodgson (1999) notes, this is misleading: planning in some form exists in all socio-economic systems. At the same time, this is not to suggest that the market always encourages creativity or enterprise. 'However, its capacity to reconcile conflicting plans and maintain a degree of diversity should not be overlooked' (Hodgson 1999, p. 32). As Jacques would agree, we must refrain from an excessive faith in the power and scope of human reason. A prominent element in much socialist thinking is the Enlightenment view that it is possible for people under the right conditions to act in harmony and rational agreement to design and construct a better society. Unless we want to return to a romanticized agrarian past, we have to accept that at present the hierarchy and inequalities associated with an advanced division of labour cannot be transcended.[2] The crucial point, then, is to assess to what extent inequalities and hierarchy can be attenuated, not that they can be transcended. Thus, to Alvesson and Willmott:

Even *within* the constraints of capital accumulation and the domination of instrumental rationality, the contradictory dynamics of modern organizations are capable of accommodating – and indeed promoting – some degree of increase employee responsibility and autonomy... (1996, p. 163).

As Sayer (1995) has convincingly argued, the irreducible causal properties of division of labour are irreducible to forms of ownership. This has been consistently played down in Marxism. Indeed, so-called 'class theory' conflates class and division of labour, thereby obscuring at a stroke the power relations and inequalities that derive from division of labour. It is worth quoting Sayer at length here:

> That class and division of labour characteristics are separate and relatively autonomous can be seen by considering the situation in non-capitalist enterprises, for these represent practical demonstrations of the relative autonomy of divisions of labour from class. Thus a cooperative could have managers and workers, manual and non-manual workers, skilled and unskilled workers, it could have variations in the amount of autonomy and discretion over work, and yet every individual could be equal in terms of ownership. To be sure, a cooperative might very well try to limit these division of labour differences, precisely to stop them overriding its members' equality in terms of ownership or class. Although power deriving from class and division of labour can interact, they are still distinct... Divisions of labour really do divide labour, though not in the same way that class does (1995, pp. 51-52).

Whether formal ownership yields actual control over property and activities depends upon the material and informational qualities of their objects. Thus, Sayer points out that the token character of 'social ownership' derives not merely from contingent forms of organization but from the fact that millions of people cannot hope to control and co-ordinate the products of property that is diverse and often dependent on arcane specialisms and information.

Thus, *pace* Jacques (2000), there are alternatives to capitalism, but they have to confront the intractability of an advanced division of labour and the varying degrees of inequality that derive from it. At the same time, we need to acknowledge, *contra* state socialist planning, the importance of the market. In brief, Hayek's distinction between 'catallaxy' and 'economy' is crucial here. However, Hayek's social ontology is individualist and whose right-wing policy implications are well documented (e.g. Willmott, 2002). Consequently, whilst recognizing the practical import of Hayek's (partially flawed) analysis of the nature of knowledge and its relation to the future, we must never lose sight of the transcendental need for state regulation and, moreover, state intervention. Indeed, any emancipatory programme enjoins assessing the extent of, and limits to, state intervention in order to offset the inequalities of (non-)capitalist economic organization.

Hayek's Catallaxy: the Denial of Social Structure

The key thinker use by neo-liberals in their drive towards quasi-marketization of the public sector in the UK context is Hayek. I have already discussed the materiality of the division of labour, which is autonomous of capitalist social relations. Hayek lends support to the *sui generis* properties of division of labour. He distinguishes between 'catallaxy' and 'economy'. His conception of economy is a restricted one, referring to clusters of economic activities that are organized for a specific purpose and have a unitary hierarchy of ends, in which knowledge of how to achieve ends is shared. A catallaxy, on the other hand, has no unitary hierarch of ends, but a mass of innumerable economies without a specific purpose. As Hayek has famously pointed out, it is the product of *spontaneous* growth as opposed to design. One of Hayek's central arguments, *contra* state socialism, is that the catallaxy eludes regulation by central control. This is due to the extraordinary division of knowledge immanent to any advanced industrial economy. Thus *the* fundamental economic problem is not calculational but epistemological, namely how to co-ordinate the actions of innumerable agents without the possibility of any adequate centralized knowledge of their needs and resources. Consequently, competition operates as a discovery procedure and the main role of markets is in generating information, through the price mechanism, as to how economic agents who are ignorant of each other may best attain their equally unknown purposes.

The salient point, then, is that the complex and evolutionary nature of the catallaxy makes its qualities unknowable to any single mind or organization. Hayek correctly takes to task the socialist vision of a collectively controlled and planned advanced economy – a 'fatal conceit', which he terms 'constructivism'. As Sayer points out, many Marxist positions have failed to acknowledge the fundamental difference between running a technical division of labour for producing a particular type of commodity and co-ordinating a social division of labour involving millions of different commodities, thousands of enterprises and billions of customers. This is not to license chaos, for although catallaxies are unplanned they are ordered. Yet, for Marx, the only good order 'must be the product of conscious collective purpose, a Hegelian legacy of humanity rising to consciousness and control over itself... Marx is resistant not only to actions having bad unintended consequences, but to unintended consequences *per se*' (Sayer 1995, p. 76). However, Hayek adopts the extreme counter-position to Marx. In brief, he reasons that because unintended consequences of actions are central to the functioning of catallaxies, one must not intervene. This is a *non sequitur* and, *inter alia*, excuses problems that can – and should – be confronted and removed (ecological problems, poverty, discrimination...). More crucially, Hayek denies that catallaxies possess emergent properties.

Absent from Hayek's image of capitalism as an unimaginably complex mass of individuals responding to one another through markets is any notion of major social structures... while modern societies and advanced economies are indeed catallaxies, they are *also* systems with grand structures... his celebration of the miracle of the market simply ignores the temporal and spatial upheavals associated with the creative destruction of capitalism. Hayek's exaggeration of 'order' is the complement of Marxism's exaggeration of 'anarchy' (Sayer, 1995, pp. 77-78).

Hayek was wrong to presume that no central planning was useful or viable. Whilst some knowledge is tacit and dispersed and cannot therefore be gathered together and processed at the centre, particular types of knowledge are usefully centralized so that they can obtained by all (telephone directory; internet...). In brief, we should reject the planned socialism versus market individualism dichotomy in assessing feasible alternatives to capitalism. As Hodgson puts it, 'Neither the individual nor the state can be omniscient. What is remarkable about both socialism and market individualism is that they both presume a high degree of capability and enlightenment on behalf of one or the other' (1999, p. 79).

To return to Jacques' not envisioning anything outside of capitalist social relations, it is worth stressing that markets and private property are necessary but insufficient features of capitalism: not all market systems are capitalist. However, of course, such systems cannot be rationally planned. Capitalist economic systems are, as Jacques rightly points out, becoming knowledge-intensive. 'One could argue that what is emerging is the *learning worker*, one whose value does not lie with what s/he knows but in the combination of discretion and skill that permit one to change what one knows' (Jacques 1995, p. 181). Current management education typically undercuts and implicitly denigrates the experiential learning that is crucial in today's fast-changing world. Thus, to Jacques:

> High value is placed on standardized curricula centered on the *textbook* – learning of others that has been frozen and packaged. Instructors know that summarizing the 'key points' of the text will generate less resistance... The experiential movement has challenged this norm, but has remained fairly marginal... Open-ended learning, as espoused by those such as Dewey or Montessori, remains uncommon (Jacques 1995, p. 184).

It is a pity that Jacques does not tease out the implications of the nature of learning vis-à-vis the impossibility of socialist central planning *and* the role of the state in developing and maintaining the 'learning economy'. Whether tacit knowledge is held individually or by a team, it cannot be widely dispersed and fully appreciated throughout the economy: there are limits to the amount of shared or widely accessible knowledge. Learning depends on ingrained familiarity, obtained through repeated routine. It is precisely for this reason that in any complex society, people have to be specialists. 'Technical knowledge is highly contextual. It is often difficult to understand the nature or value of an innovation without intimate knowledge of the situation to which it relates' (Hodgson 1999, p. 57). Consequently, the complexity and inaccessibility of dispersed tacit knowledge means that neither worker nor *manager* can know fully what is going on. This reality is not borne out in management textbooks. The increasing complexity of the global economies means that workers require more intensive training. If we are to avoid an increase in the number of what Hodgson refers to as 'McJobs', that is, low-paid, part-time and insecure, then the state, *contra* Hayek and the New Right liberals, must intervene to provide adequate levels of funding in order to meet the increasing need for knowledge-intensive workers. People have to learn how to learn and to adapt and create anew. However, such intervention is not wishful, woolly thinking, but an immanent possibility.

In turn, this means that we have to temper emancipatory demands for increased democratic participation. If we want to retain current high levels of development that derive from the diversity and immense complexity of extant socio-economic reality, then we have to assess the feasibility of increased participative democracy. As Sayer (1995) notes, democracy is recently enjoying renewed popularity on the Left. 'It is hard to resist the conclusion that democracy is often seen as an unqualified good' (1995, p. 239). For Alvesson and Willmott, 'Integral to the emancipatory intent of CT [Critical Theory] is a vision of a qualitatively different form of management: one that is more democratically accountable to those whose lives are affected in so many ways by management decisions...' (1996, p. 40). The extent of democratic accountability cannot be determined *a priori*. In a highly complex world, it is not feasible for everyone to gain the requisite specialist knowledge to be involved in many aspects of decision-making. However, this is not to suggest that we do not look for feasible ways of extending democracy wherever possible. The first-past-the-post system in the United Kingdom can be feasibly changed, for instance.

In essence, it is feasible to conceive of a post-capitalist, non-state socialist, advanced society. However, this would not concomitantly involve a considerable reduction in hierarchy and reliance on *ex post* regulation of the wider economy. In other words, there are contradictions immanent in economic organization that cannot be wished away. Indeed, it may be that in our on-going assessment of feasible socio-economic organizational forms that improvements might not be realized without creating new problems. The positing of feasible alternatives is unavoidably complex, messy and provisional.

Hodgson's Alternative Future Scenarios

However, Hodgson has proffered some plausible future causal chains, which I shall briefly delineate.

The Omega Scenario

This scenario remains within capitalism. Basically, if the growth of knowledge is thwarted, a technologically sophisticated economy may evolve in which, however, human learning and innovation have stagnated. Here, technology would be used extensively to replace humans as much as possible. Economic growth would result largely from a growing output of physical goods and automated services. The population 'would generally occupy a life of leisure, with some of them lucky (or unfortunate) enough to have a few hours' work a week in the restaurant or retail sector, serving customers who value human interaction (Hodgson 1999, p. 189).

The Epsilon Scenario

For Hodgson, the epsilon scenario could be described as beyond capitalism. Here, a form of employment contract remains, but it is a mere shell of its former capitalist self. In the work process, the degree of control by the employer over the employee is minimal. However, it is still a contract between employer and worker, but the employee retains much control of the process of work. It is an economy still dominated by private property relations and largely regulated by the market. Whilst it is not capitalist it is not socialist either.

Capitalism means more than private property and markets ... the system outlined above is not capitalism, even if it may contain capitalist 'impurities'.

> 'Market knowledgism' or 'market cognitivism' ... are some of the best labels for this system that I can come up with ... such a system requires a high social valuation of trust-based and extra-contractual relationships. A capitalist society with an ideological history of individualism ... will find it difficult to accommodate these embryonic, non-contractual forms ... The epsilon scenario may thus be blocked. Such a system could remain locked into capitalism, possibly with a relapse into the omega scenario [above] ... (Hodgson 1999, p. 213).

Alternative Scenarios

The alpha scenario for Hodgson is about the 'brave new world of McJobs, unemployment and robots'. *The beta scenario* relates to many of the actually existing developments in the advanced, knowledge-intensive capitalism of the late twentieth century. *The gamma scenario* is, loosely speaking, 'state socialism', i.e. a centrally planned economy under public ownership, with the machine-intensive technology of the second half of the nineteenth, and first half of the twentieth, centuries. *The delta scenario*, with machine-intensive production and worker co-operatives, is genuine 'market socialism', found more or less in the former Yugoslavia from the 1950s to the 1980s and Mondragon in Spain.

However, Hodgson spells out in much more detail the *zeta scenario*, which is a *further* post-capitalist development of the epsilon scenario, involving further increases in the knowledge intensity of production, of human skills, in the economic power of the workforce and in the broadening of share ownership. In this scenario, there is not necessarily common, complete and exclusive ownership of the corporation by the workforce. Knowledge is more sophisticated and enhanced. For Hodgson, the outcome of the zeta scenario would be described as 'market cogni-socialism' or 'market socio-cognitivism'. It is worth quoting Hodgson at length here:

> Despite the lack of complete common ownership, it is not necessarily less co-operative than idealized socialism ... nor necessarily any less egalitarian in its economic outcomes ... compared with the epsilon scenario, in the zeta scenario the balance of ownership of the corporation shifts crucially from the shareholders to the workers and managers ... It is not market socialism in a strict sense, nor is it any form of state

socialism ... However, such a system is socialistic and co-operative in its dominant ethos, and close in structure to ... market socialism (Hodgson 1999, p. 217).

However, Hodgson adds that markets and commodity exchange retain a crucial co-ordinating role in the system: radical theorists often ignore this.

Concluding Remarks: the Need for Normative Theory

Radical political economy has assumed (often implicitly) that contradictions and dilemmas could be successively eliminated without creating new ones. As Sayer argues, this is a modernist myth:

> There are always going to be trade-offs, though not necessarily zero-sum games, and gloomy though this may sound, we stand more chance of success being aware of this than we do imagining that they don't exist. But there is a further problem with critical social science's confident view of emancipation. This is its assumption that emancipation comes about solely or largely through removal of obstacles – be they illusions held by people ... relations of domination or material deprivation. Apparently, once we have eliminated these and people can relate to one another freely and as equals, people will be emancipated (1995, p. 236).

Sayer delineates several problems with this. One key problem is the impression of the 'good society' as a space cleared of illusions and oppressive relations, in which individuals or groups will somehow 'naturally' find liberation. The point here is that we need alternative frameworks. There is no point in changing society if we have no idea of what such a changed society could be like. Hence the need for counterfactual analysis and assessment of feasible alternatives. As Jacques reminds us, we cannot envision the 'good society' *de novo*. The problem that continues to bedevil critical social science is the lack of normative analysis, that is, critical evaluation. Given that Marxism has not developed any feasible alternatives, it is hardly surprising that critical writers like Jacques find it difficult to conceive of non-capitalist social arrangements. Sayer draws attention to political philosophy as the normative theory most relevant to political economy. As he notes, political philosophy is concerned with defining or interpreting concepts of the political good. Among others, what kinds of social practice and organization are good and why? What ought the role of the state to be? What are our responsibilities? Political theory, however, is less abstract and deals with institutions such as markets and explores their character, preconditions and consequences. In turn, this aids normative judgements of social practices. If we return to the issue of increased democracy, political theory shows here that democracy is good *and* bad: it has limitations and is vulnerable to abuses. As Sayer argues, this helps us to think about alternatives. Indeed, the nature of dispersed tacit knowledge associated with increasing specialization and the material properties of what is organized delimits the extent of democratization.

This article has maintained the need (a) for a disaggregative analysis, which is grounded in social realism, and (b) normative theory about future possibilities.

This will aid tentative assessment of feasible alternatives, which Hodgson has admirably set about doing. To reiterate, it is not being suggested that we can start afresh. There are limits to what can be changed for the better, and any immanent potentialities can be identified and debated via disaggregation and normative analysis. The latter is only possible if we recognize the stratified material nature of social reality. In other words, transcendentally the social world is composed of internal and external social relations; disaggregative analysis enables thought experiments about alternative social arrangements.

Notes

[1] In the field of organization and management studies, critical realism has had a limited impact. Notable exceptions include Clark (2000), Mutch (1999), Reed (2000), and Tsoukas (2000).

[2] As Rowlinson (1997) points out, the critique of 'tall' organizations and the call for flatter managerial hierarchies should not be confused with radical attacks upon the very existence of hierarchy.

References

Alvesson, M. and Willmott, H. (1996) *Making Sense of Management: A Critical Introduction* London, Sage.

Archer, M. (1995) *Realist Social Theory: the Morphogenetic Approach* Cambridge, Cambridge University Press.

Clark, P. A. (2000) *Organizations in Action* London, Routledge.

Hodgson, G. (1999) *Economics and Utopia: Why the Learning Economy is Not the End of History* London, Routledge.

Jacques, R. (1995) *Manufacturing the Employee: Management Knowledge from the 19th to 21st Centuries* London, Sage.

Jacques, R. (2000) 'Theorizing Knowledge as Work: The Need for a 'Knowledge Theory of Value', in C. Prichard, R. Hull, M. Chumer, H. Willmott (eds.) *Managing Knowledge: Critical Investigations of Work and Learning* London, Macmillan.

Lawson, T. (1997) *Economics and Reality* London, Routledge.

Mutch, A. (1999) 'Critical Realism, Managers and Information', in *British Journal of Management*, 10, pp. 323-334.

Ollman, B. (1971) *Alienation* Cambridge, Cambridge University Press.

Ollman, B. (1990) *Marxism: An Uncommon Introduction* India, Sterling Publishers.

Popper, K. (1979) *Objective Knowledge* Oxford, Oxford University Press.

Reed, M. (2000) 'In Praise of Duality and Dualism: Rethinking Agency and Structure in Organizational Analysis', in S. Ackroyd and S. Fleetwood (eds.) *Realist Perspectives on Management and Organizations*, London, Routledge.

Rowlinson, M. (1997) *Organizations and Institutions* London, Macmillan.

Sayer, A (1995) *Radical Political Economy: A Critique* Oxford, Blackwell.

Sayer, A. (2000) *Realism and Social Science* London, Sage.

Tsoukas, H. (2000) 'What is Management? Outline of a Metatheory', in S. Ackroyd and S. Fleetwood (eds.) *Realist Perspectives on Management and Organizations*, London, Routledge.

Willmott, R. (1999) 'Structure, Agency and the Sociology of Education: rescuing analytical dualism', in *British Journal of Sociology of Education* 20(1) pp. 5-21.

Willmott, R. (2000a) 'The Place of Culture in Organization Theory: Introducing the Morphogenetic Approach', in *Organization* 7(1) pp. 93-126.

Willmott, R. (2000b) 'Structure, Culture and Agency: Rejecting the Current Orthodoxy of Orthodoxy of Organization Theory', in S. Ackroyd and S. Fleetwood (eds.) *Realist Perspectives on Management and Organizations* London, Routledge.

Willmott, R. (2002) *Education Policy and Realist Social Theory* London, Routledge.

Chapter 8

Japan as Institutional Counterfactual: Knowledge, Learning and Power

Stewart Clegg, Tim Ray and Chris Carter

Introduction

Roy Jacques' account is that of American managerialism. This chapter questions many Anglo-Saxon assumptions about the importance of objective knowledge, the scientific method and individualism which do not sit easily in a Japanese context. Japan's institutions – defined 'as rules of the game' (North, 1990, p. 3) – privilege group-knowledge over individual knowledge and implicit understanding over explicit rules. Within Japan's institutional framework, close community relationships amongst long-term colleagues lower the marginal cost of information transfer and enable insiders to act as a group, able to ostracize and retaliate against those who break their code. This redefinition of the interface for principal-agent conflict (Jenson and Meckling, 1976, pp. 305-360) has profound implications for the way that Japan has developed knowledge 'in the context of application' (Gibbons et al., 1994, p. 3). It also underscores the importance of collective tacit knowledge (which, tentatively, we will call Mode 3 knowledge) retained within the organization as a tool for shaping future practice. A pluralist approach to the types of knowledge that mutually enable practice is used to reinterpret the Mode 1 and Mode 2 debate in the context of Japan's institutional framework. By avoiding the idea of tacit-explicit 'knowledge conversion', one can acknowledge the specificity of Japan's institutional context and consider its implications for organizational learning elsewhere.

Japan: a Distinct Industrial History

The dominant features of contemporary nation-state capitalism in industrialized countries reflect the imprinting conditions – social movements and macro-environmental forces – that framed the transition from the craft to the industrial (Lewin et al., 1999). Japan's pre-industrial history and approach to industrialization emerged from more than two-centuries of relative international isolation that saw the evolution of an extraordinarily resilient steady state hierarchical administrative and social system.

In 1603, the Tokugawa Shogunate established a government in Edo (now Tokyo) and in 1639 largely closed the country to external relations. A stable social order emerged in which embedded power relations constrained the rise of individuals with sufficient power and imagination to change the system radically. Japan was not closed off from the rest of the world during the Tokugawa period: it would better be described as 'semi-isolation' (Toby, 1977; 1984). The Tokugawa Shogunate was eventually interrupted in 1853, when Commodore Matthew Perry delivered US demands to open trade relations. Perry's 'black ships' (which have since become ingrained in Japan's collective psyche as a potent icon of unjustified foreign interference) focussed attention on the need to survive as a nation in the face of American military supremacy. Even so, prevailing power relations were able to parry many of the new uncertainties. The Meiji Restoration in 1868 – which many take to mark the birth of modern Japan – was neither a Norman Conquest nor a French Revolution; dominant groups in the old regime weakened, but subordinate or similar elements moved into their place (Mason and Caiger, 1972, p. 217). Under the slogan, 'rich nation, strong army' (*fukoku kyôhei*), the Meiji government sought to build a prosperous nation that remained free from colonization by a Western power. It took the initiative in almost every major industry and sought to minimize wasteful parallel investment (Van Wolferen, 1990, p. 493). From the outset, Japan's industrialization was 'plan-rational' (Johnson 1992, p. 19) – instead of simply setting the rules of play the Japanese government has been intimately involved with shaping the structure of industry and setting goals for innovation.

In the early days of Japan's industrialization, there was a high rate of labour mobility amongst factory workers. Employers started to strengthen links with their employees – providing various welfare benefits, company dormitories and houses at nominal rent, and other payments in kind, all of which increased the potential for soft control and surveillance of an emerging industrial workforce unused to the new disciplines, habituated instead, to more seasonal agricultural rhythms. By the end of the First World War, a system had been established whereby, each spring, large companies hired boys who were leaving school. Such recruits exhibited cherished qualities: a sense of loyalty and a willingness to accept workplace rules. In the 1920s and 1930s, uniforms for workers appeared, along with badges and insignia denoting rank. Although career-long employment did not become the norm during this era (Gilson and Roe, 1999, p. 519), the military-industrial complex responsible for fuelling imperialist expansionism accentuated the trend. It also pushed small and medium sized enterprises towards particular *zaibatsu* (groups of companies owned by a single family) thereby curtailing much of their freedom to negotiate business arrangements (Miyashita and Russell, 1994, p. 117) as they became locked into fixed supply and distribution chains, in which each firm was dependent on the one above for orders.

After the Second World War, the Allied Occupation removed Japan's military interests and unwittingly strengthened its ability to operate as a 'plan-rational' state by freeing the civilian bureaucracy from its greatest rival (Johnson, 1995, p. 29). When the occupation ended in 1952, the Ministry of International Trade and Industry was able to engineer the reformation of the military-era *zaibatsu* groups of companies into 'headless' bank-based *keiretsu* – bound together by cross-shareholdings, interlocking directorates, intra-group trade and periodic meetings of member company presidents.

Since James Abegglen coined the term 'lifetime employment' in the 1950s (but later suggested it would be better described as 'career employment' or a 'social contract'), long-term mutually binding commitment for a small labour-elite of male salaried employees has been one of the most misunderstood aspects of Japanese business practice. Many in the West have been apt to dismiss the tradition as a luxury for ineffective workers or a threat to managerial efficiency that can no longer be afforded. But efficiency, at any given instant, is not convertible into the currency of implicit obligations that sustain continually evolving 'here and now' flexibility within Japan's *workplace families*. Fingleton summarizes the perception problem succinctly.

> No aspect of Japan's remarkable economy has been so consistently underestimated as its employment system. Because the system's three main principles – lifetime employment, company unions, and seniority pay – flout free-market ideals, Westerners consider it self-evidently incapable in the long run of withstanding global competition of 'more efficient' hire-and-fire labor system of the US and Europe (Fingleton, 1995, p. 79).

To be sure, not everybody in Japan works for life. Most women remain peripheral to core business conducted in the workplace (Lorriman and Kenco, 1996, p. 74). Japanese employers also rely on various categories of temporary employees who might, for example, work full-time alongside regular employers on a *de facto* permanent basis, but with lower status and pay. Nevertheless, regular male employees in upper-level positions in the big name organizations are only dismissed in extreme circumstances. In return, these regular employees have to demonstrate a positive attitude to overtime (including unpaid overtime), accept transfers to subsidiaries when business is bad, and comply with the organization's tacitly held conventions about what constitutes acceptable behaviour. In reality, there were few alternatives, although, as Kono and Clegg (2001) report, the certain stigma that once was attached to inter-organizational career movement is no longer necessarily the case. The profile of generalist careers, which for so long sustained and defined Japanese organizations' organicism, is shifting. Many successful companies, such as Matsushita and Toyota have established specialized career tracks. Toyota has six such specialized career groups, including general management, marketing, development, production technology, production planning and new businesses, and among these groups, there are more than five career tracks. More specialized tracks are now seen to be necessary for the accumulation of considerable technological knowledge and construction of core competencies. Before the establishment of these specialized career tracks, there was an informal system in which generalist skills were emphasized. Specialized career tracks differ from a pay-for-job system and do not equate with narrow career specialization. There are no job titles, wages are paid by status and the skill level determines the status grade. This is different from the hire-and-fire system because it is based on retaining the features of the internal labour market system.

In order to protect employment and to prevent members being discharged because the jobs they do become redundant employees are trained so that skills are updated to those the organization needs. Also, these will be generic skills that other organization may need also. While in the past inter-organizational mobility was restricted, increasingly companies take great care in assisting the move of members from their own firm to others. The new conditions of employability are a modification of lifetime employment but they are not a contradiction of it, although, where ownership has changed to become vested in a foreign company the changes can be more radical. For instance, Renault now controls Nissan and is laying-off large numbers of employees. While they are seeking to do so in terms of a new contract understanding based on employability, they are insisting that employees be prepared to move geographically to find a job – something that is anathema for employees used to the old Nissan ways.

The status ladder system continues to exist: employees are promoted up the status ladder and wages are determined by status grade not by job grade. The higher ranks climb both the job and status ladders within the internal labour market system. However, under the conditions of the slow growth economy, the old system of annual wage increases with small differentials had a long term escalatory affect, increasing labour costs as the workforce aged or numbers stabilized around seniority; thus, many companies have started to change the wage system.

At Toyota, wages are composed of 30 per cent basic pay, which reflect the status grade, and 70 per cent merit pay, which reflect performance and capability. The wage could decrease depending on merit achieved. The trend is a shift from small to larger differentiation, while still keeping lifetime employment for the internal labour market. Notwithstanding recent changes in Japan's labour markets, it is difficult to sustain the position that Anglo-Saxon market rational institutional frameworks are replacing those inherited and evolved form the past. What are some of the current consequences of these?

Japan: The Consequences of History

Japan is the only G-7 economy whose traditional social values owe virtually nothing to Mediterranean origins: the others share Judaeo-Greco-Roman traditions to an extent that the differences amongst them appear less pronounced when they are compared to Japan (Dore, 1973, p. 419). Although Japan has an American-style constitution (imposed by the Allied Occupation) and a legal framework that appears to guarantee individual rights, recourse to the law remains rare: there are few lawyers and there is a pervasive reluctance to make overt acknowledgements of failures in the implicit code. Japan's low crime rate and methods of doing business normally owe more to highly aligned tacit conventions about how to read the intentions of others and act accordingly.

Given the general importance of tacit conventions in Japan's institutional framework, it would not be surprising to find them at work in economic as well as social life. Of course, the concern with tacit knowledge is hardly specific to Japan: it has been a mainstay of Western thinking since Polanyi (1967) first introduced the notion. However, recent interest in the relationship between knowledge and competitive advantage, as well as the specific emergence of Knowledge Management discourses, particularly in the wake of advances in Information Communication Technologies, have reinvigorated theorizing about the relation between work-based learning and innovation.

By closely observing actual communities and their revealed practices – as opposed to the 'canonical practice' (Brown and Duguid, 1999, p. 42) espoused by organizations – it is possible to de-construct the tensions between individual and organizational aspirations. Self-organizing communities of practice evolve from the interaction of individuals with a mutual interest in pursuing a particular agenda of problem solving activity. According to Wenger (2000), practitioners are bound together by a sense of *joint enterprise*, *mutual engagement* and a *shared repertoire*, which might included communal resources language, routines, sensibilities, tools and stories that emerge from practice. For Wenger (2000, pp. 227-228), communities of practice are 'social containers' for competencies and comprise the 'basic building blocks' that are situated within wider social learning systems.

Our argument is that Japan's 'rules of the game' effectively situate communities of practice *within broad organizational boundaries* and in the spaces that emerge from appropriate interactions with insides (such the relationship with a supplier or customer). Horizontal *keiretsu* groupings, together with fixed trading-patterns in supply and distribution chains (in which each firm is dependent on the one above for orders), continue to support Japan's post-1945 interlocking steady *state* economic structure in which new technologies tend to emerge from existing organizations. Continuous improvement innovations are mainly matters of on-the-job learning amongst organizational insiders. The lack of a labour market for specialists, coupled to the residual stigma associated with opportunistic job-hopping and head-hunting, allows organizations to act as relatively leak-proof social containers for knowledge generated through the intermingling of working, learning and innovation.

For Gibbons and his colleagues (Gibbons *et al.*, 1994) the standing of Mode 1 knowledge – produced according to the scientific method, validated by peer review and structured in terms of university disciplines – is being eclipsed by a new form of socially distributed knowledge production. Progress towards Mode 2 society involves the evolution of knowledge-trading zones or 'agora' (Nowotny *et al.*, 2001, p. 23) that imply new patterns of information transactions. Barriers between Mode 1 'knowledge silos' generated in universities and Mode 2 problems are being transgressed *in both directions*. Whereas much of science policy – in countries such as Britain and Australia – has sought to increase drip-feed flows from university research into practice, Mode 2 society implies a Schumpeterian (1976, p. 84) 'gale of creative destruction' that incessantly revolutionizes the economic structure from within. Suddenly, many universities and researchers find themselves enrolled in previously unfamiliar processes encompassing entrepreneurial competition and the *commodification* of knowledge products. As the 'rules of the game' change, organizational and national boundaries might appear less relevant as fixed points of reference. But images of global convergence, as empowered individuals generate interaction spaces across traditional boundaries, are wholly incommensurate with the evolution of expectations in Japan's distinctive knowledge-generating ecology.

Porter has noted that: 'Japanese knowledge creation has taken place in companies much more than in any other institution ... University research is limited, and interchange between companies and universities is modest compared to a number of other nations' (Porter, 1990, p. 397). While Japan leads the world in per capita R and D expenditure, this takes place mainly in private companies. Despite various attempts to reform higher education and increase public sector research funding, Porter's observations continue to reflect the situation in contemporary Japan. The power relations that embed Japanese organizations in their social context are dominated by Japan's pre-industrial precepts that privilege the collective over the individual (as the famous Japanese saying warns, 'the nail that sticks out gets hammered down'). And these precepts are spectacularly resistant to change; their collectively held implicit qualities automatically pre-empt individual efforts to change the status quo.

Within the organization, it is shared experience amongst long-term colleagues – working according to distinctly Japanese labour practices (Kono and Clegg, 2001) – that generate collective tacit knowledge, which we call Mode 3 knowledge. This Mode 3 knowledge is held-in-common by insiders and shapes subconscious influences on action (tacit knowledge cannot be consciously turned off). Mode 3 knowledge is generated in the course of shared experience and retained within the 'collective memory' possessed by insiders who are bound together through regular information transactions. Amongst organizational insiders, experiences encapsulated in Mode 3 knowledge embody the tacit dimension of what Penrose (1995, p. 78) referred to as a 'free resource', which has value in the services that it can render to insiders, but cannot be traded with outsiders. The ability of Japanese manufacturing firms to exploit Mode 3 knowledge in the realization of continuous improvement innovations is, for example, revealed in high quality, high reliability products. But the international recognition, which is justifiably bestowed upon the performance characteristics of Japan's leading brands, often overshadows the role of Japan's distinctive 'rules of the game' in enabling a different type of production process.

In the remainder of this chapter we will demonstrate the significance of situated working, learning and innovation in Japan, and elaborate its profound consequences for the evolution of universities and Mode 1 knowledge production. The acontextual generalizations that have surrounded this influential debate need to be reconsidered. With more nuanced interpretation, more appropriate policies might follow.

Knowledge in Japan

Whereas Europe's older universities pre-dated industrial society, Japan's university system has developed in tandem with its plan-rational transition from late-feudalism to economic and technological superpower. Japan's university sector stems from the foundation of the University of Tokyo in 1877. By the early 1890s, this had developed a strong emphasis on engineering (rather than science) and agriculture, forming an emphasis on applied subjects that was subsequently replicated in Japan's other Imperial Universities. But these universities were essentially agencies for training bureaucrats and were not properly equipped for research (Kiyonobu and Eri, 1974).

Since the Second World War, the number of universities in Japan has increased by an order of magnitude and the proportion of 18-year-olds who enter higher education compares well with leading Western nations. But it would be misleading to conclude that Japanese universities have come to reflect the Mode 1 ethos of their Western counterparts, as *The Economist* noted:

> Japan's universities are not places conducive to doing profound basic research. Most have rigid, hierarchical structures. Elderly faculty heads dominate the research programmes and publishing process. Intellectual dissent is discouraged. And in addition to having their ideas stifled, younger researchers often find themselves carrying out the grunt work that is done in America or Europe by technicians. Lack of money for support staff means that many people who would be better employed doing experiments are doing the washing up instead (*The Economist*, May 25 1996, p. 102).

Although prestigious employers recruit their permanent male employees from Japan's top-ranking universities, the ranking order is fixed by long-standing traditions and not directly affected by teaching standards nor research. Higher-ranking universities have harder entrance examinations and thereby select the country's elite. Graduation is a formality for those who pass the entrance examinations, while the chances of being recruited by a leading employer can be undermined by years spent in post-graduate study. Employers typically prefer first-degree graduates who can become good team players. In the course of a career, they will do many jobs and the skills of specialists could be overtaken by events as the team collectively develops new competencies in the course of collective working, learning and innovation practice through streams of continuous incremental innovation.

In comparison to its Western counterparts, Japan produces few PhDs. Although Japan's higher education profile is changing, as illustrated by rapid recent increases in MBA education (Okazaki-Ward, 2001) this is not being accompanied by the emergence of labour-market that is capable of translating these qualifications into propellants for Western-style job-hopping and building a career by moving between organizations.

Much of Japan's success with the exploitation of Mode 1 knowledge has been achieved by exploiting collective judgements in consensus-building exercises aimed at targeting exploitable areas of Mode 1 knowledge. When a desirable research objective emerges on the horizon of possibilities, Japan's coordinated policy process tends to ensure that resources are available to exploit the possibilities. Although it takes time to build a consensus, extensive consultation makes it relatively easy to implement policies once they have been agreed. The consensus has value almost exactly because it is a consensus; collective forces would act against any subsequent attempts to hi-jack or destroy the consensus.

(Hence, the decision by the United States Congress not to construct a super-conducting super-collider after such a flagship project was underway would be difficult to envisage in a Japanese context.)

During the early twentieth-century, the rise of the US electrical and German chemical industries focused Japan's attention on the need to develop an indigenous capability for sustaining progress in science-related technologies. This led to foundation of the Institute of Physical and Chemical Research or 'RIKEN', which is an abbreviation of Rikagaku *Kenkyû-jo* (meaning Physics and Chemistry Research Institute) in 1917, which marked Japan's first major research laboratory. Despite a chequered history, RIKEN has become Japan's premier centre for basic research. As the nation's economic development embraced a wider range of basic research areas, RIKEN's roots in physics and chemistry expanded to include engineering, biology, and medical sciences. It is at the vanguard of efforts to increase public-sector basic research and acts as an effective gatekeeper organization for Japanese science. In 1992, *Nature* carried a feature entitled 'RIKEN – Japan's leading light', which referred to the institute as a '... remarkably dynamic research organization that is fast becoming a truly international centre of excellence.' Since the early 1990s, the nature and extent of RIKEN's research activities have increased dramatically. Amid concerns about Japan's ageing population, a Brain Science Institute was added in 1997.

Throughout Japan's so-called 'lost decade' of economic downturn, growth in public-sector research expenditure has accelerated. The total now represents about 1 per cent of GDP, which is on a par with allocations in Europe and the United States (Goto, 2000, pp. 103-113). But Mode 1 knowledge-production in Japan has evolved in a symbiotic relationship with the evolution of practical problems. Japanese society has informed the establishment of Mode 1 research agendas according to Mode 3 mediated interpretations of need-pull criteria that emerge within the upper levels of the government, bureaucracy and industry network.

The Japanese Institutional Context

The idea of a bounded frame of reference shared by insiders has been developed by a number of authors (cf. Nakane, 1970) in terms of the Japanese concept of '*ba*', which roughly means place, with the connotation that it is the *place* or *interaction field* where purposeful activity occurs. Itami (1992) has conceptualized *ba* in terms of a bounded context, where those with a willingness to co-operate and a common agenda, interact on a regular basis. In the process, they evolve a shared 'interpretation code' that gives meaning to information signals (which might include gestures, tone of voice or indeed the absence of such signals).

The popularity of Japan's company-as-family metaphor as a frame-of-reference for organizational activities resonates with feudal moral precepts about belonging to the Japanese household (*ie*) in a total sense, which Japanese elites have not been slow to hijack and popularize – fooling many foreign observers (Harvey- Jones, 1993) if not always those who are the victims of the double-talk these elites seek to master (Mouer and Sugimoto, 1986; Sugimoto, 1997). Nonetheless, within Japan's tightly bounded work organizations, interactions amongst *insiders* do embrace myriad nested and overlapping micro *ba*. These continuously evolve and collide in the process of generative churning, as intra-organizational communities of practice are born, evolve and reform. Common sensemaking is, not surprisingly, much envied and its absence elsewhere has given rise to some famous frustrations, such as when Jerry Junkins, when CEO of Texas Instruments, remarked 'If TI only knew what TI knows' and Lew Platt, chairman of Hewlett Packard, said 'I wish we knew what we know at HP' (O'Dell and Grayson, 1998). Japan's workplace organizations usually 'know what they know' or, to be more precise, have a collective sense of what might be achieved in practice, even if some of the more breathless admirers of Japanese ways tend to overstate the matter.

Within Japanese organizations, the age-base of the promotion system enables managers to share information more easily with colleagues who form a cadre, offering a mental map of who should be treated with what degree of respect. This guides the evolution of Mode 3 knowledge and power relations. Over time, associates and subordinates develop an instinctive sense of what finds favour without anyone being told to do anything. But the integrating power that confers authority to act in certain ways also constrains that action: Anglo-Saxon notions of leadership, involving acting without regard for the group, are not on the agenda of possibilities.

The context of power relations that characterize Japanese management and organizations, and their relation to Japanese universities, whose institutional emergence and patterning we have briefly sketched, have proved to be remarkably resilient and different from the conditions that have become 'normalized' as the policy models in influential bodies such as the OECD. We will propose that these normalized assumptions are such that it is somewhat difficult to grasp the specificity of Japanese innovation in these models. In turn, this leads us to question their universalizing explanatory features.

The Knowledge Debate

While the literature on national systems of innovation has made a valuable contribution to characterizing technological change in different countries, there is a widespread assumption that knowledge is ultimately 'all of one type' and can be moved from one context to another in an unproblematic way. Similarly, the recent enthusiasm for Knowledge Management, as a fashionable weapon (Scarbrough and Swan, 2001) in the unequal struggle with information, often presupposes that all relevant knowledge can be represented as information and then be 'managed'. However, matters of intuition, emotion, judgement and skilled action can be seen as context-specific forms of knowledge that cannot be objectified in a scientific sense (Spender, 2002). Tacit knowledge possessed by individuals and groups – that is unknowable in any abstract sense – enables physical actions and mental processes.

Although Nonaka and Takeuchi's (1995) account of Japan's knowledge-creating companies prompted greater Western interest in the importance of tacit knowledge, their discussion of tacit-explicit 'knowledge conversion' is often used to justify mainstream Knowledge Management's predilection for a monist epistemology in which all relevant tacit knowledge is made explicit and thereby 'captured'. Whereas Polanyi (1967) was concerned with the difficulty of using tacit knowing as a stable alternative to positivism's ideal of objectivity, Nonaka and Takeuchi have deployed the image of 'knowledge conversion' to objectify aspects of tacit knowledge. This allows them to adopt the stance that tacit knowledge is something that 'cannot be articulated very easily' (Nonaka and Takeuchi, 1995, p. 8), which facilitates their hope that – given sufficient effort – understanding the knowledge-creating processes in Japanese companies could be made 'universal' (Nonaka and Takeuchi, 1995, p. 246). Yet, this aspiration to universal understanding is awkward given that, as Nonaka and Takeuchi themselves point out, 'knowledge ... is about meaning ... it is context-specific'(Nonaka and Takeuchi, 1995, p. 58).

Polanyi's original notion of tacit knowledge referred to something that is unknowable in any abstract sense; its existence is only implied by the ability to 'do things' in the course of purposeful activity. For example, the knowledge necessary to ride a bicycle is implied if a specific rider in a specific context does not appear to fall off. Such tacit knowledge can be used in practice without being represented in explicit terms. Indeed, if called to account for how they manage to travel such distances at such speeds and retain balance on two such narrow wheels, most riders might have difficulty. Moreover, skilled performers in a range of activities report that trying to account for their actions can intrude upon effective practice. Instinct is automatic. For example, something such as an emergency stop can be initiated before the driver is conscious of seeing a child run in front of the car; waiting for 'knowledge conversion' would imply a higher accident rate. At a group level, football teams are able to play together according to Mode 3 tacit knowledge that emerges from being coached individually, drilled as a team, and the experience of implementing these moves in the heat of playing together.

In the cognitive world, tacit knowledge is sometimes acknowledged by reference to labels such as instinct, hunches, suspicions and so on that leverage progress in explicit conceptual thinking that underpin interactions with uncertainty. Practising the solution of mathematical equations leverages a tacit feel for the activity that is not diminished by further practice; on the contrary, practice leverages the basis for improvement. Fortune favours the prepared mind, but the existence of tacit knowledge that enables eureka moments is merely insinuated by the realization of practical achievements.

The second dimension of Nonaka and Takeuchi's theory of knowledge creation concerns the question of whether group knowledge can be considered in its own right. In Nonaka's famous knowledge-creating 'spiral', modes of tacit-explicit knowledge conversion involve a growing number of individuals: 'organizational knowledge creation is a spiral process, starting at the individual level and moving up through expanding communities of interaction that crosses sectional, departmental, divisional, and organizational boundaries' (Nonaka and Takeuchi, 1995, p. 72). Thus, the distinction between *insider* and *outsider* contexts at the boundary of each community of interaction does not appear to interrupt the spiral's seamless progression to higher ontological levels.

Nonaka and Takeuchi (1995, p. 239) insist that 'knowledge is created only by individuals', which is 'organizationally amplified' then crystallized at group level. But their crystallization metaphor could be used to illustrate qualitative distinction between group knowledge and individual knowledge. (The low refractive index of crystal glass might, for example, be regarded as qualitatively different from the properties of sand and other materials from which it was crystallized.) For Spender (1998, p. 243), Nonaka and Takeuchi's emphasis on the individual presupposes a remarkably unproblematic notion of 'self' that disregards the dialectical process between the public-ness of social processes and privacy of individual intellectual and emotional processes. And public processes embody 'rules of the game' that enable and constrain the viability of individual and group actions.

Recently, Nonaka and his colleagues have adopted *ba* as a way of representing the shared context for knowledge creation. But, in contrast to writers, such as Nakane (1970) and Itami (1992), who stress that *ba* is only comprehensible as a *bounded* interaction space, Nonaka *et al.*'s (2000) approach to the insider-outsider distinction is ambiguous.

Ba sets a boundary for interaction amongst individuals, and yet its boundary is open. As there are endless possibilities to one's own contexts, a certain boundary is required for a meaningful shared context to emerge. Yet *ba* is still an open place where participants with their own contexts can come and go, and the shared context (*ba*) can continuously evolve. By providing a shared context in motion, *ba* sets binding conditions for participants by limiting the way in which participants view the world. And yet it provides participants with a higher viewpoint than their own (Nonaka *et al.*, 2000, p. 15).

At one level, the ability of *ba* to limit the way in which employees view the world and providing them with a 'higher viewpoint' is redolent of Nakane's view of the *kaisha*'s totally binding 'internal law'. But Nonaka's *et al.*'s parallel suggestion that *ba* is an open place where participants can come and go suggests a contrary message. The substantive point is that some boundaries are more important than others are and, in this respect, Nonaka *et al.* appear to abstract Japanese practice from the Japanese 'rules of the game' that make such practices possible.

In Japan's institutional framework, core employees are bound by their obligations to the organization; they are not entirely free to come and go, nor can they participate in boundary spanning communities of practice so readily as elsewhere in the West. Members of Japanese organizations (*us*) deal with the outside world (*them*) as a collective and channel their interactions towards appropriate interfaces. On this point Nonaka *et al.*'s (2000) paper concludes with a bottom-up approach to interpreting the organization's wider context and the concept of a national system of innovation that is redolent of the spiral metaphor:

> [T]he knowledge creating process is not confined within the boundaries of a single company. The market, where the knowledge held by companies interacts with that held by customers, is also a place for knowledge creation. It is also possible for groups of

companies to create knowledge. If we further raise the level of analysis, we arrive at a discussion of how so-called national systems of innovation can be built. For the immediate future, it will be important to examine how companies, government and universities can work together to make knowledge creation (Nonaka *et al.*: 2000, p. 30).

Whereas much of the Anglo-Saxon literature on national systems of innovation often treats what happens inside organizations as a *black box*, Nonaka's emphasis on intra-organizational activities appears to treat the organization's wider context as if it were a black box. This implies an extreme position in which concepts of government al learning and the nature of meaningful interaction between firms and Mode 1 university knowledge are constructed from the starting point of practice inside organizations.

A promising way of avoiding the problematic aspects Nonaka and Takeuchi's tacit-explicit 'knowledge conversion' metaphor, together with the spiral model's apparently seamless progression across bounded contexts, has been provided by Cook and Brown (1999). For present purposes, we adopt three propositions from Cook and Brown's carefully argued account:

(1) tacit knowledge is distinct from explicit knowledge, 'it is not possible, under any circumstances, for tacit knowledge to become explicit (or vice versa)' (Cook and Brown 1999, p. 397);

(2) knowledge held by an individual is distinct from knowledge held in common by a group, and;

(3) all four types of knowledge in Cook and Brown's typology interact to enable practice and, in the process, generate new knowledge. Figure 1 shows how each of Cook and Brown's knowledge types can simultaneously interact with practice or 'knowing as action'.

While the ontological status of the group remains controversial (Simon, 1990), Cook and Brown's (1999, p. 399) position is that not every action by a human collective can be usefully or meaningfully reduced to the actions taken by individuals within them. Thus, war stories that are held in common by colleagues might be used as metaphors amongst those who hold that information in common and have the ability to render it meaningful as knowledge. Similarly, in-group catch phrases are knowledge tools that can be used to convey meaning to other members of the collective. In this connection, Mode 1 knowledge might seen as be a special kind of story that is carefully validated according to the scientific method; it is possessed by collective bodies of scientists and informs their actions. In contrast, Mode 2 knowledge production 'in the context of application' is a generative process that equates to 'knowing in action': it involves all four knowledge types and, in the process, generates new types of knowledge that are possessed as tools for future practice. Figure 9.1 illustrates how the Mode 1 and Mode 2 relate to Cook and Brown's framework.

Figure 9.1 Knowledge Types and Modes of Knowing

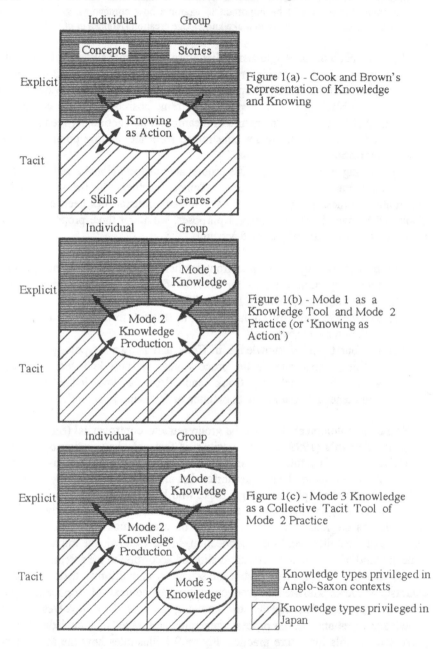

Figure 1(a) - Cook and Brown's Representation of Knowledge and Knowing

Figure 1(b) - Mode 1 as a Knowledge Tool and Mode 2 Practice (or 'Knowing as Action')

Figure 1(c) - Mode 3 Knowledge as a Collective Tacit Tool of Mode 2 Practice

Knowledge types privileged in Anglo-Saxon contexts

Knowledge types privileged in Japan

[Adapted from: Cook and Brown (1999); Ray and Little (2001); Clegg and Ray (2003)]

Whereas Mode 1 knowledge can be stored as explicit information, the retention of collective tacit knowledge – depicted as Mode 3 in Figure 9.1 – requires the continued interaction of practitioners. The ability of a rugby team to play together is shaped by collective tacit knowledge that is held in common. When the same team plays together regularly, they develop a Mode 3 *common sense* of the game that is distinct from the knowledge held by each individual player. In the process of playing, *team spirit* (which is an example of Mode 3 knowledge) and the thought processes of individual players are mutually enabling, but remain distinct bodies of knowledge. Yet, in Anglo-Saxon and other Western contexts, the team spirit that enables exceptional performance or the cost of confusion caused a lack of mutual understanding tend to be overshadowed by tangible indicators that can be measured or represented in explicit terms.

Knowledge and Power

Much of the work on knowledge and its and management ignores the issue of power. The factors that shape who can communicate with whom and on what basis cannot be divorced from the evolution of power relations. Pierre Bourdieu (1985), the French sociologist, has developed the idea of 'cultural capital' that embodies *habitus*. The *habitus* is the shared set of dispositions that orient the agents in a particular field. The dispositions derive from the competition for the field – internal conflict – and with other social fields – external conflict. Habitus can be defined as:

> the habitual, patterned ways of understanding, judging, and acting which arise from our particular position as members of one or several social fields, and from our particular trajectory in the social structure (e.g. whether our group is emerging or declining, whether our own position within it is becoming stronger or weaker) (Terdiman, 1987, p. 811).

Thus, through socialization, individual actors acquire the behaviours and habits particular to a particular environment. This emphasizes the importance of situated implicit understandings and matters of judgement. Power relations have the capacity to define what is held to be 'sacred' and what is castigated as 'profane'. To be caught within relations of power is not merely a repressive experience, in which one is simply being forbidden, prohibited, repressed or dominated: it can also be a productive experience, one that enables things to happen – as well as not happen.

Within Japanese firms, the practices of power take a different hue from some other places. Once an employee has managed to be selected by one of the big companies, then they can have a reasonable expectation that not only are they very fortunate but also that they will be taken care of for the remainder of their career with this company. And while these expectations are changing, they are not changing at a radical pace. The practice of everyday organizational power within a cocoon of basic privilege is a much more positive experience than in more exposed and bleaker situations. Indeed, elsewhere Kono and Clegg (2001) have focused on the everyday practices of power in minute detail, looking at areas such as the dual career tracks, loser-recovery systems, separate job and status ladders with many rungs and small differentials, and the explicitly gendered world of work, which all represent practices for the management of power in positive ways. In part, the negative, coercive management of power within these companies is simply not an easily available option. Consensus is built slowly, carefully, and maintained by a cohort of people who will spend about 35 years in the same company – and the company of each other. Sometimes, as doubtless seems to be the case to critical observers, the atmosphere and culture might seem overwhelmingly patriarchal and stifling but the innovative results are remarkable, nonetheless. In many ways, Japanese organizations are a case study of a specific habitus of positive power.

A central contribution of Foucault (1977, p. 27) was to observe that 'power produces knowledge... power and knowledge directly imply one another ... there is no power relation without the creative constitution of a field of knowledge, nor any knowledge that does not presuppose and constitute at the same time power relations'. Historical traditions change, because of the power to be able to conceive a difference – allied to the capacity to make a difference. In Japan, as we have explained, obligations to the group take precedence over individual rights. This includes both prohibitive powers, which prevents certain activities from taking place, and everyday ways of sense-making that permit the construction of normalcy. Japan's social etiquette stresses the subtle art of indirect communication, ritualized understatement about one's own achievements, and the significance of what is not said. The power relations that shape this sensitivity to non-decision making and non-issues effectively keep certain types of changes 'off the agenda'.

Implications

In practice, power relations can be messy and those who exercise power are to some degree the targets of that power, even if they do not perceive this to be the case. Hence, it becomes impossible to say what any individual or group 'real interests' are. The individuals and groups do not know themselves and the outside observer can do no more than project a judgement onto the subject of observation.

Japan is counterfactual in its power/knowledge relations because these are constituted in a different way by Japan's 'rules of the game' (as in North's work on institutions). First, inaction is an integral part of the system and shapes fixed parts of its structure. Certain inactions can be assumed and readily communicated because of the context of sense-making that we have outlined. For instance, the much-discussed context for the establishment of 'real' motives or interests (Clegg, 1989) cannot meaningfully be reduced to agents in a Japanese context. Collectives are the starting-point for any conceptualization of interests and motives. The ability of powerful individuals to indulge their imagination in fanciful or dramatic expressions of their power is constrained by the very processes that render them powerful. In Japan the 'rules of the game' encode almost every action with meanings that are understood by the wider collective and constrain all actions any of its members might imagine, in an argument that has parallels with Cook and Brown's conception of group-level knowledge and practice. Inaction, unconsciousness and collective organization are essential to interpreting practice in Japan's institutional framework. Japanese management is only possible because power relations are positively constituted in these complex practices.

We would argue that the direction that Japan has actually taken is neither that of Mode 1 nor Mode 2 knowledge. Mode 1 knowledge production occurs in the context of what realist philosophers of science refer to as 'standing conditions'. These comprise a definite set of contextual experimental conditions that are contrived according to the scientific method in such a way that context has no unaccountable effect. In the social world, the actors themselves interpret the 'rules of the game' locally, in situ. They are learnt in context and become reflexively automatic. From the point of view of interpreting the processes that situate Japanese working, learning and innovation practices, it appears that 'insider' (*emic*) stories and Mode 3 knowledge are privileged in a way quite distinct from classical Western 'outsider' (*etic*) accounts. Mode 1 positivist science as a tool of knowing (as illustrated in Figure 1) has contributed much to Japan's economic development, but attempts to use it as a vehicle for deconstructing Japanese organizational practices of innovation invite contradictions.

In Japanese organizations, compelling narratives, allied with positive science, will persuade rigorously, aesthetically, through the conventions of organizationally patterned discourses. Ultimately, Japanese organizations seek to understand themselves interpretively through the stories that they construct to explain reality. The questions are not concerned with objective truth, but the nature of an understanding that is intersubjectively valuable in a specific context. It is in this context, that many companies make the corporate creed very specific. Because of the risk of obsolescence in a creed, occasional updating will occur. For instance, currently Hitachi emphasizes *quality* products; Sony emphasizes *creativity* in innovation, while Honda emphasizes *youthfulness* in the appeal of its products. These creeds characterize both corporate symbolism that the company wishes to sustain and the corporate strategy that it seeks to follow. The creed stands as a condensation of what it means to share common goals (in quality, in creativity, in youthful appeal, and so on). Additionally, the creed makes clear the meaning of jobs in the enterprise: as oriented overwhelmingly to quality, to creativity and innovation, or to the youth market. The creed, as the implicit backdrop to all strategic thinking also helps create consistency in strategic decision-making. Cook and Brown's (1999) use of a pluralist epistemology, in conjunction with the epistemology of practice, provides a reasoned way of considering the processes by which practices situated in different contexts are enabled by different types of knowledge and power relationships embodied in distinct institutional frameworks.

Conclusion

The power relations that constitute Japan's implicit rules enable them to act as if they were huge gyroscopes that maintain the same spin. Outsider assumptions, about change and global convergence shifting the axis of spin, typically will fail to appreciate the role that implicit institutions and collective tacit knowledge play behind Japan's façade or public face (Porter *et al.*, 2000). Commodore Perry, the Second World War, and the lost decade since Japan's miracle growth faltered in the early 1990s, have hastened turning points in Japan's development. However, presuppositions that they are *convertible* into a new axis of spin, convergent with the assumptions of Mode 1 or 2 knowledge, should be challenged. There is a distinctive institutional component to Japanese knowledge management practices and they are not easily amenable to the representations that are dominant in much recent thinking about Modes 1 and 2 knowledge. Indeed, we suggest that, given the contextual specificities of the Japanese context, it is wiser to think of their knowledge management practices as a distinctive hybrid – which we term Mode 3.

References

Bourdieu, P. (1985) *Distinction* London, Routledge.

Clegg, S.R. (1989) *Frameworks of Power* London, Sage.

Cook, S. and Brown, J.S. (1999) 'Bridging Epistemologies: The Generative Dance Between Organizational Knowledge and Organizational Knowing' in *Organization Science* 10 (4) pp. 381-400.

Dore, R. (1973) *British Factory, Japanese Factory: The Origins of National Diversity in Industrial Relations* London, Allen and Unwin.

Fingleton, E. (1995) 'Jobs for Life: Why Japan Won't Give Them Up' in *Fortune*, March 20.

Fingleton, E. (1997) *Blindside: Why Japan is Still on Track to Overtake the U.S. by Year 2000* Tokyo: Kodansha International.

Foucault, M. (1977) *Discipline and Punish* Harmondsworth, Penguin.

Gibbons, M. Limoges, C. Nowotny, H. Schwartzman, S. Scott, P. and Trow, M. (1994) *The New Production of Knowledge: The Dynamics of Science and Research in Contemporary Societies* London, Sage.

Goto, A. (2000) 'Japan's National Innovation System: Current Status and Problems' in *Oxford Review of Economic Policy* 16 (2) pp. 103-113.

Ronald Gilson and Mark Roe (1999) 'Lifetime Employment and Labor Peace' in *Columbia Law Review* 1 (2).

Harvey-Jones, J. (1993) *Managing to Survive* London, Mandarin.

Itami, H. (1992) 'Firm as an Informational "Ba" (Interactive Field)', in: Ijiri, Y. (Ed.) *Information and Internationalization* Pittsburgh, Carnegie-Mellon University Press.

Jacques, R. (1996) *Manufacturing the Employee: Management Knowledge from the 19th to the 21st Centuries* London, Sage.

Jensen, M. and Meckling, W. (1976) 'Theory of the Firm: Managerial Behaviour, Agency Costs and Ownership Structure' in *Journal of Financial Economics* 3 pp. 305-360.

Johnson, C. (1992) *MITI and the Japanese Miracle: The Growth of Industrial Policy 1925-1975* Tokyo, Charles E. Tuttle.

Johnson, C. (1995) *Japan: Who Governs? The Rise of the Developmental State* New York, W. W. Norton and Co.

Kiyonobu, I. and Eri, Y. (1974) 'The Japanese Research System and the Establishment of the Institute of Physical and Chemical Research' in Nakayama, S. Swain, D. and Yagi, E. (eds.) *Science and Society in Modern Japan* Massachusetts, MIT Press.

Kono, T. and Clegg, S.R. (2001) *Trends in Japanese Management* London, Palgrave.

Lewin, A. Long, C. and Carroll, T. (1999) 'The Coevolution of New Organizational Forms' in *Organization Science* 10 (5) pp. 535-550.

Lorriman, J. and Kenjo, T. (1996) *Japan's Winning Margins* Oxford, Oxford University Press.

Mason, R. and Caiger, J. (1972) *A History of Japan* Rutland, Charles E. Tuttle.

Miyashita, K. and Russell, D. (1994) *Keiretsu: Inside the Hidden Japanese Conglomerates* London, McGraw-Hill.

Nakane, C. (1970) *Japanese Society* Berkeley, University of California Press.

Nature (1992) 'RIKEN – Japan's Leading Light' in *Nature*, 359, 15 October 1992, p. 578.

Nonaka, I. and Takeuchi, H. (1995) *The Knowledge Creating Company: How Japanese Companies Create the Dynamics of Innovation* New York, Oxford University Press.

Nonaka, I. Toyama, R. and Konno, N. (2000) 'SECI, *Ba* and Leadership: a Unified Model of Dynamic Knowledge Creation' in *Long Range Planning* 33 (4).

North, D. (1990) *Institutions, Institutional Change and Economic Performance* Cambridge, Cambridge University Press.

Nowotny, H. Scott, P. and Gibbons, M. (2001) *Rethinking Science: Knowledge and the Public in an Age of Uncertainty* Cambridge, Polity Press.

O'Dell, C. and Jackson-Grayson, C. (1998) 'If Only We Knew What We Know: Identification and Transfer on Internal Best Practice' in *California Management Review* 40 (3) pp. 154–74.

Okazaki-Ward, L. (2001) 'MBA Education in Japan: Its Current State and Future Direction' in *Journal of Management Education* 20 (3) pp. 197-234.

Penrose, E. (1995) *The Theory of the Growth of the Firm* Oxford, Oxford University Press.

Polanyi, M. (1967) *The Tacit Dimension* London, Routledge and Kegan Paul.

Porter, M. (1990) *The Competitive Advantage of Nations* New York, Free Press.

Porter, M. Takeuchi, H. and Sakakibara, M. (2000) *Can Japan Compete?* London, Palgrave.

Scarbrough, H. and Swan, J. (2001) 'Explaining the diffusion of Knowledge Management The Role of Fashion' in *British Journal of Management* 12 (1).

Schumpeter, J. (1976) *Capitalism, Socialism and Democracy* London, George Allen and Unwin.

Spender, J.-C. (1998) 'Pluralist Epistemology and the Knowledge-based Theory of the Firm' in *Organization* 5 (2).

Spender, J.-C. (2002) 'Knowledge, Strategic Problems, and The Theory of The Firm' in Bontis, N. and Choo, C.W. (eds.) *The Strategic Management of Intellectual Capital and Organizational Knowledge* New York: Oxford University Press.

Terdiman, R. (1987) 'The Force of Law: Toward a Sociology of the Juridical Field' in *Hastings Law Journal* 38.

The Economist (1996) 'Science and Technology: Back to Basics in Japan' in *The Economist* 102, May 25.

Toby, R.P. (1977) 'Reopening the Question of Sakoku : Diplomacy in the Legitimation of the Tokugawa Bakufu' in *Journal of Japanese Studies* 3 (2) pp. 323-63.

Toby, R.P. (1984) *State and Diplomacy in Early Modern Japan: Asia in the Development of the Tokugawa Bakufu* Princeton, Princeton University Press.

van Wolferen, K. (1990) *The Enigma of Japanese Power: People and Politics in a Stateless Nation* London, Macmillan.
Wenger, E. (2000) 'Communities of Practice and Social Learning Systems' in *Organization* 7 (2) pp. 225-246.

Chapter 9

'He Came, He Saw, He Re-engineered': New Managerialism and the Legitimation of Modern Management Practice

Kirstie Ball and Chris Carter

Introduction

In *Manufacturing the Employee* (1996), Roy Jacques examines, through Foucauldian method, the discursive and practice based shifts in the late nineteenth and early twentieth centuries which precipitated the development of modern American Management Knowledge. In this paper, we seek to examine, using a method of discourse analysis which has been based on Foucauldian thought, changes in the last twenty years which mark further shifts in key aspects of management knowledge and practice to form what we term 'new managerialism'.

That the last twenty years or so has been a period of great change for organizations is hardly a profound comment. From the 1980s to the present, there has been an explosion in the production and dissemination of a number of highly popular managerial concepts; these initiatives, such as TQM and BPR, highlight a number of themes, which include, inter alia, a move away from bureaucracy, a flattening of the organizational structure, teamwork, an emphasis on creating the 'right' culture, and an elevation of the importance of the role of charismatic leadership. This wave of managerial ideas marks a departure from the traditional American System of Manufacture, whose rise is documented by Jacques, and as such we refer to it as the discourse of new managerialism, with it setting the tone, and acting as a *'regime of truth'* (Foucault, 1972) for what constitutes 'good practice'.

It is necessary to explain why we consider the latest managerial ideas to constitute a break with the past, for instance, do they not just constitute the latest nostrums in a teleology that spans back to Taylor's work a century ago? Whilst we acknowledge that there are some parallels between Scientific Management and contemporary ideas, there are also fundamental differences, not just in content, but also in the institutional frameworks that support, reinforce and circulate the discourse of new managerialism. We argue that the 'surface of emergence' (Foucault 1972), or the conditions that allowed the discourse and practice to emerge, were a product of the crisis of western capitalism experienced with the collapse of the 'golden age of capitalism'. The loss of confidence in the existing

American System of Manufacture, was arguably borne in part from the growing competition from Japan and the South-East Asian economies. This, combined with a New Right political agenda, which encouraged globalization, pursued privatization, and was accompanied by rapid developments in the field of information technology, served to create the conditions of uncertainty that led to the emergence of a robust discourse of new managerialism. In a similar manner to the institutions described by Jacques, modern occidental management practice was legitimated by the emergence of various institutional seats of management knowledge: the business school, the management consultancy, the popular management text, and most importantly for the purposes of this paper, the newly privatized utility companies and the UK national health service, as well as private sector organizations. The 1980s privatization wave in the UK hugely transformed the way in which public sector bureaucracies were managed, with the UK government investing millions in research which documented, analysed and precipitated further this transformation. Public sector management emerged as a cognate discipline in business schools, with issues of competency, responsiveness, competitiveness and flexibility being at the heart of these 'new' private sector giants.

In this paper, we seek to complement Jacques' work by extending his arguments about the construction of management knowledge to the recent past, and extending his method to examine the live talk of an executive in a newly privatized public utility who explicitly constitutes his practice through the language of new managerialism. At this point, it is also worth noting ontological issues which arise from examining live talk or 'discourse', against the background of movements in grander scale 'Discourses' (Hodgson and Ball, 2004 (this collection); Alvesson and Kärreman, 2000) which emanate from epochal shifts. Whilst we recognize that new managerialism is a Discourse in the Archaeological sense, delimiting a field of knowledge, we also argue, using genealogical method, that this will emerge and disperse locally, occurring in everyday talk and text, or 'discourse'. Put briefly, the genealogical method is concerned with how broader movements in power/knowledge relations feature in local scenarios, with the analyst mapping the lineage of social relations at different nodes in the institutional and pan institutional web of power. This assertion is based on Foucault's observations that power/knowledge acts in a capillary fashion: in other words, that it does not emanate from a central source, but rather is dispersed around the dense web of institutions and individuals which constitute society. Thus, power relations can be constructed from individual instances, reactions to local circumstances, which interconnect from the bottom up to form an ensemble of power relations in society. On the other hand, grand movements in fields of knowledge emerge when these power relations become strategically codified in key institutions (Foucault 1990), of the kind in which we see the Discourse of new managerialism located. Therefore, like Jacques, we seek to observe local constructions of grander scale ideas, and the resistance with which they are met; but unlike Jacques, we are able to focus on live talk.

Talking New Managerialism

The method we choose to examine live talk is compatible with, and partly inspired by genealogical notions: Potter and Wetherell's (1987) interpretive repertoires. Interpretive repertoires attempts to identify the different lexicons of themes, concepts and ideas used by individuals in different sites, and the interplay between them (Potter and Wetherell, 1987; Wetherell 1998). Located firmly within 'critical discursive social psychology' (Wetherell 1998) this approach focuses on 'practices that produce persons, notably discursive practices, and seeks to put these in a genealogical context' (1998: 405) Effectively, they examine the way in which individuals construct and identify social relations within their worlds, observing the identity work and ideological practice through which this is achieved (Wetherell 1998). They advocate a reading of interview texts which emphasizes the constructed nature of accounts – in other words what interviewees say should not be read as indicative of some external, measurable context. Individuals use their battery of repertoires to make their reality seem real to the researcher: the *accounting* function in the context of the research interview is emphasized (Shotter 1989). Potter and Wetherell bolster the genealogical compatibility of interpretive repertoires by drawing on the work of Shapiro (1992). Shapiro's notion of historically located 'proto-conversations' which enable present conversations, allows for the identification of interpretive repertoires and the rendering of 'normal' and 'transparent' modes of conversational exchange problematic, viewing them through a genealogical lens. This is not dissimilar to Jacques (1996:19) distinction of 'what can be said' from 'what is said'. The researcher needs to search for the origin of these surface irregularities and tensions in speech practices which occur within the space of one, or a series of, accounts as simultaneously historically and currently located. The idea is therefore, that individuals use their interpretive repertoires to position themselves and others in relation to a subject of conversation (in this case, the executive's managerial practice), and that this positioning has a broader basis. In closely examining the talk of our executive, we attempt to be sensitive to subject positioning in broader discourses, whilst recognizing the local nature of the study itself.

The following pages show that the executive used five repertoires throughout his account, which ally to aspects of new managerialist discourse as embodied in the its texts and institutions:

- The **charismatic** repertoire: concerning the executive's potency as a leader;
- The **anachronism** repertoire: concerning the executive's potency to dismiss all that is 'old' and 'outdated';
- The **inevitability** repertoire: concerning the executive's lack of power over changes which were dictated by circumstance;
- The **external alliances** repertoire: concerning the executive's self legitimation through links external to the organization;
- The **empowerment** repertoire: concerning the relationship the executive has with his 'followers'.

An Executive's Tale

Our executive is Mike Clark (a pseudonym), the Metering Executive, head of the Metering function at CoastElectric, a British Regional Electricity Company. Privatized in 1990, the company underwent a series of organizational changes. In 1993, it moved towards a functional organizational structure. The corollary of this change was for different tasks to be explicitly identified, rather than, as had been the case, being one constituent part of the general operations. This meant that the Metering Function (consisting of the fitting, maintenance, and reading of electricity meters) went from being part of the Services, Fixing and Testing Department to being a separate entity within the two Engineering Regions, still under the control of the Regional Engineering Managers. In 1994, however, the Metering functions were taken out of the 'Main Engineering Business', and a Senior Management position, titled 'Metering Executive', was created; the brief for the Metering Executive was to *'create a separate metering business within the organization'* (named CoastMeter). Clark, the then Customer Services Manager, was appointed to this high profile role. This section will examine Clark's representation of the process of forging 'a separate metering business', and explore the discursive resources he uses in legitimating his position and reality in CoastMeter.

Clark's account features stories and anecdotes, which refer to his dealings with trade unions, the workforce, his management team, his foremen, and a management consultancy firm, the IPD and other business associates in securing the organizational changes he designed. Pursuing a unitary employee relations framework, contracting out metering staff, making foremen into managers, and changing outdated organizational psychologies and ideologies are just a few of the changes that feature in this account. Throughout his narrative, he is at pains to illustrate his potency in implementing them, and hence his commanding position in local relations of power. These notions of potency are explored through the previously described discursive resources he employed, beginning with the charismatic repertoire.

The Charismatic Repertoire

Upon becoming Metering Executive, Clark had various ideas about how the organization was to change in response to strategy, the environment, and, of course, his own leadership. Using the charismatic repertoire, Clark refers to his dynamism as a leader, and in doing so, presents an alternative version of himself as a 'charismatic maverick'. He constructs his ideation behaviour as unusual, enigmatic, but extremely powerful in his sphere of influence at managerial level:

> Well I get my ideas in the bath. So when I go into a meeting and say to my managers 'I've had a bath' they all groan. I had a bath, and now I have always approached the CoastMeter as if it was my own company. If it succeeds I succeed. Now what I wanted to do was to get that kind of psychology going amongst the staff.

In his dealings with trade unions, relations are far more hostile. Believing that the union would oppose most proposed changes to working conditions, he contrived, in negotiations, that metering staff would be imminently contracted out. Of course, the trade union was opposed to this but in particular, they disliked the way he approached the negotiations themselves, calling him an 'evil bastard'. Clark's account belittles the union officials, as childish, irrational, unprofessional, and stupid. Throughout the account, he adopts a unitary frame of reference, where states his intention to align employees, ideologically and psychologically with the organization, rather than with the union. Positioning himself as the determinant of these intangible and personal aspects of his workers further serves to reinforce his superiority in local relations of power . In the following extract, he describes the Machiavellian guile he used to force the union to negotiate these new terms and conditions, thereby claiming another powerful, intangible personal characteristic for himself in the charismatic repertoire:

I had my masterstroke... Of course they hadn't heard of it, and they couldn't argue, they had been completely outmanoeuvred. In fact, the trade unions are now employing a sense of urgency to talk to me. I have told them that the present levels of performance are unacceptable, and that I will get quotes from contractors. Now the Union has rejected this, as the full-time officers have told me they would. But they have come back to me saying 'we'll talk about other ways of doing this'. Now this was a good job, as it would have been very difficult to go out to tender at the moment, and contractors may not have been cheaper. But the Union did not know this. We have made huge advances over the last two years, there would have been a riot two years ago for our current proposals.

This (successful) manoeuvring is illustrative of his personal guile. Furthermore, by contending that 'they were completely outmanoeuvred', he alludes to his superior personal and intellectual skills. This 'personal guile' surfaces again as he recounts how, through the contrived threat of contracting-out work, he was able to achieve an agreement that working conditions could be changed. His argument that CoastMeter had made 'huge advances' in employee relations, equates the destabilization of the union position as progress. Effectively, he had made the union climb down from their original position, in which they refused to negotiate with Clark; the shakiness of the trade union's position in Clark's eyes is explained further below.

Anachronism Repertoire

The link developed above between change and 'huge advances' is a common theme within Clark's discourse, and supports the incidence of the anachronism repertoire. This repertoire highlights the status quo as being an anachronism, outdated, and in need of change. For instance, in the quote below, Clark identifies that there was an 'old psychology' among some of his staff which had to be overcome:

I really had to get over the old foreman psychology of 'I'm a man manager, I'm not doing projects'.

Elaborating on this 'problem' Clark argued that:

Basically their (foremen) attitude was 'I don't break wind unless they tell me to'.

The two quotes above signify that Clark regarded the foremen as being inflexible, and un-dynamic: in other words, rather unlike the way he has portrayed himself. Similarly, Clark's contention, in the next excerpt, that, 'we have to have different working patterns', points to the present work organization as being anachronistic, this is further reflected by his identification of two alternative ways of organizing the work, which serve to negate the pre-existing work practices.

We have to have different working patterns. Now there are two ways of doing this we either have 1) Variable Working hours or we have 2) Job and Finish. Basically, Variable working hours mean you work for five hours go home for four hours and then come back to work for five hours. Job and finish, means that you just do the job when you like. This is actually outside the current trade union agreement.

The representation, in the excerpt above, of the current working practices being anachronistic seems to legitimate him breaking the existing trade union agreement. Furthermore, it also raises the question as to whether the trade union itself is to be regarded as an anachronism. Clark seemingly confirmed that this is the case when he elaborated on his relationship with the trade union, claiming that:

I'm afraid the trade unions are dinosaurs, they are ideologically opposed, saying we can't have that as it is a split shift. They give the members all the crap about it being against all we have fought for over the last 50 years. They have a huge angst over all of this, which is of course against their member's wishes. We have now reached the stage where the access rate is not up, and we need to get the cost down.

In the above excerpt, Clark clearly represents the trade unions as being an anachronism, the way in which he does this is two fold, firstly, he refers to their tradition as being 'crap', secondly, he labels them as working against the wishes of their members. All these serve the ultimate goal of him accounting for his perceived potency in the breaking down resistance to first of all contracting out status for the staff, and second his ideas *per se*. However, unitary imperatives, old hat and self claimed personal skills aside, there are elements in the organization over which Clark has no control, and he neatly gives way to these other 'driving forces for change', and he uses them to reinforce his position in the inevitability repertoire.

Inevitability Repertoire

In the following extract, he commences establishing the need for and the inevitability of organizational change, articulating a direct causal link between the external environment and CoastMeter:

> On taking over it was clear we had to change. I decided to approach restructuring by asking 'what does the future offer?'. To this, I came to the conclusion tighter regulation, developments in IT and the possibility of competition.

Much of the reorganization and pressure for change within CoastElectric was directly attributed to the future liberalization of the domestic electricity supply market. Clark argued that in its current form, CoastMeter was uncompetitive, something he attributed to the relative (against the contract price) inefficiency of the meter readers. This is shown in the excerpt below:

> Sometimes the competitive market is supposed to start in 1998, then it goes to year 2000 and then back to 1998. The psychology of all this means we are not in a stable environment. The costs of meter reading are analysed, and basically our position is we will contract out meter reading unless the unit costs of our Meter Readers measure against the contract price. We have set three measures for this: 1. The number of calls made per day, 2. The access ratio (i.e. the percentage a meter reader is actually able to gain access to enter a property and read the meter), and 3. The cost per meter read. We have gone from 200 meter readings a day to 245 on average. The cost per meter read had gone from 78p last June to 64p now, so that is about a 20 per cent cut. The access ratio remains at 73 per cent. Now we want the figures to improve and are setting much higher targets.

In presenting change as inevitable, and with a sense of considerable momentum, Clark has plenty of discursive resources to enable his organizational mission, and his role in it as central, and potent. In self positioning as relatively powerless against 'bigger' forces, he also acts as an organizational interpreter and harnesser of these forces. This is notwithstanding that this inevitability within the CoastMeter environment eventually led to forty redundancies, something which Clark again equates with progress. Clark is notably 'silent' about them, viewing them as an inevitable part of the organizational change process.

External Alliance Repertoire

As well as deriving legitimacy for his plans from his relative powerlessness over the external environment, Clark is proactive in presenting the importance of his various, specific external alliances, and enrolling them in his mission: other successful business people, management consultants, negotiating experts and professional bodies. The common factor amongst all these external alliances is the specialist knowledge they can provide to Clark, which, again (and according to Foucault) reinforces his position in local power relations. For example, in striving to create unitary employee relations and ideological alignment amongst his staff, he asked an owner-manager friend to talk to them:

> I needed to get the right kind of psychology among the staff, what I decided to do was to get a friend of mine, who runs a successful business, manufacturing squash courts, and toilet cubicles for airports, to come and talk to us as an owner manager. He came and talked about Business Planning, Transport, Finance and Industrial Relations. This went down very well and from this I got them to ask, what have we got to do? They then invented their own training requirements.

Notions of entrepreneurialism as being the 'right psychology' precipitated the staff 'inventing' their own training requirements, and frames his unifying disciplinary strategy. Despite this, he still thought their salaries were too high, and legitimated change in the organization by, again, describing how he employed another external alliance, this time, Humana Management Consultants, and their knowledge of the 'market' wage rates of ex public sector employees:

> Clark A: 'Our wages are 60 per cent above the market rate, so we need to incentivize staff, so they increase their productivity by 60 per cent.
> Carter Q. 'How do you determine the market rate?'
> Clark A. 'Humana Management Consultants calculated the market rate. The rate was based on their research. The wages for that kind of job is £7,000, we pay £13,000'.

The need for an increase in the output of the meter reading staff is represented as being necessitated by the prevailing 'market rate', when this rate was, in fact, based on a report by a management consultancy. The data generated by Humana Management Consultants are elevated to the status of 'objective fact', and subsequently this implies that the CoastMeter meter readers need to be disciplined by the market. The 'market rate' had important implications for Clark's staff in that, in order to retain their jobs they had to be 'incentivized'. In continuation of his negotiations with the union, Clark also explains:

> I was specially trained by an American negotiating expert who had worked as a Middle East peace negotiator. He trained me in a new technique whereby the approach is based on 'Ethics and Integrity'.

He once again makes use of an external alliance with specialist knowledge, in this case to draw attention to his superiority to the trade union. The phrase 'I was specially trained' denotes his personal importance, this is further emphasized when we are informed that his trainer is no less than an 'American negotiating expert' who had worked as a 'Middle East peace negotiator'. This admission connects, however tenuously, Clark's proposed changes in CoastMeter with geo-political world events, and the charismatic guile with which he out-manoeuvred the union earlier in his account, the conclusion of which he describes in the following extract:

> I attended an IPD annual conference, of which I'm a Fellow. There was a talk by John Monks the chief of the TUC about employers and unions working in partnership. I was

profoundly influenced by this. At the next meeting with the Full-time officers I said 'of course you will be all aware of the proposals from your leader John Monks'. Of course they hadn't heard of it, and they couldn't argue.

This excerpt clearly demonstrates yet again how Clark draws on external alliances to justify a particular position. In this instance, he decontextualized a speech made by a leading trade unionist, at an IPD conference, in order to legitimate his arguments. Moreover, his mention that he was a 'Fellow' of the IPD, and that he was at their 'annual conference' links him into a broader, professional managerial network.

Empowerment Repertoire

Apart from the contracting out, unitary employment relations framework and 'psychological changes' outlined by Clark, the final change for CoastMeter employees was for the foremen: they were to become managers, and hence 'empowered' as such. Their 'anachronistic' psychology was outlined earlier, but the detail of what was to constitute their 'empowerment' is outlined below:

> An anxiety remained on how to deal with and who could help them get the requisite skills. We pushed as much as we could down to the foremen, who were now Metering Managers, even getting foremen to handle dismissal interviews. We had to take a step from this as things were getting a bit personalized, but my point was I don't want to be wasting my time with a dismissal interview.

The involvement of the Foremen in an increased range of tasks is indicative of the devolution of managerial work which, provides more time for Clark to concentrate on 'strategic issues'. This point is illustrated by Clark's assertion that he does not want to waste time on dismissal interviews. On closer consideration of his comments, the main individual to be empowered by this change is Clark , rather than the newfound Metering Managers, who appear to simply have a heavier workload, completing more mundane and unsavoury managerial tasks. Thus, Clark uses the empowerment repertoire, again, to demonstrate his strong position in local relations of power.

Discussion

The CoastMeter case highlights how an executive in an organization constructs an identity as someone who cunningly and entrepreneurially leads through change, surfing the environment for opportunity. He uses themes pertaining to (1) Charisma, (2) Anachronism, (3) Inevitability, (4) External Alliances, and (5) Empowerment to position his narrative.

Beginning with his position as an enigmatic, unconventional, creative thinker, Clark uses the charismatic repertoire to present his skill as something which is beyond the grasp of his colleagues and adversaries in the organization. This is also evident in the executive's legitimation of his position through his use of external alliances. The external alliances are varied, but nonetheless their prime function remains the same, namely, to provide support from without for the Executive's position within. This supports our assertion that a dense, network of new managerialism is in existence; actors and institutions within the network of new managerialism possess 'Authorities of Delimitation' (Foucault 1972) which establishes that they possess a particular knowledge and authority, the corollary being that their statements are accorded value. Statements were made on CoastMeter by management consultants, and an entrepreneur, this is coupled with Clark, the executive in the case, elevating his own status as a speaker by, inter alia, highlighting his ties with a professional body, and a world negotiating expert.

The 'External Alliances' repertoire provides a critical understanding of how an executive or a manager may mobilize for enacting organizational change, however, it does not fully explain why the particular change is required, or how change is to be represented in the organization. This is a role fulfilled by the 'Anachronism', and the 'Inevitability' repertoires. The 'Anachronism' repertoire attempts to fix meaning (Clegg and Hardy 1996), demonstrating why the status quo is no longer an adequate means of organizing. The 'Inevitability' repertoire suppresses the notion that there may be an alternative to the changes proposed, it also acts as a mechanism to link changes in the external environment to the need for changes to the conditions of employment.

But how can we relate this to Jacques work, and to the grander discourses to which he alludes? The notion of a grander discourse of new managerialism, which exists and circulates in different institutions, is strongly supported in the CoastMeter case. This is not just because of external alliances either. Identifying with charismatic leadership practices, using empowerment language and practice, harmonizing adversarial employment relations ideologies, aligning individual's goals with those of the organization, leveraging the knowledge of extra-organizational 'experts' and distinguishing, privileging and radicalizing current and future organizational practices from those used in the past are all evident across the new managerialist literature, especially in the more evangelical accounts of Peters and Waterman (1982), Hammer and Champy (1993) and Karaoke accounts of leadership practice. Clearly, Clark's ideological practice clashes heavily with those of other organizational members with whom he is involved. The intense nature of power struggle and political manoeuvring around the pluralist trade union members and 'old school' employees are more than highlighted in the text, and it is these tense, competing discourses in local discontinuous sites that the genealogical method exactly aims to capture.

Furthermore, that we have found evidence of new managerialist Discourse in a local site is highly significant. The discursive resources drawn upon by Clark closely resonate with key, popular new managerialist texts, new managerialist institutions are interpellated, and identities are actively constructed which, as Clark's political manoeuvring demonstrates, have material consequences for those in and around the organization. The strategically codified new managerialist Discourse indeed occurs at capillary level, and constitutes local power relations. In this case, power/resistance is observed in Clark's desire to unify ideologies and create the 'right' psychology amongst his staff, to make the union climb down and negotiate on his terms, and to redesign jobs. In all of these scenarios, Clark uses his repertoires to carefully construct the strategies he designed to achieve the desired outcomes. They are derived from new managerialist Discourses to claim potency and superiority in governing power relations, and to silence local competing discourses.

Conclusion

In this paper, we used Jacques' analysis as a basis for an investigation of current changes in management knowledge and practice. We postulated that the emergence of new institutions, such as the professional managerial body, the business school, the rise of the management consultancy, the popular management text, and the implementation of managerial approaches in newly privatized public utilities marked a departure from the American System of Manufacture, the rise of which was documented by Jacques, and the introduction of a broad 'new managerialist' discourse. Using the genealogical method, we examined instances of this discourse at a local institutional site: a newly privatized electricity company. We found thematic concurrence between the speaker's interpretive repertoires and those expressed at a broader pan institutional level, which, according to the genealogical method, is highly significant, particularly when tied to the history of the organization in question, and that of the individual we interviewed. The case itself highlights, to a considerable extent, the power and political struggles involved within and between organizations in establishing this new ideological practice. Jacques' analysis does not afford such detail, partly because of the lack of systematic management research documentation earlier this century, which is symptomatic of the embryonic nature of management knowledge as a field in itself. Indeed, this paper is a product of the very processes which Jacques set out to examine. One question remains: what would have Jacques' managers said at the time their discursive and practical frameworks began to shift? We will never know.

References

Alvesson, M. and Kärreman, D. (2000) 'Varieties of discourse: On the Study of Organizations through Discourse Analysis' in *Human Relations* 53 (9) pp. 1125-49.
Billig, M. (1992) *Talking of the Royal Family,* London, Routledge.
Clegg, S. (1989) *Frameworks of Power,* London, Sage.
Clegg, S. and Palmer, G. (1996) 'Producing Management Knowledge', in Clegg, S. and Palmer, G. (eds.) *The Politics of Management Knowledge,* London, Sage.
Deetz, S (1992) 'Disciplinary Power in the Modern Corporation', in Alvesson, M. and Willmott, H. *Critical Management Studies,* London, Sage.
Edley, N. and Wetherell, M. (1999) 'Negotiating Hegemonic Masculinity: Imaginary Positions and Psycho-discursive Practices', *Feminism and Psychology* 9(3) pp. 335-356.
Foucault, M. (1977) *Discipline and Punish* Harmondsworth, Penguin.

Foucault, M. (1990) *The History of Sexuality Vol. 1* Harmondsworth, Penguin.

Hammer, M. and Champy, J. (1993) *Reengineering the Corporation: A Manifesto for Business Revolution* London, Nicholas Brearly.

Hodgson, D. and Ball, K. (2004) 'Problematizing Discourse Analysis: Can We Talk About Management Knowledge?' in Hodgson, D. and Carter, C. (2004) *Management Knowledge and the New Employee*, Aldershot, Ashgate.

Jacques, R. (1996) *Manufacturing the Employee: Management Knowledge from the 19th to the 21st Centuries* , London, Sage.

Peters, T. and Waterman, R. (1982) *In Search of Excellence*, New York, Harper and Row.

Potter, J. and Wetherell, M. (1987) *Discourse and Social Psychology: Beyond Attitudes and Behaviour* London, Sage.

Thompson, J.B. (1988) *Studies in the Theory of Ideology*, Cambridge, Polity.

Shapiro, M. (1992) *Reading the Postmodern Polity* Minneapolis, University of Minnesota Press.

Shotter, J. (1989) 'Social Accountability and the Social Construction of "You"', in Shotter J. and Gergen, K. J. *Texts of Identity* London, Sage.

Weber, M. [1924] (1947) *The Theory of Social and Economic Organization* (trans. A.M. Henderson and T. Parsons; ed. T. Parsons), New York, Free Press.

Wetherell, M. (1998) 'Positioning and Interpretive Repertoires: Conversation Analysis and Post Structuralism in Dialogue', in *Discourse and Society* 9(3) pp. 387–412.

Chapter 10

'Plus Ça Change ...': Enforced Change and its Influence on Employees' Assumptions

Julian Randall

Introduction

Examining history to seek insight into worker identity and its significance in society is not new among commentators of industrial history (Barley and Kunda, 1992). At various times individual workers have been described as hands – mere cogs in the wheel of organizational mechanism – and their efforts have been co-ordinated into the performativity of efficiency and productivity factors (Taylor, 1913). At other times they have been regarded as the critical means of motivation whereby corporate creativity can somehow be mobilized (Peters and Waterman, 1985). For others, there has been an erosion loss of previously held autonomy and status (Jacques, 1996) for others a loss of character and diminution in the value of self-worth (Sennett, 1998).

For Jacques, the employee is a relatively recent emergence with a history of little more than a century (1996, p. 11). The industrial giants whose names are remembered in the car and steel sectors made their mark at the end of the Nineteenth Century. The build up of large organizations drew in many workers whose lives would previously have been situated in small towns and small businesses. For Jacques, such workers would have served an apprenticeship in a small business and then have expected to build up such a business elsewhere for themselves. They would have been what he calls 'men of character'. What Jacques sees replacing this world of self-sufficiency and development at work is a world where the worker becomes a wage slave and a 'hireling for life' (1996, p. 48). What then happens is that a new discourse is opened up, which reinforces a new social contract, what he calls the 'rise of the capitalist-labour account' (1996, p. 55). The management discourse now becomes a manager-employee discourse in which the efforts of the wageworker are defined in terms of 'outcomes, outputs and inputs'.

This new discourse becomes what Jacques describes as a 'truth-trap'. It is reinforced by the 'hypothesis-testing methodology to the near exclusion of the history and sociology of knowledge'. In the words of the author:

Within this method-driven community of knowers, 'research' means 'data', which is easily confused with meaning. Attempts to contextualize the role of empirical inquiry are mistakenly seen as attacks on empiricism. The metanarratives within which knowledge to date has been produced cannot be examined because it is believed to be a transparent framework, not an expression of values. Expression of this metanarratives is the key goal of this book (Jacques, 1996, p. 17).

It is similarly the key goal of any research that seeks to penetrate beneath the surface of apparent change into the thought and feelings of those who suffer change at work and have little alternative but to accept that change. Examination of such events is always difficult because access is not always possible to researchers at the time of the change and we are left with narratives some time after the event. It is therefore always an opportunity not to be missed to research for meanings attributed by subjects at the time of enforced change at work.

Identity and Discourse

We may agree with Jacques that in certain academic traditions, the focus has been on the quantifiable elements of organizational life, perhaps to the detriment of the meaning that is inherent in discourses, which frame organizations (Goffman, 1959). Indeed, data itself has no inherent significance unless it is informed by a perception of what is valuable or important in the interpretation attributed by the subject. Organizations as narrative construction suggest, some might say, require a context (Touraine, 1995) and that context will often be enforced change. However, the content of the change also invites further examination to ascertain if possible, what that change has meant to those who have suffered it.

A more qualitative approach to research in organizations would accept that how organizations are constituted can be accounted for by analysing the way in which individuals explain, interpret and evaluate their experience at work. It is multi-disciplinary in nature and can include the 'analysis of metaphor, language games, stories, poetry, narratives, rituals and myths, rhetoric, texts, drama, conversations and sense making' (Oswick, Keenoy and Grant, 2000). Within this tradition we can identify two approaches to the study of discourse: 'interpretive' and 'critical' Heracleous and Hendry, 2000). In the former, the discourse expresses and also creates social relations and practices. Discourse in this sense is capable of forming our identities and social beings (Reed, 1998). Discourse, therefore, would be seen not simply as a linguistic device but as central to the 'social construction of reality' (Berger and Luckmann, 1967). From such discourses, therefore, arise the development of shared meaning and common identity for organization members (Heracleous and Hendry, 2000, p. 1255).

Enforced Change and Basic Assumptions

Thus far we may accept that discourses can be seen as meanings derived from experience at work and arising within the everyday interactions of those who share experience at work. Actors interpret their experience and share it with others. They make sense of what they find and may share this too (Louis, 1980a and b; Weick, 1979; Silverman, 1997). But not all discourses are simple sense making as some sort of process of uncritical assimilation and compliance. What managers require of workers may be uncongenial, unacceptable or unethical. But the wage slave may have no options than to comply. Managers have an instrumental power and exhibiting resistance could have terminal consequences. The managerial discourse can in this context be seen as an imposition of power over individuals who might not have chosen to adopt practices at work had they had a choice. In such cases 'power and knowledge are quite clearly articulated in discourse' (Foucault, 1976, 133). The critical stream of research into organizational discourse follows Foucault in seeing a decentring of the subject and the rejection of human agency as focal in discovering how knowledge is institutionalized shaping social practices and setting new practices in play (Alvesson *et al.*, 2000; du Gay, 1996).

However, the resistance that may be occasioned in groups or individuals can become the focus of what Foucault described as 'reverse discourse' where minorities are made stronger and empowered by a hostile managerial discourse and work out their own explanation, interpretation and meaning in resistant evaluation. It is in that context that the present research has sought to make a contribution to research (Randall, 2001). What individuals experience as changing perception and how each evaluates the experience of enforced change at work would seem to offer a unique opportunity to discover how discourse changes and the stages that are inherent in reconstructing work experience in different ways.

Enforced Change and Resistant Evaluation

Mergers and acquisitions have multiplied by a function of four times between 1984 and 1992 (Hunt and Downing, 1990). And every enforced change in an organization is likely to bring challenge to the individuals involved. Only in the nineties did more evidence appear that suggested that all was not well with the subjects of such change. Cases studies began to illustrate that even where individuals were involved in change they did not always accept it or adapt to it as the rhetoric suggested they would do if correctly handled (Storey, 1989 and Alvesson, 1995). Indeed, some writers began to question whether the theoretical basis of HRM's claims was not beginning to look flawed to the point of being impossible to achieve (Blyton and Turnbull, 1992). Retail assistants required to behave in certain customer-focused ways described their response to enforced change and coping with the threat of management action in the face of failure to comply (Ogbonna, 1992).

The starting point for this research was the basic assumptions that individuals hold about themselves, their work and their career prospects in the face of enforced change at work. If subjects differ significantly in their evaluation of an enforced change event, perhaps a difference in their taken-for-granted assumptions about these aspects of their working lives may account for the meaning they attribute to such change and the value they ascribe to events.

But if basic assumptions are like internal criteria – used to adjudge what is experienced and attribute meaning and value in this way, it begs the question how do basic assumptions themselves ever come to undergo shift or change within the individual and what sort of experience might trigger this internal change? It seemed to the present author that if it were possible to identify such change of basic assumptions during enforced change at work, then it might be possible to identify a change of interpretation and a reconstruction, which signals a new discourse free from the trammels of past beliefs supporting Jacques' employee discourse.

Research Methods

The qualitative approaches of ethnomethodology offer researchers seeking to uncover the discourses of individual subjects in the narratives and texts used to describe personal experience and evaluate its significance. From the phenomenological sociology of Alfred Schutz and the symbolic interactionism of George Herbert Mead and Erving Goffman comes this concern to understand encounters in their own terms. For ethnomethodologists, the attempts by lay actors to make sense of the social world represent mechanisms through which social structure is created and sustained (Hassard, 1990, p. 98). The analysis of transitions has attracted the attention of large-scale surveys seeking to pinpoint differences between subjects (Nicholson and West, 1988) and also 'transformation' in which individuals undergo stages of reframing into the required assimilation of interpretive schema following change (Isabella, 1990).

Our own approach has been to let individual subjects have a voice as they reflect on the impact of enforced change and their responses to it as they interpret and reinterpret the significance, meaning and value they may attach to enforced change We have examined the narratives of 32 individuals subjected to enforced change at work giving an opportunity of examining what individuals say about the meaning they ascribe to such imposed change at work. So, we have sought to use their narratives to uncover what they believe should or should not have happened during that experience.

Our subjects were drawn from three organizations with whom the researcher happened to be working at the time that enforced change impacted on the organizations examined. These included a Government Department sited in a local divisional office, a Local Authority team of health workers subjected to compulsory competitive tender and pharmaceutical company site subject to takeover and threatened close down of the site, which did not in the end take place.

The interviews conducted were an hour and a half in length and allowed the individuals to identify and explain the nature of the change and the surprise that this had or had not engendered. The contributors to the literature on surprise and sense making emphasize that significance of allowing individuals the opportunity of explaining what has surprised them that happened and also what has not happened. This is sometimes referred to as confirmed and disconfirmed elements in a change experience (Louis, 1980). Interpretation requires a belief or assumption that an event will or will not happen and may even include what should or should not happen – sometimes referred to as 'ethicality' (Townley, 1994).

Further questions were included to explore more fully the explanations individual subjects offered for different outcomes of their experience of enforced change. Particularly we included questions on whether subjects thought they had survived enforced change and if so how; how they felt about a similar future change event recurring and questions relating to the relational elements of the psychological contract (McNeil, 1985) and their perceptions of the employer-employee relationship (Rousseau, 1998; Guest, 1998).

Our subjects had been employed in their organization for periods ranging between 17 and 37 years. Several of them had reached very senior positions in their organization. The purpose of our research was to examine the basic assumptions threatened by enforced change at work and whether they were still as firmly held as prior to the change or whether they had been abandoned and other assumptions adopted in their place. It seemed to us that therein lay an opportunity to identify perhaps the beginnings of different employer-employee discourse and what the implications of this might mean both for the individual and their possible future evaluation of enforced change.

Traditional Basic Assumptions

For many individuals the prospect of a long service in one organization may be an outdated notion. But there are still individuals and groups who retain a belief in security and an acknowledgement that long service and good conduct should equate to the rewards of a life of dedication and service properly granted. The disbelief and shock for such individuals is almost palpable:

> It came like a bolt out of the blue. I remember being called to the collector's office and told that the two departments were to be amalgamated and that there was a choice of manager to be made between __ and me. I said jokingly, 'I suppose this means I could be redundant' and to my surprise I was told, 'Yes, it does'. So now the total guarantee of security was gone.

For managers in the pharmaceutical industry the change to a clinical research organization meant the loss of personal projects responsible for developing compounds and a new world of jobbing consultancy work in which time and cost had to be negotiated with clients on the run. Worse still a system of productivity metrics was introduced in which all staff were monitored and targeted for results. Failure to meet these results were followed by withdrawal of privileges such as air travel to meetings, training courses until such time as the targets were met. PhD chemists were not used to such treatment and did not respond as well as they new owners had hoped:

> Had I known how it would turn out I would have taken the parachute. I felt very bitter about that. It all came to a head at a meeting with my boss and the Managing Director. They explained that they needed me to be committed to the studies that – wanted. Then we were moved to new building, gave up manufacturing and QC. Pre-clinical was taken over by ___, a microbiologist who knew nothing about our business.

For such subjects there was an experience of betrayal and bitterness and even disbelief. For most there were only two options: stay and put up with it or go elsewhere. Both options were taken, but not quiescently or in total compliance. Several chemists moved to a competitor whose working practices equated to the life they had previously known. In another case, a deputy director forced to move to a new headquarters 50 miles from his previous office continued to leave his home town at 8.45am travelling to his new destination by 10.30am and then leaving for the return journey at 3.30pm so that he would be back exactly where he would normally have been at 5pm. The energy once reserved for the job is now placed elsewhere: 'as far as loyalty and trust are concerned, all my energies are put into my family and friends rather than push myself at work.'

Not all basic assumptions are retained, however. From one manager came the retort:

> I had always thought that the directors were a sophisticated bunch. They would look after the needs of the managers. Well, that didn't happen and I had to think again about the quality of our senior managers.

For many subjects there continued to be retained basic assumptions about the duties and obligations that organization should discharge for them and a withdrawal of good will and attendant reduction of effort or adherence to contract working only.

Alternative Discourses

Not all subjects experienced the extreme responses expressed by those retaining basic assumptions of dependence on the organization for security, career and prospects. In contrast, we have identified subjects who seem not to have had such basic assumptions of dependency on traditional managerial discourses at all. They define their identity in terms of a discourse of control over their career destiny. In the words of one female senior manager:

Overall changes have not haven't taken me by surprise. I suppose you could call me naïve but adaptable. I would try anything, as long as I knew what I was doing and got a reward for it. I can do anything I want and that's what I feel about myself.

Such subjects sometimes describe joining the organization as a chance encounter. They would have been equally content to join other organizations – some have done. But from the time that they undertook to start working, their commitment to the job was firmly in the context of where it would lead next – and not necessarily within the organization. The focus of their attention is summarized in one word: marketability. So, in the face of imposed change they do not express the same anger and feeling of being betrayed. They don't mention feeling devalued or denigrated or marginalized. They may well be equally condemnatory of careless management behaviour during the change and equally judgmental about promises made and not kept. But for them there remains the challenge, willingly accepted, of making change work to their own personal benefit.

Indeed, change can signal opportunity and opportunity brings the chance of proving that there are more challenges to take on. Another female manager heard the CEO's address that if you have an idea, you just do it and extended her site job into responsibility for the UK site in Health and Safety:

> I thought, 'Why shouldn't Edinburgh be the centre for H and S in the whole country?' That was the thing Dennis (COE) said, 'If you see something, go after it'. And I took it with both hands. It's been hard work but I like hard work. It's true you set your own standards. I hear people complain and I can't understand it. How can they get in such a mess?

For other subjects, too, enforced change bought opportunity and the chance of bettering themselves. In two cases a Private Finance Initiative scheme to fund departments in-house led to external providers working with the internal staff. Two individuals left the service and joined the external provider. For them the lessons are clear:

> I should have moved eight years ago. I should have been more self-sufficient. I should have managed my career.

So not all subjects of enforced change at work either had or retained a discourse of dependence on the organization to provide their job, work and career prospects. But interestingly, neither are such subjects uncritical of the way enforced change was handled. One young chemist ended up with a department of 21 having been in charge of a research group of just four prior to the changes:

> I was at ___ for 4 years. I had a good boss. He was switched on and taught me the value of hard work. He taught me to realize that the company is not going to lead you along. If you want it, you do it.

But his attitude to the organization was:

Loyalty, I don't think it can exist to the same extent. Companies don't matter anymore. This happened quite recently where a friend of mine working for a local firm was told, 'You're no longer required'. And I said to him, 'Don't take it personally. It's not you'. You can have this trust but it takes a blow and then you never trust again. But for the individual the result is you will have clearer goals about what you want to achieve.

Such are the basic assumptions of many subjects who might be described as the successful survivors of enforced change. The advice they give others does not reinforce the managerial discourse.

Basic Assumptions and Reconstruction

For some subjects the experience of enforced change is, as the last speaker suggested, a chance to reassess how they interpret who they are and what this means in terms of the employer-employee discourse. For one such female enforced change brought a move from training into a section devoted to fraud at a time when she was about to lose her marriage and be left with a young son to look after and the search for a new home. She relates that experience as follows:

My house, marriage and job were all moving under me so I had to find security for myself. The Springboard course came along (assertiveness for female employees) and I got a lot out of that. I had to ask myself what I wanted to attain, what my goals were. I am very practical and logical. I am always thinking about things and I thought, 'For twenty four years my mother had a miserable marriage. She would have been better off without my Dad'. I decided what was the right thing to do: I had to control my own destiny. But I still feel angry about the way things were done. But I proved I could do it. I feel happier now. I know I can survive. I had some doubts. But I had to be strong.

For subjects who abandon traditional discourses of compliance and passivity there is the option of re-examining just how dependent they are on that employer-employee discourse. Once they have proved that it doesn't have to dominate their working lives and that other options are quite possible, there is a new assessment and a difference discourse of self-sufficiency. For another female subject there was the option of taking self-employment as a trainer and continuing to do work within the organization. Her own beliefs have now changed:

People put in long hours. But their contract is not with the organization; it is with other people in the organization. An organization is essentially inhuman – by that I mean that it doesn't really exist. What we've got is senior management devising a policy and then imposing it, passing it down to other people. I always said after the takeover, 'I don't care whose name is over the door. I just work for these people'.

Both these subjects may well have survived to stay in the organization. Their unsuspecting managers could be forgiven for believing that they have accepted the inevitable and are now settled back into ready compliance of a revised managerial discourse. Following them through the different responses based on their assumptions about change has enabled us to examine in detail whether such confidence would be well placed or not. For we would agree with the view that:

> there is some danger in assuming that compliance reflects 'a new identity' because even in the case of prisoners who appear to conform to the rules of prison life, this does not extend to the point of identifying with the values of the guards or of passing off an opportunity to escape, should it present itself (Knights and McCabe, 1999, p. 221).

Basic Assumptions and the Psychological Contract

The initial stimulus, which triggered the present research, was the assertion by one subject who had endured a very harrowing experience during enforced change at work that she 'felt stronger' as a result. This led to the quest to discover why she interpreted events in this way when her peer group workers were expressing very negative views. We accepted that in explaining their experience, subjects would express a number of opinions about what they thought should and should not happen to them in such a situation. This was the first step in our research approach and it indicated that there can be quite distinct expectancies lying behind personal interpretation, which predate the event itself and may well have been unchallenged until something different from their original expectancy occurs (Louis, 1980a and b). Once these basic assumptions about change had been expressed it became possible to examine the implication of what holding such views might imply in related areas of perception and interpretation.

The statement of feeling stronger also raised the question of whether subjects felt more self-sufficient, particularly at the prospect of a further experience of enforced change at work. Did they attribute their survival to chance, or was there some defining factor that might have accounted for their apparent success compared with others? Is reconstruction of basic assumptions, then, dependent on a self-appraisal, which transcends the present work or is there a different focus of self-perception that triggers optimism about future working prospects?

Finally, the opinions expressed by our subjects seemed to have implications for the continuing debate about the psychological contract as an expression of the traditional employer-employee discourse. Is loyalty and trust still alive in the perception of our subjects and would they seek to find it in another organization or abandon it altogether? We found, again that subjects whose basic assumptions were independent of the organization did not construct such a discourse in the first place. Whereas those that remained dependent on such a managerial discourse, were more likely to have abandoned any hope of finding it again and felt duly betrayed as a result. A few, who were offered employment elsewhere, were prepared to express a tentative hope in its restitution. However, some subjects who had done well under the enforced change with new promotion and responsibility, continued to harbour doubts about a restoration of the traditional managerial discourse of mutual care between employee and employer.

All of these conclusions beg the question, how do individuals come to construct a particular discourse? We have seen that there are suggestions offered in past experience which subjects suggest has been salient in forming beliefs and expectancies: a significant manager, past experience of change, a parent in self-employment, were sometimes cited as significant factors. Our own research has focused on the effect of enforced change on previously held basic beliefs themselves. The subjects we have identified as reconstructing what they had previously believed reinterpret their identity quite differently as a result. To move from dependence on a discourse to independence is a significant step for any individual to take. We have identified different factors that can give rise to such a transition. It might be an offer of employment by an outside agent, a significant family loss, the reassessment of life through marital breakdown. For all of them there can be no return of a traditional belief in or dependence on the traditional employer-employee discourse.

We have not attempted to generalize these findings. We acknowledge that the number of subjects is too few. Neither have we attempted to make any comparison between organizations. This would be a macro level consideration outside the scope of our research. What we can offer here are pointers for future research. We would suggest that where links have been demonstrated between basic assumptions about work and responses about self-perception and self-sufficiency, there is scope for examining their links across a broader band of subjects undergoing enforced change at work.

Whether organizations can continue to draw on the traditional assumptions laid out in the theories of psychological contract and by extension the theoretical assumptions of Human Resource Management depends on individuals at work continuing to link such beliefs to their self-perceptions of value, meaning and trust. We believe that there are now enough indicators to suggest that such beliefs and assumptions either no longer exist or do not link together in the way that companies and their managers have come to expect.

Deconstruction and Reconstruction

If we list the factors which individuals attest they have been deprived of it makes a formidable list of all that appeared to be promised to them by employing organizations: autonomy; status and respect; career prospects; fairness; involvement; listening; a friendly culture; variety of job and location; supportive manager; valued contribution; significant work results; achievement and good work procedures are all mentioned by subjects whose basic assumption is that the organization owes them this.

For most of them, came a violation of all those valued aspects of their perceived employment rights and instead a regime which brought a closer monitoring of their labours; an imposition of profitability metrics; a world of instant response to failure to achieve targets by deprivation of the very things that they know they need to achieve value-added performance. They are confronted by a bricks-without-straw situation, which brings with it the requirement to comply with a newly imposed managerial discourse and at best accommodation to new demands until something better comes up or an active search for another organization that will offer them the same supporting and nurturing environment, which they believe they had before imposed change shattered the reality.

In contrast, we have identified subjects who never held the basic assumption about the organization being a provider of security of tenure and future career prospects. Autonomy for these subjects is expressed not in terms of the work they do and their freedom to do it as they wish. Their autonomy is expressed in terms of their ability to take advantage of change to further their own career interests. The basic assumptions here expressed as advice to others, for example, comes across quite definitely: 'I can see opportunity and take it'; 'you have to promote yourself'; business is business'; 'I had no peer group'. The focus of their commitment is not to some previously existent Garden of Eden at all. It is the next opportunity to break out of a managerial discourse and get on with improving career prospects and employability elsewhere that dominates their accounts.

At this point we can refer to the long search for the essential element of commitment in the theory of Human Resource Management. It has been the object of such a quest both by managers and gurus alike (Huczynski, 1993). It is questionable whether the assurances of organizational commitment can any longer be sustained, if indeed it ever existed (Coopey and Hartley, 1990). What we can say here is that if feeling good about the organization depends on the traditional beliefs of loyalty, trust and job security, then enforced change imposed on subjects who have bought into this belief brings about immediate repudiation of such feelings of trust and a subsequent withdrawal of good will.

Similarly, for those looking for progression though the grades and an upward progression path through the organization, the prospects do not look promising. What we can support from the present research is that many subjects no longer look for the organization to plan their career and offer the promise of progression through the ranks. Independent subjects are well able to look for it from their own resources. So, for them there is an internalized quest for job opportunity and employability. Not all of them will consider stepping outside the organization immediately. The confidence to make a successful career outside the organization may have to wait for a job offer, say, form an external provider. Internal politics is the continued focus of their career aspirations.

It is more typical of subjects who have reconstructed their basic assumption of dependence on the organization to embark on the newfound career outside the organization. That may be because the trigger has been an outside offer of employment but can equally be the survival of a personal or family tragedy, which proves to them that they assert themselves without the need of dependence on an organization. If they can do it in their personal life, they see no reason why they should not do it in their working life, too.

The spectre of the organization seeking to reinvent itself through transformation of work processes and required supporting attitudes will probably be a constant however it is packaged and promoted. It rests on an assumption that job satisfaction and organizational commitment can somehow be secured (Curry *et al.*, 1986; Shore and Martin, 1989). However, employee responsiveness is always mediated by their assessment of the reasonableness of such calls in relation to how they are treated with regard to job security, conditions of work, promotion prospects, etc. As the effects of the results of enforced change at work impact on individuals, it becomes apparent to them that 'commitment is often expected from but not given to employees' (Kamoche, 1998). Side by side with that demonstration comes reinforcement for many 'that the idea of a 'career' is constructed and reconstructed while the practices related to this notion are deployed and individuals survive or fail' (Hatchuel, 1999).

It is our contention that such reconstruction of the managerial discourse is more likely when enforced change triggers a reassessment of the basic assumption of dependence on the organization. For many of our subjects enforced change at work brought about that shift in expectancy of continuing dependency and career support and for them there is no way back to a discourse of compliance to organizational assurances of continued security of employment.

Discipline and the Internal Response to the Management Discourse

The view of the organizing of work as dominance of the individual by those who want to control society is central to writers who see capitalism as the hegemony of the few who own the means of labour over the many who have only their labour to offer (O'Neill, 1987; Braverman, 1974; Burawoy, 1979). From this interpretation of labour processes comes the concept of power in its instrumental and social forms, which govern relationships between owners of capital and those who invest their labour (Lukes, 1986; Barnes, 1988). New managerial strategies derive from the apparently humanized exercise of this power dispensed in ways that would take individuals with it so that they would be less aware of the covert dominance inherent in the relationship (Child, 1985; Friedman, 1977).

In Foucault's view language and categories imposed at the very opening of relations govern the disciplinary nature of the discourse between the parties to the relationship thereafter (1977; 1980; 1984). This imposed dominance could mean a monitoring of subjects in a constant panopticon (Fox, 1989) whereby the organization and its managers could exercise control without being seen by the subjects themselves (Clegg, 1989; Deetz, 1992; Jackson and Carter, 1998). But, even with sophisticated techniques of observation, this compliance would still depend on putative benefits for the individual. The danger to the organization is the dawning of awareness that there may, in fact, be nothing in the promises made of reward for obedience (Jermier, Knights and Nord, 1994; Clegg, 1998) and that the Emperor really does have no clothes. The dilemma for organizations is that they depend on monitoring behaviour and assuming from correct performance that the subject has acquiesced. But it may be that the subject is a good deal more adept at offering compliance and that his or her acquiescence does not denote acceptance or assimilation at all (Henriques, 1984; Rose, 1990).

Enforced change at work enables us to examine how far internal compliance is still intact – if it was ever present in the first place – and how far the individual has radically changed his or her perception of the disciplinary relationship and if so, how this change has occurred. We have at this point to abandon the internal quest in subjects who are still dependent on the organization to offer the promises looked for from the relationship. The focus of their anger is the organization for reneging on the promises they thought were part of the discourse. Apart from looking for an alternate organization to offer a restored service, they still accept little or no responsibility for their own destiny nor is there any evidence of reconstruction of their basic assumptions about their employment rights.

However, for subjects who were independent of the organization then the factors which they attribute to their successful survival of enforced change is similar to the literature: effort, ability and political astuteness together, sometimes, with a supportive manager. Such subjects affirm that: 'it's all about effort and achievement'; 'proving you can do the job'; ' control of the situation and the effort you put in'; 'it's all about what you want to achieve for yourself'. Such subjects compare themselves with their dependent colleagues: 'it's the self sufficient against the whiners' and if they don't get what they want, then: 'look elsewhere'. The whole experience of enforced change confirms for some: 'there is a broad range of things I could do' and the bottom line is: 'I am more marketable'.

For those subjects who have reconstructed their basic assumptions from dependency on the organization to a new discourse of self-reliance, there is a difference emphasis: 'I had to do it for myself'; I had an offer and it gave me prospects'; 'I had to take control of my life'. Not all received a job offer, some experienced the change through personal circumstances: a failed marriage; a son charged with a serious crime; a breakdown in health and recovery are typical examples. Perhaps such an experience triggers a more objective personal assessment and makes subjects more philosophical about their survival prospects. Survival and self-assessment enable them to view themselves in a more self-sufficient light. A breakdown in the managerial discourse means that the power on which they depended has been replaced by a discourse of self-sufficiency independent of managers and their empty promises.

But the internal change experienced within has to relate to outside assessment of what is now possible in terms of risk-taking. Here we have examined two elements of self-sufficiency: cognitive control and behavioural coping ability (McCarthy and Newcomb, 1992). We have identified subjects who feel confident and experience no risk in making the move outside, compared with subjects who have proved their confidence but still feel uncomfortable about stepping outside the organization. What has emerged is a distinction based on competence proven in a job but continued feelings of dependence on the organization for employment, compared with subjects who have been offered assurance by an outside agency that their competence is recognized and so are ready to take the step outside the organization. For some, experience and success in a new job does not bring self assurance: 'you're only as good as your next piece of business' remains a basic assumption; for other, more independent subjects, their confidence reinforces the self-sufficiency to survive more change within the organization and sometimes reinforces a feeling of marketability without putting it to the test. Only those subjects who have had their self-sufficiency validated by an outside agent or experienced and survived significant personal disaster seem to embark on such a risk with confidence.

Reconstruction and Knowledge Management

Managing knowledge is a logical extension of panopticon in a world whose technology offers a new opportunity to observe while remaining unobserved. The prospects look encouraging and ought in theory to offer better opportunities for control than ever. There are those who see in the management of knowledge a new opportunity to assert control techniques and re-establish hegemony over the important human resource. 'The wide use of teams in BPR and process improvement efforts has given senior management newfound faith in the ability of skilled knowledge workers to understand, re-shape and improve their own work' (Neef, 2000, p. 15).

The evidence of this belief being justified does not look too encouraging. Workers in manufacturing seem to have the ability to see the hidden agenda in managers' attempts to inveigle them into team working schemes of production (Ezzamel, 1998; Knights, 2000). White-collar workers can be as resistant to such schemes, seeing them as a ploy to get more functional flexibility for less money (Procter and Currie, 2000). Even more disturbing for the proponents of this new managerial control discourse are findings that IT surveillance in the pharmaceutical sector may be as far away from establishing panopticon as ever (McKinlay, 2000). It would seem that the tacit knowledge required by those who work in any organization is the very thing that makes them employable and that they know this very well. Enforcing change on individuals increase this alienation from the company, make individuals more aware of their own marketability or even reconstructed in a discourse that causes them to feel independent of organizations for continued success at work.

'Social practices are constantly examined and reformed in the light of incoming information about those very practices – thus constitutively altering their character' (Giddens, 1991, p. 38). We would maintain that the present research has offered a closer examination of this inner re-examination process during the experience of enforced change at work. The prospects for the management of knowledge do not look encouraging for managers banking on reasserting their traditional managerial power discourse using such techniques.

The Future of Work and the Psychological Contract

The simple prescriptions of future working patterns have attracted the attention of writers from different traditions, both researchers and popular management gurus. The promise of unitary control, which the theory of Human Resource Management seemed to offer, promised linkage between efficiency and effectiveness whilst harnessing the good will and motivation of the worker. A concerted approach to the tools of Human Resource Development would enable the HR department to co-ordinate the incentives to consolidate the commitment of individuals and consensus in groups and teams (Purcell, 1987; 1989). These flexible styles of working would affect the status of individuals within the organization and core workers might find themselves in sub-contract or consultancy mode (Handy, 1989).

This new flexibility could well be seen as another example of enforced change at work. As such it could have repercussions for both employment and the organization (Morris and Blyton, 1991; Blyton and Turnbull, 1992). Early evidence suggested that some brown-field sites attempting radical change among their traditional workforce encountered significant levels of resistance (Storey, 1989, 1995). Even the incentives offered to make workers feel part of the world of capitalist shareowners failed to emerge quite as its prophets had foretold (Dunn, 1990). If the managerial discourse was now beginning to be deconstructed, how would organizations reassert the managerial discourse (Christie, 1994; Marcotte, 1995)? If people are indeed the most important asset of the company and they are being alienated by enforced change at work, what is the chance of retaining the control once taken for granted in the management discourse (Ehrlich, 1994; Stewart, 1991)?

We have referred above to the discussion on whether psychological contract is a valid concept or a realistic basis for discussing the interactive relationship between the individual and the employing organization (Rousseau, 1998; Guest, 1998). It is not our intention to reopen that debate here. However, we do accept that the elements of the contract as laid out in its transactional and relational factors are worth re-examining to identify the effects of enforced change. It is less important to discover whether the assumptions made by workers can be reciprocated by the organization and therefore whether a contract can be said to exist at all (Guest, 1998). What matters is how individuals who have believed that their employment contract was underwritten in this way will respond to enforced change at work, which appears to threaten previously held expectancies.

In this regard, we have identified subjects who have held such beliefs of life long commitment to a professional position in return for loyalty, trust and promotion and heard how they respond to what they see as its breach. We have observed that such subjects are likely to have served most of their employment with the organization and are now reaching the last fifteen years of economically active life. Their response is predictable: a feeling of anger at betrayal; withdrawal of good will; unwillingness to leave until they have got as much as they can out of the organization and willingness to consider alternative outlets for their energies, official or unofficial. It is a sobering thought that these managers are now its senior executives – responsible for motivating the younger, more dependent employees. How far such subjects will willingly reinforce the managerial discourse is a question that ought to be considered by those who institute enforced change at work.

One thing rarely emphasized in current research is the existence of subjects who do not appear to hold any of the elements of the psychological contract as they are traditionally described or the traditional management discourse of dependence. Mostly younger subjects in this study feel no loyalty and trust and even view with cynical acceptance the fact that senior managers will lie about job security amid enforced change and then leave with significant emoluments, leaving fellow workers to fend for themselves. The focus of their own efforts will be to look after their own career prospects and advise friends: 'don't take it personally'; 'use the organization as it used you'. They may not be confident enough to leave or see any opening for alternative employment elsewhere. However, in the meantime they have learned that the only thing that is important is to become more employable and that means identifying knowledge, skill and experience 'that will make me marketable'.

Finally, there are subjects whose basic assumptions have changed completely from dependence to feeling independent of the organization for their future career prospects. Some have been headhunted; others have survived their own tragedies or seen parents wrestle with self-employment, sometimes with catastrophic results. They can cope, they are self-sufficient, they are not afraid of a repeat of the experience of enforced change at work and they are willing to risk moving out altogether, when they feel ready to do so. Most of all they are confident and seem unlikely to drop back into any belief of need in others – organizations or individuals. Taken together, the independents and reconstructed subjects account for two-thirds of the subjects interviewed in this research. Given that the other third is already discontented but determined to stay on in an alienated state, we would be entitled to ask: who does believe in the promises of HRM or any similar managerial discourse anymore and more importantly, who now controls the workplace, workers or managers (Edwards, 1979)?

Human Resource Management R.I.P.

The theory of Human Resource Management suggests that its aim 'is not merely to seek compliance but to strive for the much more ambitious objective of commitment' (Storey, 1995). This goal is connected with the need to succeed for 'commitment and loyalty of employees determines the firm's ability to maintain competitive advantage' (Purcell, 1989). In the pursuit of this aim, then, HRM is a 'cultural filter which embraces the uncertainties of employee existence, imposes order and meaning on them and provides the employee with a predictable, secure and carefully projected and rewarded understanding of organizational life' (Keenoy and Anthony, 1993, p. 243). Ideally, it is 'an internalized, complex set of practices which provide common sense, self-evident experience and personal identity' (Alvesson and Willmott, 1992).

What individuals believe about their work and its value is part of a set of socially assumed expectations and in absorbing such values both knows and becomes known. The Foucauldian analysis of this process suggests the individual becoming more controllable, the more he or she is known. The on-going interaction of knower and known makes it easier to manipulate and manage the subject and this discursive practice makes knowledge of the individual possible in the reproduction of power relations (Rose, 1990). What is deemed as important here is the control of the 'processes through which meaning is produced' (McNay, 1992).

We have attempted to assess what happens to this process of acquired or imposed meaning during the events surrounding enforced change at work. In doing this we have accepted that when confronted with the most unwanted outcomes in the context of their working career, individuals are faced with the position that 'as soon as one can no longer think things as one formerly thought them, transformation becomes very urgent, very difficult and quite possible' (Townley, 1994, p. 17). In this research we have sought to examine how individuals evaluate what is most important to them. We have accepted that the 'constructs we employ to make sense of organization are moral imperatives' (Hassard and Parker, 1993, p. 18). In getting individuals to reveal these we have examined the process of deconstruction of basic assumptions in which the unthinkable must be thought and the basic assumptions reconstructed or abandoned.

Our subjects have exhibited different assumptions about the organization. Some have demonstrated traditional assumptions about job security, career prospects, loyalty and trust. Others seem never to have held such views but work rather from an independent manipulation of opportunity taken and benefit derived from whatever occurs at work. For others, a new set of assumptions is triggered offering self-sufficiency and independence of previous indebtedness to the organization for career prospects and future employability. For each subject, there can be no return to the easily held promises of the past. The main loser would seem to be the dominant managerial discourse, which looks for organizational commitment and in return offers the benefits of the psychological contract. Enforced change at work would seem to have made that contract untenable as far as most individuals are concerned.

In their description of emancipatory studies, Alvesson and Willmott (1992, p. 454) suggested that 'the challenge for the critical ethnographer is to simultaneously concentrate on local actors' meanings, symbols and values; to place these within a wider political, economic and historic framework; and to prevent such a framework from pressing the material into a particular theory and language (a dominating voice)'. We would suggest that we have attempted to contribute to that challenge in the present research. We would further suggest that we have demonstrated that 'individuals are not mere objects in truth games. They are self-referencing and self-creating subjects and the new concept of truth games is one based upon evolving relationships between truth, power and self – a genealogy of how the self constitutes itself as subject' (McKinlay and Starkey, 1998, p. 243).

The present research accepts that the small number of subjects from three organizations is not sufficient to sustain the belief that radical change has occurred for most individuals in their experience of enforced change at work. However, it was our intention to seek to identify different responses to such change and examine how far traditional assumptions in dominant managerial discourses had been affected. We believe that sufficient links have been identified between these factors in our subjects to justify further research focused on the same links involving a larger number of subjects across more organizations affected by enforced change at work.

Postscript to the Manufactured Employee

We began this chapter with Jacques' offering of the employee as a type of new social contract, a contract that made the managerial discourse of domination and control much easier to reinforce. The assertions of Human Resource Management reinforced the belief that organizational commitment was a goal which managers could strive to achieve and thereby reinforce that discourse (Guest, 1987). More recently, the proponents of Business Process Re-engineering promoted similar claims for the more stringent and deliberate changes imposed by management dictat, guaranteeing performativity and justifying more ruthless means of achieving it (Hamel and Prahalad, 1994; Champy, 1995). It would appear from such rhetoric that the wage slave is firmly governed by constant reinventions of servitude connected to compliance. According to this appraisal, the panopticon is alive and well and can view the individual via the very instrument of work now common to all knowledge workers – the personal computer. They know what you in-put, how fast and when. They know whether you have accessed Internet sites and which they were. They have a record of your e-mails. So, even knowledge workers are in thrall to the dominant managerial discourse.

But just when hope of escape seems unlikely, hopes of emancipation seem to be offered. If we are right to identify taken-for-granted basic assumptions as being the criteria used by individuals to interpret imposed change and attach meaning and value to its outcome, then the signs that the managerial discourse is intact must be questioned. Our evidence suggests that a deconstruction of the basic assumptions held by that discourse is quite likely and that reconstruction may embrace assumptions perhaps unthinkable before the change took place. Further, we can say that there is in all three workforces that we examined clear evidence that younger subjects may not share the discourse at all and that the focus of their own perceptions will not include the customary expectancies reinforced by a controlling discourse. Jacques' himself seems to accept that the previous certitude may be undergoing significant change:

> It may be too early to know what the core issues of postindustrial society will be, but it is probably safe to say that they will not be those central to US society a century ago. Perhaps, if these artefacts of the industrial US can be understood as temporary formations in the river of social life, researchers and practitioners can loosen our obsessive grasp on these temporary constructions to focus instead on the changing currents (Jacques, 1996, p. 191).

We would suggest that changes in individual basic assumption occasioned by enforced change at work offer a means of examining such change through the petits récits referred to by Lyotard (1976). They have implications for the meso-discourse of HRM and for the mega discourse of poststructuralism they offer evidence that the key managerial discourse can no longer be relied upon to make sense of the employment experience (Alvesson and Kärreman, 1998).

The man of character whom Jacques admired and thought had been replaced by the 'hireling for life' or 'wage slave' is sometimes seen as a victim cynically manipulated by the forces of capitalism, which bring about a 'corrosion of character'. Indeed, in his book of the same title Sennett offers a final paragraph, which is at once sad but also dimly hopeful:

I have learned from my family's bitter radical past; if change occurs it happens on the ground, between persons speaking out of inner need, rather than through mass uprisings. What political programs follow from those inner needs, I simply don't know. But I do know a regime, which provides human beings no deep reasons to care about one another cannot long preserve its legitimacy (Sennett, 1998, p. 148).

Just when the prospects for the employed wage slave looked bleak, the prospects of a different discourse begin to emerge. The voices may be disparate and they may be small. But they are not isolated and ironically the strategies of enforced change may well have brought about an alternative discourse which is no where near as amenable to control as managerialism once assumed.

References

Alvesson, M. (1995) *Cultural Perspectives on Organizations*, Cambridge, Cambridge University Press.

Alvesson, M. (2001) 'Knowledge Work and Ambiguity: Image and Identity', in *Human Relations* 54(7) pp. 863–886.

Alvesson, M. and Kärreman, D. (2000) 'Varieties of Discourse: On the Study of Organizations through Discourse Analysis', in *Human Relations* 53(19) pp. 1125–1149.

Alvesson, M. and Willmott, H. (1992) 'On the Idea of Emancipation in Management and Organizational Studies', in *Academy of Management Review*, 17(3).

Barley, S.R. and Kunda, G. (1992) 'Design and Devotion: Surges of Rational and Normative Ideologies of Control in Managerial Discourses', in *Administrative Science Quarterly* 37 pp. 363–399.

Barnes, B. (1988) *The Nature of Power*, Cambridge, Polity.

Berger, P.L. and Luckmann, T. (1967) *The Social Construction of Reality*, London, Penguin.

Blyton, P. and Turnbull, P. (1992) *Reassessing HRM*, London, Sage.

Braverman, H. (1974) *Labour and Monopoly Capitalism*, New York, Monthly Review.

Burawoy, M. (1979) *Manufacturing Consent: Changes in the Labour Process under Capitalism*, Chicago, University of Chicago Press.

Champy, J. (1995) *Re-engineering Management: the Mandate for New Leadership*, London, Harper Collins.

Christie, I. (1994) 'Flexibility – its Discontents: New Perspectives on the Future of Work', in *Policy Studies* (Winter) 15(4) pp. 22–33.

Coopey, J. and Hartley, J. (1991) 'Reconsidering Organizational Commitment', in *Human Resource Management Journal* 1(3) pp. 18–32.

Curry, J.P. *et al.* (1986) 'On the Causal Ordering of Job Satisfaction and Organizational Commitment', in *Academy of Management Journal* 29 pp. 847–858.

Deetz, S. (1998) 'Discursive Formations, Strategies, Subordination and Self-Surveillance' in A. McKinlay and K. Starkey (eds.) *Foucault, Management and Organizational Theory*, London, Sage.

du Gay, P. (1996) *Consumption and Identity at Work*, London, Sage.

Edwards, R.C. (1979) *Contested Terrain: The Transformation of the Workplace in the Twentieth Century*, London, Heinemann.

Ezzamel, M. Willmott, H. and Worthington, F. (2001) 'Power, Control and Resistance in "The Factory that Time Forgot"' in *Journal of Management Studies* 38 (8) 1053–1079.

Foucault, M. (1977) *Discipline and Punish: The Birth of the Prison*, Harmondsworth, Penguin.

Foucault, M. (1980) *Power/Knowledge: Selected Interviews and Other Writings 1972–1977* (ed.) C. Gordon: Brighton, Harvester Press.

Foucault, M. (1984) *The History of Sexuality: An Introduction* Harmondsworth , Penguin.

Fox, S. (1989) 'The Panopticon: From Bentham's Obsession to the Revolution in Management Learning', in *Human Relations* 42 pp. 717–739.

Friedman, A. (1977) *Industry and Labour: Class Struggle at Work and Monopoly Capitalism* London, Macmillan.

Giddens, A. (1991) *The Consequences of Modernity*, Cambridge, Polity Press.

Goffman, E. (1959) *The Presentation of Self in Everyday Life*, New York, Doubleday.

Guest, D.E. (1987) 'Personnel and HRM', in *Personnel Management* (January).

Guest, D.E. (1998a) 'Is the Psychological Contract Worth Taking Seriously?', in *Journal of Organizational Behaviour* 19 pp. 649–664.

Guest, D.E. (1998b) 'On Meaning, Metaphor and the Psychological Contract: a Response to Rousseau', in *Journal of Organizational Behaviour*, 19 pp. 673–677.

Hamel, G. and Prahalad, C.K. (1994) *Competing for the Future*, Cambridge, Harvard University Business Press.

Handy, C. (1989) *The Age of Unreason*, London, Hutchinson.

Hassard, J. and Pym, D. (1990) *The Theory and Philosophy of Organizations*, London, Sage.

Hatchuel, A. (1999) 'Foucault, Management and Organizational Theory', in *Human Relations* 52 (April).

Henriques, J. *et al.* (1984) *Changing the Subject: Psychology, Social Regulation and Subjectivity*, London, Methuen.

Heracleous, L. and Hendry, J. (2000) 'Discourse and the Study of Organization: Towards a Structural Perspective' in *Human Relations* 53(10) pp. 1251–1286.

Hunt, J.W. and Downing, S. (1990) 'Mergers, Acquisitions and HRM', in *International Journal of Human resource Management* (September) 1(2) pp. 195–209.

Isabella, L.A. (1990) 'Evolving Interpretations as a Change Unfolds: How Managers Construe Key Organizational Events', in *Academy of Management Journal* 33(1) pp. 7–14.

Jackson, N. and Carter, P. (1998) 'Labour as Dressage', in A. McKinlay and K. Starkey (eds.) *Foucault, Management and Organizational Theory*, London, Sage.

Jacques, R (1996) *Manufacturing the Employee: Management Knowledge from the 19th to the 21st Centuries*, London, Sage.

Jermier, J. Knights, D. and Nord, W. (1994) *Resistance and Power in Organizations*, London, Routledge.

Kamoche, K. (1998) 'Human Resource Management and the Appropriation Learning Perspective', in *Human Relations* 51.

Keenoy, T. and Anthony, P. (1992) 'HRM: Metaphor, Meaning and Morality', in P. Blyton and P. Turnbull, *Reassessing HRM*, London, Sage.

Knights, D. and McCabe, D. (1999) 'Are There No Limits to Authority? TQM and Organizational Power', in *Organization Studies* 20 (2) pp. 197–224.

Louis, M.R. (1980a) 'Surprise and Sense Making: What Newcomers Experience in Entering Unfamiliar Organizational Settings', in *Administrative Science Quarterly* 25 pp. 226–251.

Louis, M.R. (1980b) 'Career Transitions: Varieties and Commonalities', in *Academy of Management Review* 5 pp. 329 – 340.

Lukes, S. (1986) *Power*, Oxford, Blackwell.

Lyotard, J.F. (1976) *The Postmodern Condition: A Report on Knowledge*, Minneapolis, University of Minnesota Press.

Marcotte, D.E. (1995) 'Declining Job Stability, What We Know and What it Means', in *Journal of Policy Analysis and Management* 14 (4) pp. 590-598.

McCarthy, W. and Newcomb, M. (1992) 'Two Dimensions of Perceived Self-efficacy: Cognitive Control and Behavioural Coping Ability', in R. Schwartzer (ed.) *Self-efficacy: Thought control of action, London*, Hemisphere.

McKinlay, A. (2000) 'The Bearable Lightness of Control: Organizational Reflexivity and the Politics of Knowledge Management', in C. Prichard, R. Hull, M. Chumer and H. Willmott (eds.) *Managing Knowledge: Critical Investigations of Work and Learning.* London, Macmillan.

McKinlay, A. and Starkey, K. (1998) *Foucault, Management and Organizational Theory*, London, Sage.

McNay, L. (1992) *Foucault and Feminism: Power, Gender and the Self*, Cambridge, Polity Press.

Morris, J. and Blyton, P. (1991) *A Flexible Future? Prospects for Employment and Organization*, Berlin, W de Gruyter.

Neef, D. (1997a) *The Knowledge Economy, Resources for the Knowledge-Based Economy*, Boston, Butterworth Heinemann.

Nicholson, N. and West, M. (1988) *Managerial Job Change: Men and Women in Transition*, Cambridge, Cambridge University Press.

Nicolini, D. and Meznar, M.B. (1995) 'The Social Construction of Organizational Learning: Conceptual and Practical Issues in the Field', in *Human Relations* 48 (7) pp. 727-746.

Ogbonna, E. (1992) 'Organizational Culture and HRM: Dilemmas and Contradictions' in P. Blyton and P. Turnbull (eds.) *Reassessing HRM,* London, Sage.

O'Neill, J. (1987) 'The Disciplining Society: from Weber to Foucault', in *British Journal of Sociology* xxxvii (1) pp. 42-60.

Oswick, C. Keenoy, T. and Grant, D. (2000) 'Discourse, Organizations and Organizing: Concepts, Objects and Subjects', in *Human Relations* 53 (9) pp. 1115-1124.

Peters, T.J. and Waterman, R.H. (1982) *In Search of Excellence*, New York, Harper and Row.

Purcell, J. (1987) 'Mapping Management Styles in Employee Relations', in *Journal of Management Studies* 24 pp. 533-548.

Purcell, J. (1989) 'The Impact of Corporate Strategy on HRM', in J. Storey (ed.) *New Perspectives on HRM,* London, Routledge.

Randall, J.A. (2001) 'Enforced Change at Work, Reconstruction of Basic Assumptions and its Influence on Attribution, Self-sufficiency and the Psychological Contract', Unpublished PhD, University of St Andrews.

Reed, M. (1998) 'Organizational Analysis as Discourse Analysis: a Critique', in D. Grant, T. Keenoy and C. Oswick (eds.) *Discourse and Organization,* London, Sage.

Rose, N. (1990) *Governing the Soul: the Shaping of the Private Self*, London, Routledge.

Rousseau, D.M. (1998) 'The Problem of the Psychological Contract Considered', in *Journal of Organizational Behaviour* 19 pp. 665-671.

Sennett, R. (1998) *The Corrosion of Character*, New York and London, W.W. Norton.

Shore, L.M. and Martin, H.J. (1989) 'Job Satisfaction and Commitment in Relation to Work Performance and Turnover Intentions', in *Human Relations* 42 pp. 625-638.

Silverman, D. (ed.) (1997) *Qualitative Research: Theory, Method and Practice*, London, Sage.

Stewart, R. (1991) *Managing Today and Tomorrow*, London, Macmillan.

Storey, J. (1989) *New Perspectives in HRM*, London, Routledge.

Storey, J. (1995) *Human Resource Management: A Critical Text*, London, Routledge.

Taylor, F.W. (1911) *The Principles of Scientific Management*, New York, Harper.

Touraine, A. (1997) *What is Democracy?* Oxford, Westview Press.

Townley, B. (1994) *Reframing HRM*, London, Sage.

Weick, K.E. (1979) *The Social Psychology of Organizing*, Reading, MA: Addison-Wesley.

Chapter 11

Contesting Critical Strategies for the New Millennium: A Conversation with Roy Jacques

Campbell Jones, Shayne Grice and Roy Jacques

Introduction

In *Manufacturing the Employee: Management Knowledge from the 19th to 21st Centuries* (1996), Roy Jacques outlines what he describes as a discursive history of the emergence of the category of the employee. Drawing on poststructural theory and particularly on the work of Michel Foucault, Jacques provides an innovative account of the meaning of the employee, and outlines the potential redundancy of certain conceptions of management and organization as we move into a postindustrial or knowledge-based economy. Here, in an effort to extend and refine a number of themes emerging from his work, Jacques engages directly in dialogue with Campbell Jones and Shayne Grice. His two interlocutors press him to clarify his position and to defend it from charges from a number of angles. Spurred on by Jacques' suggestion about the prohibitions of mainstream management theory which forbid certain questions, Jones and Grice here make an effort to test the limits and prohibitions of Jacques' work. In the resulting conversation, the three discuss and debate a wide range of issues beginning with Jacques personal background, the emergence of his intellectual interests and his conception of knowledge, management and postindustrialism. The discussion opens on to questions relating to the potential contribution of poststructuralist histories in relation to alternative critical accounts of management, and pose central challenges to issues relating to strategies of critical engagement and the choices made in those engagements.

Campbell Jones:

In your book *Manufacturing the Employee* you propose to write a 'history of the employee'.[1] To some people this might sound like a peculiar project. Could you explain what you were trying to achieve, and the influences that would lead you to ask this kind of question and to pose it in the way that you did?

Roy Jacques:

Academically, the prime influence in my formulating the problem this way would be the major earlier works of Foucault, where he takes a concept and shows how its meaning has changed so much over time that it is hard to say that the concept has any essential meaning.[2] I call my book a history of the employee because, in the American case, 'the employee' appeared as an exotic foreign term – *l'employé* – at a significant time, when relationships of power structuring work were undergoing systemic change. The normalization of this term during roughly the years 1870 to 1920 was coincident with the sedimentation of a historically and culturally specific set of relationships, associated with a specific set of assumptions about the abilities, values and perceptions of the person at work. This is important to me as a management scholar because it is this object of analysis, 'the employee', that is posited as the problem that needs to be solved. Within management literature, the social production of this object has been lost over time, and 'the employee' has come to mean 'any person at work'. This inappropriately universalizes historically specific assumptions about work and the worker. To question this naturalization, I attempted to bring to light the relations of power sustaining this dominant representation and to make them available as objects of inquiry.

A more experiential answer to your question is that I got into academia largely as a result of questions I began to have as a practising manager. It seemed to me that certain people in organizations were getting a lot of reward relative to their contribution and certain others were making a lot of contribution relative to their reward. As *naïve* as it may sound, I was surprised by this. Like many, I had grown up socialized to have a meritocratic view of what to expect in large organizations. In my managerial experience I also came to believe that the nominal purpose of the organization – the provision of goods and/or services – could be done far more effectively if these issues were addressed. For me, then, concerns with social justice and organizational effectiveness were intertwined with each other.

Shayne Grice:

But for many management theorists, issues of organizational effectiveness and justice are issues that demand a focus on the present rather than the past. The fact that you turn to history for an understanding of the present positions you quite differently from most management theorists. Could you briefly explain how you position yourself in relation to history, and what you see us learning from history?

Roy Jacques:

Well, I think that history and a constructionist perspective, of whatever kind, more or less go hand in hand. Social life in general, and business in particular, is a constructed reality, meaningful only within a social context. To take a solid-looking aspect of business, the machine, it is important to understand it not as a physical truth, but as a social one. Yes, it's demonstrably made of certain materials, the materials have certain properties and it has certain objective capacities in terms of speed and so on. But the significance of these objective facts is derived from a *social* medium.

How does something fall into the category of presumed-true or presumed-false? That is an interesting and critically useful social question. It is here that we have a very important link with history. History is our best resource for understanding how we come to presume that certain things make sense and certain things don't. By helping us to understand the production of the social world in which we become subjects, history helps us to better understand to what extent we want to accept the assumptions we grew up with and to what extent we want to question them.

In the case of *Manufacturing the Employee*, I take the idea of the 'employee'. It's not even treated *as* an idea in most management writing. The employee is treated as a self-evident concept, and we go on to prescribe about that entity. It's ironic that I never set out to do historical work. I did an historical study in order to understand contemporary organizational phenomena. This study is 'deconstructive' in a general sense, in that it is not aimed at better understanding the workplace itself, but at better understanding how the workplace has come to be represented in certain ways.[3] I did this because I believe these representations currently constitute a barrier to understanding. Understanding these deeply entrenched assumptions about the person at work required gaining a better sense of where these assumptions came from. For me to understand the governing logic of the workplace today, it was less useful to look at what's going on in today's workplace because today's workplace is not the *source* of that logic, it is only the site of its reproduction.

Shayne Grice:

I would like to press you more on the issue of your 'constructionist perspective' in general and your turn to poststructuralism in particular. You are arguably one of the most coherent 'users' of poststructural theory within the management academy. Could you explain what is it about poststructural theory that you find helpful for understanding management?

Roy Jacques:

In my work, to the extent that I'm talking about poststructuralism, I'm talking about the influence of Michel Foucault. My encounter with his work was stimulated by studying with Linda Smircich and Marta Calás. Foucault's work catalysed many things that had been growing in an inchoate form for some time in my way of seeing the world. It also suggested – forgive me if I say it – a methodology. Foucault provided a workable set of techniques for conducting and analysing field observation. His work also suggested ways of understanding organizations which were useful to my thinking as a manager.

Hypothetically, I could have got some of these insights from other sources. Had I done a serious reading of volume one of *Capital* when I was still a manager it might have helped me to see how much of the dissonance I experienced came from failing to realize the degree to which systems of organizing are systems of power. But as it happened, I studied Foucault before I studied Marx. The greatest contribution Foucault's work made to my perspective was that, over time, I went from looking at organizations as instrumental systems to looking at them as social systems of power relations. This way of seeing helped me to formulate the problems that had bothered me as a manager in ways that were immensely useful. I could better see the origins of these problems and the forces sustaining them. I could also better see where one might work to influence those forces.

Business school people make much noise about creating 'practical theory' and 'useful knowledge'. As a former manager, I have to say that the most practical things I found in business school were poststructuralist and feminist theory—not from the perspective of social criticism, but from the perspective of managing and organizing. This is why I said in my book that there is nothing so practical as a good poststructuralist feminist theory.[4] Suppose I returned to my old software development job, spending my days trying to figure out how to get a piece of software out the door before a deadline. Of the things I have studied in twelve years since leaving that environment, what would help me function more effectively? Almost everything that would be of use to me has come from one or another strand of critical theorizing, especially poststructuralism and feminism. Correspondingly, I have learned very little that is of use from the canon of organization studies. In fact, one of the main reasons I enrolled for a PhD in organization studies was to learn why my two years of MBA study had given me almost nothing of use in the workplace. The mainstream is obsessively attached to measurable knowledge that can be stated in testable hypotheses. This doesn't seem to have been very useful, since half a century of efforts have produced very disappointing results. That's unfortunate, because I have found powerful, useful concepts, but in areas marked FORBIDDEN.

Shayne Grice:

Yes, recognizing that certain areas are perpetually out-of-bounds is an important observation. And it seems especially pertinent in reflecting upon how the postindustrial, and more recently, the Knowledge Society, has been represented within management studies. Much of this work seems to be written under the influence of what Stuart Hall calls the 'tyranny of the new'.[5] In this 'state of emergency', there is a demand to forget or ignore what we have known and focus instead on that which is 'new' and 'fantastic'. Peter Drucker's *Post Capitalist Society* offers one of the most vivid, and influential expressions of this tyranny in action. For Drucker, the Knowledge Society is saturated with good news and represents a radical break from the past. Whatever insights one may have gleaned from Marx's reading of capitalism, and its relations of exploitation, we are told that they have little relevance in the brave new world. The tyranny of the new calls for us to rejoice in the 'good news' today and to have faith in the coming of the good news in the future. It is a story of salvation in which the logic of development reigns supreme. While Balibar notes that what we are seeing is the simultaneous deployment of all the historical forms of exploitation rather than their elimination Drucker assures his audience that we shall soon see 'poor, backward, Third-World countries transform themselves, virtually overnight, into fast-growth economic powers'.[6] How comforting! This propensity for management writing to ignore its complicity with relations of exploitation is a problem that clearly has not disappeared in accounts of the Knowledge Society. How do you deal with this problem in your work?

Roy Jacques:

A lot of what I'm interested in is much less applicable to situations where the worker still looks like the exploited proletarian of *Capital*. I have not personally been as bothered by work experiences I found openly oppressive or alienating as by white collar situations that I worked in such as sales, customer service, computer programming or management. There, you still get the boot in the face, but you are asked to smile afterward and say thank-you for being offered the opportunity to self-actualize. As a result, the kind of workers I've focused on have been in what we might call 'knowledge-intensive' situations. This may also partially explain why Labour Process Theory is not prominent in my work. I haven't looked very much at people on the shopfloor, which is largely the focus of Labour Process Theory. In the situations I have chosen to study, I have found that whether I read *Capital* or an introductory Organization Behaviour textbook, I have some very fundamental problems with the assumptions that I find reflected there. Of course, I would not argue that the proletarianization of labour, especially in industrializing contexts, is less important than the management of discretionary, knowledge-intensive work. It is simply a different problematic than the one I have chosen to study.

Campbell Jones:

In your book you talk about the way in which you depart from both managerialist and critical approaches, and argue that *both* managerialist and critical ways of narrating history are problematic. You offer a 'third way' which you call a 'poststructuralist' or 'discursive' history.[7] When I hear talk of a 'third way', I can't help recalling Peter Drucker's outrageous claim that Taylorism represented a 'third way' between capitalism and socialism.[8] This raises a number of problems. In my reading there is in fact a marked continuity between poststructural theory as it is practised by Foucault, and critical theory, as it is practised by Marx, but more specifically by writers such as Benjamin or Adorno. By contrast, the same continuity doesn't exist between Foucault and managerialist theory. Foucault is a critic. So if we say that we could reject both managerialist and critical histories and accept this poststructuralist or discursive position then we might be carving up the terrain in a way which is a little dishonest to start with.

The second problem relates to your representation of the managerialist and critical traditions. In your book you represent and discuss managerial writers – Rosabeth Moss Kanter, Drucker, and so on – but you do not seem to have given equal weight, one might say, to certain aspects of the critical tradition. In relation to the critical tradition, I am thinking in particular of work on the labour process. In *Manufacturing the Employee* we find only passing reference to Braverman in a footnote, with major contributions following Braverman such as the work of Michael Burawoy, Andrew Friedman, Richard Edwards not even being mentioned. Also missing are the later contributions to the debate, including consolidations around the work of Paul Thompson or the annual review books which are put together by, among others, Knights and Willmott.[9] It seems strange that this work is somehow erased in your book, particularly when a considerable amount of Labour Process Theory tries to provide histories of management, management strategies, management processes. It seems strange that it would be erased – not even mentioned in so far as it could be mentioned, criticized and dismissed – when the managerialist literature is given such a full treatment. It seems to me that those critical works would have been quite useful in filling in certain absences in your 'third way'.

Roy Jacques:

This raises a really important point about how I would like this book to be read and discussed. If this should turn into a case of whether Jacques, 1996, got it right or wrong *in toto,* I would find that terribly depressing. There is nothing useful that can come from a discussion like that. I hope there are points where people will be reading and say 'oh this is an insightful comment'. But there are also huge areas of ignorance that I represent, and it would not be useful to try to mask them. I wrote from a context and I wrote within certain boundaries of knowledge and ignorance. Both of those are extremely important in assessing what one can do with this work.

Now your initial question, if I recall, had to do with my characterization of managerialist and critical histories. Within the boundaries of mainstream North American management discourse – against which I was writing – 'history' generally means either a *naïve* social Darwinism of 'organizations just evolved' or a critical position defined by relatively few people, with little in-depth knowledge of the currents of thought to which you're referring. So I am not attempting to characterize all historical perspectives, but to speak about two concrete discursive constructions situated in North American – and, to some extent, British – management theory in the mid-1990s. To the extent that we're talking about other sites, it would be appropriate to bracket my work as only partially applicable or maybe even applicable only by analogy. I would defend the book as making meaningful statements about the communities of management knowledge it was written to analyse. At the same time, you justifiably point to many currents in critical thinking and to subtleties and complexities of relationships that I would not want to see ignored.

You aren't going to find *Manufacturing the Employee* addressing everything. What we're discussing has become much clearer for me as I've worked outside of the North American canon, here in New Zealand, subsequent to the books publication. You two, for instance, define organization studies far differently than it is defined discursively within the Academy of Management. As far as I'm concerned, it would not just be a legitimate project, but would show respect for my work and further it, for others to identify what I overlooked or misrepresented.

Campbell Jones:

It seems that you don't engage with the kind of methodological or substantive issues that are raised by what used to be called 'historical materialism'. If an historical materialist were to read your work, they would probably point out at least two major omissions. The first is a tendency towards *idealism* in your work, that is, you talk about discourse and language as if they construct material reality, and any emphasis on material reality effecting possibilities of language, discourse and ideas is written out of the picture. The second problem is the absence of *conflict* in your book. A historical materialist will argue that one of the central motifs of history is conflict, some kind of relation of struggle. The classic statement of this, of course, is to suggest that the history of all societies has hitherto been one of conflict, an uninterrupted, sometimes open, sometimes hidden fight.[10] In your work, class conflict seems to be so enormously hidden that no-one can see it. Where is the struggle in your book? Where is the conflict? Where are the bodies being decimated? Where is the violence that is inflicted on the subjects of work today, during this century and in the last century?

Roy Jacques:

First of all, to be a bit *cliché*, Marx is a spectre haunting my book. I came to doctoral study generally unread in social critique, although I've worked hard to fill this gap. During the last year while doing a careful re-reading of volume one of *Capital*, I have been embarrassed to note at least a few points which were influential in my thinking long ago, but which had completely lost the connection to Marx by the time I sat down to write. In addition, I believe that you've made an analogous argument in your work about Foucault relative to Marx. I think that whatever failings you would attribute to Foucault in this regard, you can assume are reproduced by me. Also, in addition to whatever limitations he had, I've added some of my own.

Nevertheless I'm more and more convinced of the need for producing a discursive formation about work in which the central metaphor for work is the production, application, capitalization and sale of knowledge. I think that understanding 'knowledge work' is a far more general and far more difficult problem than we usually treat it to be. That is what led me to quote Naisbitt on the need for a 'knowledge theory of value'.[11] I don't find Naisbitt at all interesting other than that one phrase. Today, whether we proceed from neo-classical economics or from Marxian theory, we inherit a common-sense which assumes that relations of production are about capital and labour. Today, although relations of capitalist exchange are becoming more and more robust, many of the relationships mediating between technology, the body and power in the workplace are in a state of flux extreme enough to be treated as some form of disjuncture. If we want to influence the critical power/knowledge relationships structuring what will be done, for what purpose it will be done and who will benefit from it in the workplace, we find these relationships revolving on an axis of knowledge, not of labour...

Campbell Jones:

So it's not labour that makes value, is that what you're trying to say?

Roy Jacques:

Yes. I don't think that Marx adequately distinguished between labour as a motive force analogous to, say, electrical energy, and labour as the knowledge of how to use that force. When I say it was inadequate, I don't think it was inadequate for his purposes. I think that because of changes since his time, it has become more important to analytically distinguish these two aspects of labour power. The idea that an hour of generic labour has an inherent value is no longer adequate to our needs in understanding the production or distribution of value.

Shayne Grice:

The way that you are talking, it sounds like you are about to reproduce the myth that a company like 3M succeeds simply because of the 'innovativeness' of a small cadre of brilliant people sitting around making up ideas. Such a reading seems to be curious, given the way that poststructural theory has demonstrated the importance of examining the construction of relations between centre and outside. In the case of 3M, the fact is that there are a whole bunch of people who slave away on machines in factories making, packaging and delivering post-it notes. This is the harsh reality of how 'knowledge work' ends up getting done to most people! The relationships between these two groups – knowledge workers and 'the rest' – are neither random nor natural. They are part of what used to be called 'the division of labour'. To focus on one group at the exclusion of the other erases these linkages at exactly the moment that these relationships are radically deepening. When we ignore the realities of the division of labour and focus on 'knowledge workers', don't we commit the idealist erasure of the material reality of those who are actually making the post-it notes?

Roy Jacques:

I am not trying to valorize a knowledge-bearing caste. It is simply that I feel the need to understand the relations of power that govern the circulation of knowledge. I am attempting to understand *knowledge* as the medium of work. The problem is that a system for analysing the relations of knowledge capitalization does not yet exist, and it is not merely analogous to the capitalization of labour. I think that you are right that I am close to falling into the dangers that you are warning me about, and I know that at other times you have found this problem with *Manufacturing the Employee*.

I think where we disagree is that I believe we need to walk this dangerous path in order to build effective arguments in a knowledge-based mode of production to defend the very workers whose interests you are identifying. I think the underlying problem was clearly seen by Marx and many other social theorists early in the history of mechanization. It is the reduction of any human being to the role of chattel. This is a social inequity, full stop. Marx did a superb job of pointing out the marginalization of those who possess labour relative to those who possess capital. What we have accelerating today is a double marginalization where labour power is also marginalized in relation to those who get to use the knowledge component of their labour power more than others.

Shayne Grice:

Could we consider the way that you are constructing 'labour' here? It strikes me that your slippage between human being, labour and labour power is highly problematic. In particular, your suggestion that knowledge workers somehow represent a third way (again) between labour and capital actually perpetuates the most rudimentary of binaries between mind and body, civilized and savage, man and beast. This is perhaps of no great surprise. These binaries have a long history in management thought, as you are well aware. And they are certainly present in the work of Drucker and Naisbitt that informs much of your theory of the Knowledge Society.[12]

Roy Jacques:

To what you have said, you could add a Taylorist head/hand dualism to that of mind/body. It is precisely my intention to *question* these dichotomizations. If either the mind or the body have a meaningful organizational existence, it is in their relationship to each other as manifest in social practices. I am not advocating that we create social castes on this basis. I am observing that it is the deployment and capitalization of knowledge that determines value, and that this is difficult to understand with reference to a theory of labour power.

Campbell Jones:

But surely, you can't be taking this to be a failing of Marx, or to count as a meaningful criticism against Marx? Right from the beginning of *Capital* Marx tries to explain the historical emergence of 'abstract homogeneous labour', and the distinction between the groups controlling labour and those being controlled?

Roy Jacques:

Perhaps the greatest barrier to discussing Marx today is that one has to first identify oneself as being a Marxist or not. Among Marxists, Marx's system must remain central, however much it is revised and elaborated. Among non-Marxists, his thought is seldom taken seriously. I find myself in the middle ground where I think the guy has great value, but I can't take that value systematically enough to claim a Marxist position.

Campbell Jones:

Here, as in your book, I think that you have homogenized and simplified both Marx and the Marxist tradition. In your book, all the Marxists who would count today as being worthy of serious consideration are entirely ignored or erased. Where is Étienne Balibar? Where is Althusser? Where is Terry Eagleton? Where is Spivak? Where is Stuart Hall? Where is Ernesto Laclau?[13] If we want to criticize Marxism today, these are the people that we need to take seriously. When you dismiss Marxism in your book without having engaged with people such as these, don't you commit a category error of the worst sort?

Roy Jacques:

This has come up in our earlier discussions and to a certain extent I agree with you. This has been partly a question of boundary choices and partly a deficiency on my part. What we keep coming back to is that what you define as your primary interests diverge from what I find as my primary interests. The global division of labour is *relevant* to the issues I have studied, but not *central* to them. They could be made central by others in their studies.

Campbell Jones:

You seem to be saying: 'you do this critical work, I'll do this work, and never the twain shall meet'. In this situation, your form of 'incommensurability' argument seems to implicitly *support* the current global division of labour, which is being increasingly ordered around a privileged elite First World doing knowledge work and an underprivileged Third World doing largely proletarianized work. Surely we should be interrogating these relationships?

Roy Jacques:

I think it's an inevitable, practical problem, not one of incommensurability. We...

Campbell Jones:

It isn't inevitable that some would study elite work and only study it in abstraction from the relations of power and domination in which they are fundamentally implicated. That's not a fundamental condition of knowledge!

Roy Jacques:

No, but that's a caricature of my point. If we are going to produce useful knowledge we can't always be holding the whole universe in our hands.

Campbell Jones:

I'm not asking you to hold the whole universe in your hands. What I'm pointing out is a fundamental omission in your construction of knowledge work.

Roy Jacques:

OK, and I'm trying to acknowledge the legitimacy of your argument while defending my choice to have drawn different boundaries than those you would choose. I think if I were to characterize myself – you know I am sometimes represented as a radical Organization theorist, as a postmodernist...

Campbell Jones:

In this room as a conservative and an objectivist and a rationalist and all kinds of other things as well!

Roy Jacques:

[Laughs]

Shayne Grice:

Perhaps we should explore this problem in terms of the way that Burrell and Morgan's reading of the notion of paradigms has worked in organization studies.[14] While it was initially received as a somewhat radical intervention, it seems that today Burrell and Morgan's framework operates in quite the opposite way. Instead of offering positions from which to launch critique, it seems that today it mainly works to reinforce a particularly noxious version of relativism. It says: 'everyone in this pluralist, crazy, postmodern world has a position and no one position is better than any other. Some people choose to look at labour relations – they're in that box, they're 'radical structuralists'. Their work is legitimate, but I'm over here in a different paradigm'. This culminates in the postmodern ethos in which 'anything goes'. In effect this reinforces Kuhn's incommensurability thesis, but in a form of cynical relativism. The casualty of this move is to relegate questions of paradigm to ones of individual choice, thereby undermining the problem of the relation between paradigmatic formations and power.

Campbell Jones:

Indeed. In organization studies there is a kind of myth that until the 1970s organization studies was the victim of some kind of 'theoretical closure' but that now we are liberated by a new 'theoretical pluralism'. This story is continually repeated – it is rehearsed by Michael Reed and others, and bemoaned by people like Jeffrey Pfeffer.[15] The problem is that in earlier times there were a number of people who are outside that community who are ostensibly looking at the 'same problem', but were looking at it in very different ways. If we look at the kinds of things that were being done by Marxists or feminists at almost any point in time, there exists an enormous critical literature.

Roy Jacques:

OK, fine. But since the 1970s we have seen considerable importation of much of that theory, which is surely of some significance. But still in your comment comes the importance of recognizing that I'm being very North American and you're being very Antipodean. For me as a North American who has been living in New Zealand for a few years, I guess when it comes to organization studies I still think more as a North American and that's largely bounded by the Academy of Management. Perhaps in England if you were to look at who was being legitimated in the 1970s you have things like the Aston studies, a little earlier you have the Tavistock stuff that was grounded in a pretty positivist view of the world. You do get some contestation within those limited areas, but I think it's important, and admittedly, not all of organization studies was hypothesis-testing.

Campbell Jones:

Yes, but my argument is that in the sixties – which is when the Aston project was in its kind of heyday – there *were* other voices saying different things. In the sixties a certain form of feminism was making massive progress throughout the West in terms of rights for female workers and recognition of the legitimacy of alternate claims about the nature of gender and subjectivity. Such social movements are neither marginal nor minor. They are not something *outside* the 'dominant discourses', but they are significant statements that are made about organizations. When we include these statements – when we redefine the territory in terms of 'the set of things said about work organizations in the sixties' – then the suggestion that there was theoretical closure is shown to be somewhat hasty. The ideological function of this story about the move from closure to pluralism is to show how organization studies is more open and free today. We can then all live happily every after...

I don't want to introduce another theoretical reference, but I can't help thinking about Derrida's comments on the way that the 'framing' of paintings operates.[16] He suggests that the act of putting a border around a painting is not external to the art object, but is essential to the construction and capturing of that aesthetic space, the physical and conceptual space that *is* the painting. Derrida poses the question of the border and framing, and asks how those borders operate in ways that are unmistakably political. They are not political in the sense of people fighting in the streets, but political in the sense of the politics of knowledge formation, which is, of course, no less political.

Roy Jacques:

I think we can agree on that. One of the most important things that we could be doing with the status of knowledge development in organization studies is recognizing the importance of framing as a productive aspect of every argument. For instance, to most constituencies outside of nursing I continually need to defend my argument that nursing is professional work. The signifier 'profession' is the one that comes closest to appropriately recognizing the complexity, skill demands, training needs and discretion required in the work. However, within nursing, I want to emphasize how the signifier 'profession' colonizes nursing with reference to industrial and patriarchal norms developed by science, management and medicine. It is not that nurses really *are*, or *are not*, professional. Whether they are depends on the framing and the appropriateness of any frame depends on the context.

Shayne Grice:

Could I use this to draw us back to the question of the Knowledge Society. I still have some serious problems with your proposal that we need a 'Knowledge Theory of Value' which will replace all earlier critical vocabularies. In the context of the relativity of paradigms, your exclusive focus on knowledge could easily operate as an alibi for ignoring the systematic relationships between the so-called Knowledge Society and the increasing division between knowledge work and manual labour, its global divisions and the inequalities that these divisions produce. The acceleration of relationships of marginalization is exactly one of the defining characteristics of the postindustrial world, but I don't see enough of a critical edge in what you are proposing.

Roy Jacques:

I'm still struggling to better articulate this problem of the changing relations in the postindustrial world, and the critical vocabularies we need to understand it. But remember, the central discursive icons on which the discourse of industrial organization has been built do not, by a long shot, cover everything that happens in the workplace. They refer to the things which have been defined – by those with the power to do the defining – as central problems. More and more, as I am immersed in trying to understand what we might call 'knowledge intensive' work, I am increasingly convinced that another language will have to be constructed, just as the present language was once constructed. But we need a language in which the key signifiers are congruent with the key relationships through which power, voice, marginalization are being determined.

Campbell Jones:

I suppose that if we're going to create this language, then I would be all for jettisoning many of the terms that prevail within the management community. In their place we could centralize terms like 'global environmental devastation', 'massive global inequalities in the division of labour', 'continuation and extension of Western exploitation of the remainder of the world'. Those kind of categories would need to be foremost in that language.

Roy Jacques:

Well this returns us to the question of strategies and audiences. We don't need *one* language. Rather, we can perhaps think of a variety of ways to plug in to and hopefully influence the emerging dominant language. If we're talking within Western business schools, there are different discursive boundaries to negotiate with. To compromise with the tyranny of common sense is the price of engagement, but it also does violence to one's beliefs. I'm regularly subjecting my beliefs to this kind of violence. It's fair for others to criticize my choices as long as I presume to proselytize – this is something for which we should all be accountable. But I hope that today I've clarified some of my reasons for making them.

For a number of years I have been trying to resist what Donna Haraway refers to as 'the God trick'.[17] If I ask the godlike question 'can I change the world?' it sets me up for certain failure. Even those who we identify as world leaders are produced by world events more than they are producers of them. What I *can* change – and see its effects – is my direct relationships. So, what is happening between us right now? What is happening between me and my circle of friends? What is happening between me and the people with whom I interact in the Academy? If I ask myself 'can I change the direction of management knowledge?', 'can I change the norms of the workplace?', these questions are too big. If I can stay focused on what I can do in the context of my relationships – and I admit that it's a very, very difficult thing to do – then there is hope.

For these reasons, I have made a choice to try to speak within the North American business school. Now, I realize that these groupings and boundaries are irrelevant to both of you in your work. This is a difference of strategies for engagement, not necessarily a difference in how we see the world. It may be that you are more optimistic about possibilities for change than I am. I sincerely hope that time shows you to be right, and to show that I have chosen too conservative a strategy!

Notes

1 Roy Jacques (1996) *Manufacturing the Employee: Management Knowledge from the 19th to 21st Centuries* (London, Sage).
2 Michel Foucault (1961/1988) *Madness and Civilization: A History of Insanity in the Age of Reason* (New York, Vintage Books); (1963/1994) *The Birth of the Clinic: An Archaeology of Medical Perception* (New York, Vintage Books) and (1966/1989) *The Order of Things: An Archaeology of the Human Sciences* (London, Routledge).
3 See also Sarah Jacobson and Roy Jacques (1997) 'Destabilizing the Field: Poststructuralist Knowledge-Making Strategies in a Postindustrial Era' in *Journal of Management Inquiry*, 6(1) pp. 42-59.
4 Roy Jacques (1996) *Manufacturing the Employee: Management Knowledge from the 19th to 21st Centuries* (London, Sage), p. xii. cf. Kurt Lewin (1952), 'Problems of Method in Social Psychology' in Dorwin Cartright (ed.) *Field Theory in Social Science* (London, Harper & Row).
5 Stuart Hall (1996), *Critical Dialogues in Cultural Studies* ed. David Morley and Kuan-Hsing Chen (London, Routledge), p. 133.
6 Étienne Balibar (1991) 'Class struggle to classless struggle?' in Étienne Balibar and Immanuel Wallerstein *Race, Nation, Class: Ambiguous Identities* (London, Verso), p. 177. cf. Peter Drucker (1993) *Post-Capitalist Society* (New York, Harper-Collins), p. 12.
7 Roy Jacques (1996) *Manufacturing the Employee*, pp. 14-16.
8 Peter Drucker (1968) *The Age of Discontinuity* (London, Pan), p. 331.
9 Harry Braverman (1974) *Labour and Monopoly Capital: The Degradation of Work in the Twentieth Century* (New York, Monthly Review Press); Michael Burawoy (1979) *Manufacturing Consent: Changes in the Labour Process under Monopoly Capitalism* (Chicago, University of Chicago Press); Richard Edwards (1979) *Contested Terrain: The Transformation of the Workplace in the Twentieth Century* (New York, Basic Books); Paul Thompson (1983) *The Nature of Work : An Introduction to Debates on the Labour Process* (London, Macmillan); David Knights and Hugh Willmott (1990) *Labour Process Theory* (Basingstoke, Macmillan).
10 Karl Marx and Frederick Engels, (1848/1968) 'The Communist Manifesto' in *Marx-Engels Selected Works* (Moscow, Progress Publishers), pp. 35-36.
11 John Naisbitt (1982) *Megatrends* (New York, Warner), p. 17. For further development of this argument see Roy Jacques, 'Conclusion: Theorizing knowledge as work: The need for a "Knowledge theory of value"' in Craig Pritchard, Richard Hull, Mike Chumer and Hugh Willmott (eds.) (2000) *Managing Knowledge: Critical Investigations of Work and Learning* (Basingstoke, Macmillan).
12 Peter Drucker (1993) *Post-Capitalist Society* (Harper-Collins: New York), cf. Jacques, (1996), p. 183 n.77. For a more detailed comment on the deeply engrained nature of this opposition between nature and culture, see Jacques Derrida (1967) *Of Grammatology* (Baltimore, John Hopkins University Press), pp. 95-268.
13 See, for example, Étienne Balibar (1995) *The Philosophy of Marx* (London, Verso); Louis Althusser (1969) *For Marx* (London: Verso); Terry Eagleton (1996) *The Illusions of Postmodernism* (Oxford, Blackwell); Gayatri Chakravory Spivak (1996) 'Scattered speculations on the question of value' in *The Spivak Reader* ed. Donna Landry and Gerald Maclean (New York, Routledge); Stuart Hall (1996) *Critical Dialogues in Cultural Studies* ed. David Morley and Kuan-Hsing Chen (London, Routledge); Ernesto Laclau (1990) *New Reflections on the Revolution of Our Time* (London, Verso).
14 Gibson Burrell and Gareth Morgan (1979) *Sociological Paradigms and Organizational*

Analysis (London: Heinemann).

[15] Mike Reed (1992) *The Sociology of Organizations* (London, Harvester Wheatsheaf); Jeffrey Pfeffer (1993) 'Barriers to the Advance of Organizational Science: Paradigm Development as a Dependent Variable' *Academy of Management Review*, 18(4), 599-620.

[16] Jacques Derrida (1987) *Truth in Painting* (Chicago: University of Chicago Press).

[17] Donna Haraway (1988) 'Situated Knowledges: The Science Question in Feminism and the Privilege of Partial Perspective' in *Feminist Studies*, 14, pp. 575-599.

Index